R
333.95
END
V.10

DISCARD

Endangered Animals

VOLUME 10

Tree-Kangaroo, Goodfellow's – **Zebra,** Mountain

Grolier
EDUCATIONAL

Published 2002 by Grolier Educational, Danbury, CT 06816

This edition published exclusively for the school and library market

Produced by Andromeda Oxford Limited
11–13 The Vineyard, Abingdon,
Oxon OX14 3PX, U.K.
www.andromeda.co.uk

Copyright © Andromeda Oxford Limited 2002

All rights reserved. No part of this publication may be reproduced, stored in a retrieval system, or transmitted in any form or by any means electronic, mechanical, photocopying, recording, or otherwise, without the permission of the copyright holder.

Principal Contributors: *Amy-Jane Beer, Andrew Campbell, Robert and Valerie Davies, John Dawes, Jonathan Elphick, Tim Halliday, Pat Morris. Further contributions by David Capper and John Woodward*

Project Director: *Graham Bateman*
Managing Editors: *Shaun Barrington, Jo Newson*
Editor: *Penelope Mathias*
Art Editor and Designer: *Steve McCurdy*
Cartographic Editor: *Tim Williams*
Editorial Assistant: *Marian Dreier*
Picture Manager: *Claire Turner*
Production: *Clive Sparling*
Indexers: *Indexing Specialists, Hove, East Sussex*

Reproduction by A. T. Color, Milan
Printing by H & Y Printing Ltd., Hong Kong

Set ISBN 0-7172-5584-0

Library of Congress Cataloging-in-Publication Data

Endangered animals.
    p. cm.
    Contents: v. 1. What is an endangered animal? -- v. 2. Addax - blackbuck -- v. 3. Boa, Jamaican - danio, barred -- v. 4. Darter, Watercress - frog, gastric brooding -- v. 5. Frog, green and golden bell - kestrel, lesser -- v. 6. Kestrel, Mauritius - Mulgara -- v. 7. Murrelet, Japanese - Pupfish, Devil's Hole -- v. 8. Pygmy-possum, mountain - Siskin, red -- v. 9. Skink, pygmy blue-tongued - tragopan, Temminck's -- v. 10. Tree-kangaroo, Goodfellow's - zebra, mountain.
   ISBN 0-7172-5584-0 (set : alk. paper) -- ISBN 0-7172-5585-9 (v. 1 : alk. paper) –
ISBN 0-7172-5586-7 (v. 2 : alk. paper) -- ISBN 0-7172-5587-5 (v. 3 : alk. paper) –
ISBN 0-7172-5588-3 (v. 4 : alk. paper) -- ISBN 0-7172-5589-1 (v. 5 : alk. paper) –
ISBN 0-7172-5590-5 (v. 6 : alk. paper) -- ISBN 0-7172-5591-3 (v. 7 : alk. paper) –
ISBN 0-7172-5592-1 (v. 8 : alk. paper) -- ISBN 0-7172-5593-X (v. 9 : alk. paper) –
ISBN 0-7172-5594-8 (v. 10 : alk. paper)
   1. Endangered species--Juvenile literature. [1. Endangered species.] I. Grolier Educational (Firm)

QL83 .E54 2001
333.95'42--dc21

00-069134

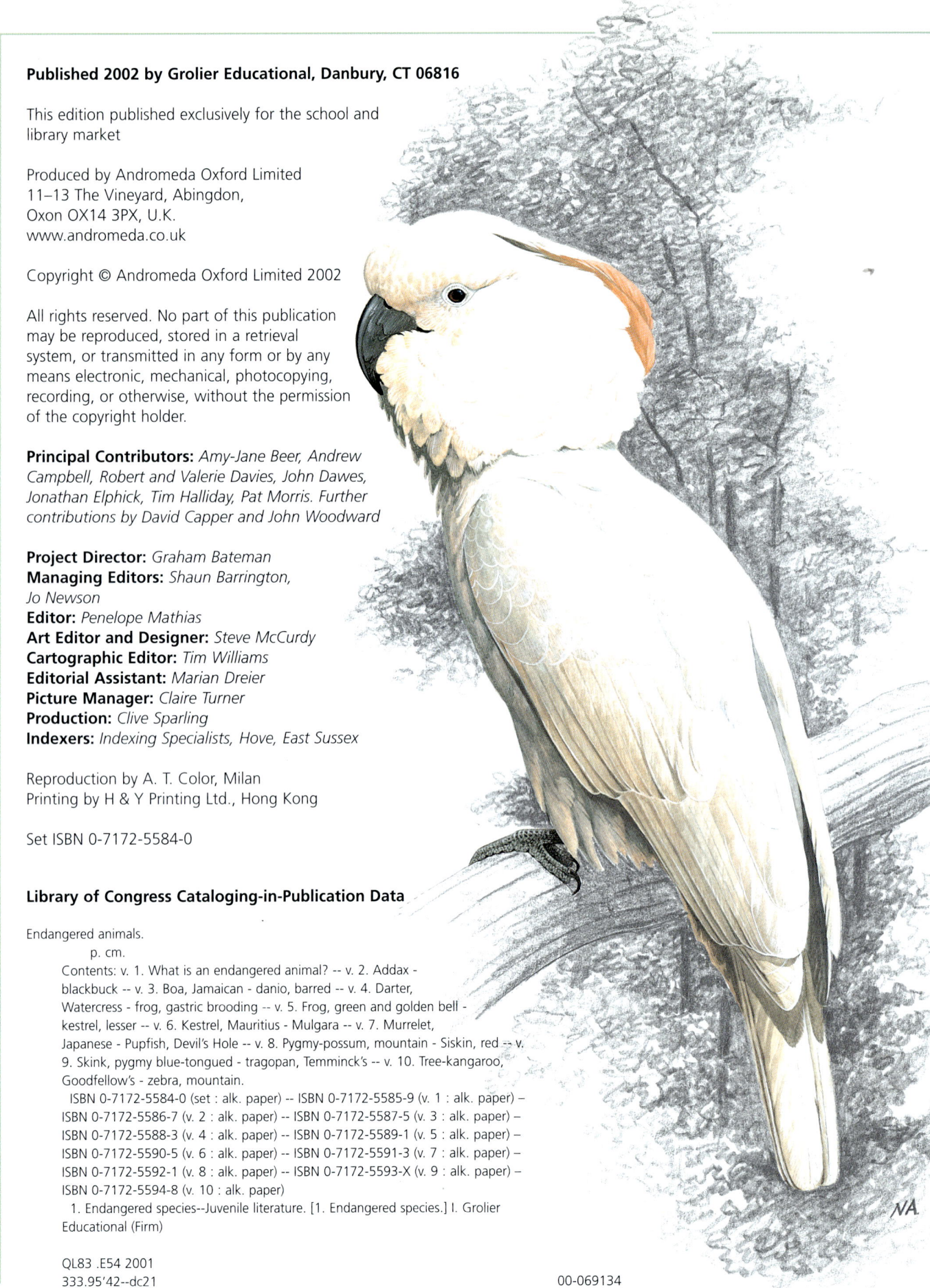

Contents

Tree-Kangaroo, Goodfellow's	4	**Warbler,** Aquatic	36	**Wolf,** Red	72
Tuatara	6	**Warbler,** Kirtland's	38	**Wolverine**	74
Tuna, Northern Bluefin	8	**Whale,** Blue	40	**Wombat,** Northern Hairy-Nosed	76
Turaco, Bannerman's	10	**Whale,** Fin	42	**Woodpecker,** Ivory-Billed	78
Turtle, Alabama Red-Bellied	12	**Whale,** Gray	44	**Woodpecker,** Red-Cockaded	80
Turtle, Bog	14	**Whale,** Humpback	46	**Worm,** Palolo	82
Turtle, Chinese Three-Striped Box	16	**Whale,** Killer	48	**Worm,** Velvet	84
Turtle, Hawksbill	18	**Whale,** Minke	50	**Wren,** Zapata	86
Turtle, Pig-Nosed	20	**Whale,** Northern Right	52	**Xenopoecilus**	88
Turtle, Western Swamp	22	**Whale,** Sei	54	**Yak,** Wild	90
Turtle, Yellow-Blotched Sawback Map	24	**Whale,** Sperm	56	**Zebra,** Grevy's	92
Vanga, Helmet	26	**Whale,** White	58	**Zebra,** Mountain	94
Vicuña	28	**Whiptail,** St. Lucia	60	Glossary	96
Viper, Milos	30	**Wildcat**	62	Further Reading and Websites	99
Vireo, Black-Capped	32	**Wolf,** Ethiopian	64	List of Animals by Group	100
Vulture, Cape Griffon	34	**Wolf,** Falkland Island	66	Set Index	102
		Wolf, Gray	68	Picture Credits and Acknowledgments	112
		Wolf, Maned	70		

About This Set

Endangered Animals is a 10-volume set that highlights and explains the threats to animal species across the world. Habitat loss is one major threat; another is the introduction of species into areas where they do not normally live.

Examples of different animals facing a range of problems have been chosen to include all the major animal groups. Fish, reptiles, amphibians, and insects and invertebrates are included as well as mammals and birds. Some species may have very large populations, but they nevertheless face problems. Some are already extinct.

Volume 1—What Is an Endangered Animal?—explains how scientists classify animals, the reasons why they are endangered, and what conservationists are doing about it. Cross-references in the text (volume number followed by page number) show relevant pages in the set.

Volumes 2 to 10 contain individual species entries arranged in alphabetical order. Each entry is a double-page spread with a data panel summarizing key facts and a locator map showing its range.

Look for a particular species by its common name, listed in alphabetical order on the Contents page of each book. (Page references for both common and scientific names are in the full set index at the back of each book.) When you have found the species that interests you, you can find related entries by looking first in the data panel. If an animal listed under Related endangered species has an asterisk (*) next to its name, it has its own separate entry. You can also check the cross-references at the bottom of the left-hand page, which refer to entries in other volumes. (For example, "Finch, Gouldian **4:** 74" means that the two-page entry about the Gouldian finch starts on page 74 of Volume 4.) The cross-reference is usually made to an animal that is in the same genus or family as the species you are reading about; but a species may appear here because it is from the same part of the world or faces the same threats.

Each book ends with a glossary of terms, lists of useful publications and websites, and a full set index.

Tree-Kangaroo, Goodfellow's

Dendrolagus goodfellowi

One of the few kangaroos living outside Australia, Goodfellow's tree-kangaroo of New Guinea is typical of several species that are threatened by hunting and habitat loss as logging and mining operations steadily encroach on their forest home.

Many people are surprised to learn that there are any kangaroos living as native species outside Australia. Goodfellow's tree-kangaroo is one of several that are found across the Torres Straits in Papua New Guinea. Like most other marsupials, Goodfellow's tree-kangaroo is largely nocturnal. It emerges from dense clusters of silkwood trees at dusk and gets around by means of a peculiar, rocking, hopping gait using both front and back legs. The tree-kangaroo does not use its tail as an extra limb to aid balance, so it is unable to take long series of bounding hops like its more familiar cousins. Relative awkwardness on the ground is the price the animal pays for surprising agility in the trees. By spending a good deal of their time off the ground, tree-kangaroos are relatively safe from predators and able to reach abundant food sources that are inaccessible to their earth-bound relatives.

The tree-kangaroos' unusual lifestyle made them very successful in the past, when their forest home extended from the highlands of eastern and central Papua New Guinea—where they are now found—down to sea level. The main factor controlling the population was the weather, which is extemely variable in this part of the tropics. The tree-kangaroos coped by having a variable reproductive rate. The females do not tend to breed when conditions are poor. However, since they are not tied to a particular breeding season, they are able to raise one baby every 10 or 11 months in a run of good years. Although unusual, Goodfellow's tree-kangaroo is, nevertheless, a successful and viable mammal species. As recently as the 1960s, before guns became widespread in Papua New Guinea, it was hunted using dogs and spears or arrows. Such traditional hunting took its toll, but had little effect on the total population. The rarity of tree-kangaroos today is a result of more recent developments.

Changing Landscape

The landscape of Papua New Guinea has changed dramatically in recent decades. Much of the lowland rain forest has already been cleared, and logging activities are now encroaching on the highlands, too. Papua New Guinea is also

DATA PANEL

Goodfellow's tree-kangaroo (ornate tree-kangaroo)

Dendrolagus goodfellowi

Family: Macropodidae

World population: Unknown, perhaps only a few hundred

Distribution: Eastern and central Papua New Guinea

Habitat: Lowland and montane (mountainous) rain forest up to about 10,000 ft (3,000 m)

Size: Length head/body: 21–30 in (55–77 cm); tail: 27.5–35 in (70–85 cm); females up to 20% bigger than males. Weight: 14–18 lb (6.5–8 kg)

Form: Small, slender kangaroo with shorter back legs and longer front legs than terrestrial species; fur short and reddish brown, fading to creamy-yellow on underside and feet; coat marked with 2 pale dorsal stripes and pale rings on tail

Diet: Leaves and fruit

Breeding: Single young born at any time of year after 3–5 week gestation; incubated in pouch for 10–12 months. Lives up to 14 years in captivity

Related endangered species: Other species of tree-kangaroo, including Doria's tree-kangaroo *(Dendrolagus dorianus)* VU; Scott's tree-kangaroo *(D. scottae)* EN; Bennett's tree-kangaroo *(D. Bennettianus)* LRnt

Status: IUCN EN; not listed by CITES

See also: Habitat Loss 1: 38; Money Problems 1: 88; Rock-Wallaby, Prosperine 8: 36

rich in mineral reserves, and huge mining and oil-extraction operations have added to the devastation. The settlements that spring up around the mining and logging industries mean that more land has to be cleared to grow crops to feed the people. Tree-kangaroos have always been prized for their meat, and with new roads and settlements appearing throughout the forest, more colonies are vulnerable to hunting than ever before. In some places tree-kangaroos have taken to eating cereal crops planted alongside their forest habitat, giving hunters an excuse to kill yet more of an increasingly endangered species. Goodfellow's tree-kangaroo has been wiped out of the areas surrounding even very small settlements in a short space of time. With logging and mining constantly eating away at the edge of the forest, the species' range is shrinking fast.

Goodfellow's tree-kangaroo *does not look or act much like the kangaroos and wallabies of Australia. It has traded the convenience of a hopping lifestyle for the security and plentiful food resources available in the trees.*

Tree-kangaroos do have some refuges in national parks and appear to be doing well in areas where they and their habitat are properly protected. The simple answer to the tree-kangaroo's problems would be to designate large areas of forest as protected land. However, much of the real power in Papua New Guinea lies not with the government but with the multinational corporations exploiting the country's mineral and timber resources. For such organizations conservation of a little-known marsupial is not a priority.

Tuatara

Sphenodon punctatus

The tuatara is a unique lizardlike reptile and the sole surviving member of a group common in Mesozoic times. Now one of the rarest reptiles in the world, it is struggling to survive on small islands off the coast of New Zealand.

In spite of their appearance, tuataras are not lizards. Sometimes referred to as "living fossils" because they have changed little from their ancient ancestors, they are the sole surviving members of an ancient group of reptiles, the Rhynchocephalia ("beakheads"). These animals developed before dinosaurs and were once found on every continent except Antarctica. The fossil record shows that all other species of Rhynchocephalia died out 65 million years ago. When New Zealand separated from other land masses, the tuatara survived because of the absence of major predators. Now, however, it is one of the rarest reptiles in the world.

Unlike lizards, tuataras do not have eardrums or a copulatory (reproductive) organ, and there are certain differences in the skeletons. They can produce a croaking sound and are thought to be able to see in the dark. Their eyes are similar in structure to a crocodile's or turtle's. One feature shared with lizards is the "third eye" in the skull. This scale-covered gland is connected to the brain and is sensitive to light, but cannot actually "see." The scientific name *Sphenodon* means "wedge tooth." Unusually, the tuatara's teeth are fused to the jawbone. (In most reptiles teeth can be replaced.)

Home Sweet Habitat

Once common throughout New Zealand, tuataras are now restricted to 30 cool, damp islands off the northeastern coast of North Island and in the Cook Strait area. Tuataras were last seen on the mainland of New Zealand in the 1860s. The summer temperature on the islands habitats rarely goes above 70°F (21°C) with about 80 percent humidity. Unlike other reptiles, tuataras thrive at low temperatures and are active at just above freezing.

DATA PANEL

Tuatara (Cook Strait tuatara)

Sphenodon punctatus

Family: Sphenodontidae

World Population: 25,000–30,000

Distribution: Islands off North Island and in the Cook Strait area, New Zealand

Habitat: Cool, damp, rocky islands with soil cover, shrubs, and low vegetation

Size: Length: male up to 24 in (60 cm); female up to 18 in (45 cm). Weight: male up to 2.2 lb (1 kg); female less

Form: Stout-bodied reptile. Spiny crest along back is more prominent in males. Coloration is mainly olive green, sometimes slate gray or pink with overall light speckling. Male usually has a dark patch on each side of the head

Diet: Insects, invertebrates, lizards, chicks and eggs of seabirds, occasionally their own young

Breeding: Females may not breed until they are 11–18 years old; maturity is based on size rather than age. Mating to egg hatching takes 2 years. Eggs laid every 4 years; clutch size 6–15 eggs

Related endangered species: Brother's Island tuatara (*Sphenodon guntheri*) VU

Status: Not listed by IUCN; CITES I

See also: The History of Reptiles 1: 73; Dragon, Southeastern Lined Earless 4: 38

The tuatara's habitat has open areas between scrubby growth. The reptiles particularly like a good depth of soil. They dig burrows, but occasionally share those of seabirds. The seabirds are important to the island habitats: their droppings help sustain the vegetation and support the insects on which tuataras feed. On sunny days tuataras bask outside their burrows; the males display by raising their crests and bob their heads to intimidate others. Open areas can become an arena for disputes between males.

Recognizing the unique nature of the tuatara, the New Zealand government made it a strictly protected species in 1895. The Wildlife Act of 1953 enforced complete protection. The tuatara is listed by CITES, which forbids trade in the animals or its products, and access to the islands is strictly controlled. Even so, smuggled specimens have been found in confiscated consignments in the United States.

Enemy Territory

In spite of protection, tuatara numbers have declined. The two main reasons are habitat destruction and predation by rats. Several of New Zealand's reptiles and amphibians are in decline as a result of habitat destruction. Large areas of native vegetation are under cultivation, huge pine forests planted for timber are a prominent feature, and in many parts the vegetation has been destroyed by sheep and goats. Rats have been the tuatara's main enemy. The Polynesian rat arrived with Maori people; brown rats came with European settlers. On some islands where rats have been introduced there are no young tuataras. Rat-eradication programs are part of conservation projects. Another problem is that small islands can only house a limited population of tuataras. There is a proposal to reintroduce tuataras on mainland North Island, but providing a rat-free environment on the mainland would be difficult.

Meanwhile, captive breeding is underway; artificial incubation is already showing some success, and hatchlings have been raised to maturity in five years by providing optimal conditions. However, there has been no second-generation breeding, and release into the wild will not be without its problems.

Tuatara means spiny (tara) back (tua) in Maori. The distinctive spiny crest along the reptile's back is less prominent in females.

Tuna, Northern Bluefin

Thunnus thynnus

Tuna are the long-distance specialists of the fish world, covering several thousand miles a year on their migrations. They are also among the fastest-swimming fish in the world. Some populations are now endangered as a result of the world demand for tuna meat.

Tuna are fish built for speed. Every aspect of their body form is suited to maximum performance in the water. Their body is fusiform (pointed at both ends) with a stiff, sickle-shaped caudal (tail) fin perfect for producing maximum thrust. The bluefin tuna also has several features designed to reduce water resistance. Its scales are tiny and lie tightly against the skin, so minimizing friction. Its large eyes are well-bedded within their sockets, so the outer layer lies flush with the skin surface. The two dorsal (back) fins and the single anal (belly) fin fit into grooves when they are folded, while the series of finlets between the fins and the tail allow water to flow between them. The pectoral (chest) and pelvic (hip) fins are small and have a stiff front edge, which prevents them from collapsing when they are extended at high speeds.

A striking feature of the tuna's body is the deep-red color of the muscle tissue. This characteristic is found in the family Scombridaea that includes other high-speed species such as mackerel, bonitos, and their relatives. Red muscle has a rich blood supply that is typical of a species constantly on the move. The blood supplies the high levels of oxygen that the fish need and gives them plenty of stamina.

However, tuna would be unable to maintain their constant day-and-night swimming at speed were it not for a further adaptation. Unlike the majority of fish whose internal body temperature matches that of their environment, a tuna's countercurrent blood circulation allows it to maintain a high internal body temperature whatever the water temperature.

All-Consuming Demand

Bluefin tuna have been fished for about 100 years. Originally only sport fishermen and a few small-scale

DATA PANEL

Northern bluefin tuna (Atlantic bluefin tuna)

Thunnus thynnus

Family: Scombridae

World population: Disputed: about 40,000 in the western Atlantic (no equivalent data available for the eastern Atlantic)

Distribution: Atlantic. On eastern side from Norway to Mediterranean Sea, along western African coast to Cape Blanc. On western side from Newfoundland south to Brazil. Seen in central and northwestern Pacific

Habitat: Open oceanic waters

Size: Length: 15 ft (4.6 m). Weight: up to 1,320 lb (600 kg)

Form: Fusiform (spindle-shaped), streamlined body. Coloration deep blue above, with purple or green iridescence (colors that shimmer as observer changes position); silvery sides and belly

Diet: Fish (including herring, mackerel, and whiting); also squid

Breeding: Spawning occurs in the Gulf of Mexico, the western Atlantic, and in the Mediterranean Sea in the east. Western stocks spawn from mid-April to mid-June; their eastern counterparts breed from June–August. Female can release about 30 million eggs

Related endangered species: Albacore tuna (*Thunnus alalunga*) CR; bigeye tuna (*T. obesus*) VU; southern bluefin tuna (*T. maccoyii*) CR; Monterrey Spanish mackerel (*Scomberomorus concolor*) EN

Status: IUCN DD (western population CR; eastern population EN); not listed by CITES

See also: Hunting **1:** 42; Research **1:** 84; Cod, Atlantic **3:** 54; Cod, Trout **3:** 56

enterprises supplying fish for human consumption fished the species. But starting in the 1930s—and continuing for the next 30 to 40 years—sport fishing soared in popularity.

Then in the 1970s a new commercial dimension was added to the sports angling industry, arising out of the fast-expanding demand for fresh (deep-frozen) tuna meat in Japan. The market for raw tuna provided by sushi and sashimi enthusiasts led to 40 percent of the global tuna catch being sent to the Japanese market. A major factor leading to the rapid expansion was the improvement in air freight and transport that began in the 1970s and made possible transglobal overnight deliveries of fresh-caught tuna.

Allied to major changes that had occurred within the commercial fishery—which had also led to ever-greater catches—the fishing of large tuna by sport anglers for profit as well as sport led to dramatically declining yields in the space of a few years. Total Atlantic harvests of bluefin tuna plummeted from a peak of 38,600 tons (35,000 tonnes) in 1964 to less than half—18,500 tons (16,800 tonnes)—by 1972. By the early 1980s catches in the western Atlantic had dropped even further to about 6,600 tons (6,000 tonnes). A report by the International Commission for

Northern bluefin tuna *are superbly adapted to their environment in shape and structure. The deep blue color on the back and pale-colored belly also makes them hard for predators to see from above or below.*

the Conservation of Atlantic Tunas (ICCAT) has estimated that by the early 1990s the population of adult bluefins in the western Atlantic had dropped to just 13 percent of its 1975 level.

Population Conundrum

It is clear that fishing controls need to be introduced to protect the northern bluefin tuna. However, differences of opinion, disputed scientific data, a lack of faith in ICCAT's ability to enforce quotas, demands for higher-than-stated quotas for the western Atlantic mean that there is no consensus on population levels. The picture is made even more complex by the migration of some stocks across the oceans.

Meanwhile, tagging programs, aerial surveys, captive breeding, and genetic analysis are some of the methods being used to establish the status of the bluefin tuna on both sides of the Atlantic. This should pave the way for enforcing realistic fishing controls.

Turaco, Bannerman's

Tauraco bannermani

One of Africa's most threatened birds, the beautiful Bannerman's turaco lives in tiny remnants of mountain forest in a small part of western Cameroon.

Bannerman's turaco belongs to a distinctive family of mostly pigeon-sized, fruit-eating birds found only in the forests and woodlands of sub-Saharan Africa. Turacos have a number of unique features. Their plumage is remarkable in that it contains two copper-based pigments that are not found in any other animals, let alone other birds. One—turacoverdin—produces the glossy green of the birds' plumage. The other—turacin—is responsible for producing the sudden, dramatic flash of brilliant crimson when a turaco opens its wings. Turaco plumage is also distinctive in that the head and breast feathers mainly lack barbules—minute hooks that interlock and make the feathers look smoothly joined—so the feathers resemble hair.

Although quite large and brightly colored, Bannerman's turacos are very shy. Their green plumage camouflages them against the background of the forest foliage, and the birds are more often heard than seen. Their loud, harsh barking calls can carry as far as half a mile (1 km).

Like other turacos, Bannerman's turacos spend almost all their life in the trees, descending to the ground only to drink or bathe. They are poor fliers, taking to the air only when necessary to move from one tree to another; bursts of flapping of their short, rounded wings alternate with clumsy glides. In the trees, however, they are extremely nimble, running and moving around among the branches with agility.

A Unique Habitat

Bannerman's turaco is restricted to small areas of forest in parts of western Cameroon—the Bamenda Highlands and nearby Mount Mbam. It lives in dense forest covering slopes, crags, and crater rims of the mountains in areas outside the main forest between 5,900 and 8,500 feet (1,800 and 2,600 m). There the trees are shrouded in mist, and dense thickets are covered with mosses and lichens. The turaco can also survive in degraded or secondary forest, provided that there are enough tall fruiting trees. It is likely that the birds migrate to altitudes of between 7,200 and 8,500 feet (2,200 and 2,600 m) in the breeding season, where they take advantage of seasonal fruit.

The area where Bannerman's turaco lives is a center of biodiversity, with many unique animals and plants; but it is also a resource for many local people. As pressure on this special habitat has increased, all of its wildlife has come under threat. The forest is regularly cleared for growing crops, grazing livestock, and supplies of firewood and timber. During the dry season forest fires add to the destruction.

The species' habitat had already been markedly reduced by 1985. In 1994 researchers recorded Bannerman's turacos in several remaining fragments of forest in the Bamenda Highlands. They were encouraged that the birds seemed able to survive in extremely small areas of forest. Follow-up surveys in 2000 revealed that some of the fragments had almost entirely vanished, with only a few pairs of the turacos surviving in them. The species was upgraded to Endangered status as a result. At present the total area occupied by the birds is estimated to be less than about 200 square miles (500 sq. km), and it is thought that individuals in forest fragments are at imminent risk of extinction. The species is likely to become completely extinct unless the largest remaining montane forest area, Kilum-Ijim, can be saved.

See also: Categories of Threat **1**: 14; Saving the Habitats **1**: 88; Nuthatch, Algerian **7**: 16; Swallow, Blue **9**: 42; Warbler, Aquatic **10**: 36

TURACO, BANNERMAN'S

DATA PANEL

Bannerman's turaco
Tauraco bannermani

Family: Musophagidae

World population: 2,500–10,000 birds

Distribution: Bamenda Highlands and Mount Mbam, western Cameroon

Habitat: Montane forest at altitudes of 5,600–9,700 ft (1,700–3,000 m)

Size: Length: about 17 in (43 cm). Weight: 7–9 oz (200–250 g)

Form: Large bird; crest, crown, and nape bright crimson; yellow bill red along top; face and chin gray; mantle, lower back, and most of wings golden-green, outer 3 secondary wing and primary feathers crimson; rump black with green gloss; uppertail coverts and tail purple-blue, outer edge of tail feathers green; sides of neck and breast green; belly and undertail coverts black. Juvenile duller

Diet: Mainly fruit and berries of *Podocarpus milanjensis* trees; also figs

Breeding: March–June (early rainy season); nest a flimsy platform of twigs hidden in tree or shrub among tangled creepers or dense foliage; usually 2 white eggs incubated by both sexes

Related endangered species: Prince Ruspoli's turaco *(Tauraco ruspolii)* VU; Fischer's turaco *(T. fischeri)* LRnt

Status: IUCN EN; CITES II

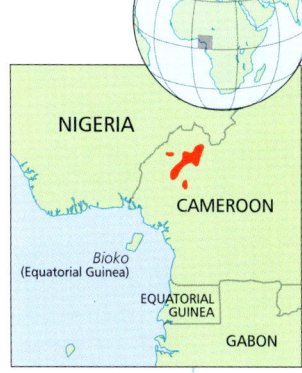

Conservation

Conservationists have set up the Kilum-Ijim Forest Project. It is run by a partnership of international and other agencies and coordinated by BirdLife International, a global partnership of conservation groups working together in over 100 countries and dedicated to saving birds. The project has helped local people in Kilum-Ijim preserve forest boundaries, adopt sustainable farming methods, and enhance soil productivity. The organizations have set a number of targets, including restoring and protecting areas of natural forest. The cornerstone of the project is the involvement of local people. In 2000 such community-based conservation programs were extended to other remnants of forest in the Bamenda Highlands.

Bannerman's turaco has feathers that are loose and hairlike. Its golden-green plumage provides camouflage in the forest.

Turtle, Alabama Red-Bellied

Pseudemys alabamensis

In 1987 the Alabama red-bellied turtle was designated an endangered species by the United States Fish and Wildlife Service. Its reliance on clean water and sandy beaches has made it vulnerable to habitat destruction.

The distribution of the Alabama red-bellied turtle is limited to quiet backwaters, pools, tributaries, and rivers in the Mobile Delta in Mobile and Baldwin Counties. The turtle seems to prefer shallow- to medium-depth water with a good growth of aquatic plants and a layer of silt into which it can dive if disturbed. Today red-bellies are found in scattered areas, although they once had a wider range. Urban development, drainage, and other human activities have restricted the turtles' territory.

Red-bellies are semiaquatic (adapted to a life both on land and in water). They spend much time basking in the sun to maintain a suitable body temperature and enter the water to forage on aquatic plants.

The species has not been thoroughly studied, and knowledge of various aspects of its lifestyle is still limited. Even its life span is unknown, although like many other chelonian species (turtles and tortoises of the order Chelonia) it may be able to live for 50 years or more. The number of eggs laid is also unknown; if it is the lowest estimate—between three and nine per year—then recovery of the species could be slow and difficult. However, one reason why turtles have been an evolutionary success is their longevity rather than rapid breeding rates.

At the Mercy of Humans

Red-bellied turtles have many natural predators such as alligators, the fish crow, racoons, and large fish. The turtles are also at the mercy of other creatures; crows and pigs destroy nest sites, and fire ants (an introduced pest) have been found in turtle nests attacking the eggs. However, humans have had by far the greatest effect on red-bellied turtle numbers. Adult turtles and their eggs used to feature in the human diet. During the Great Depression of the 1930s turtles of various species in many areas were eaten as an essential rather than a luxury item.

Habitat destruction is perhaps the greatest threat. Waterside sites with loose, sandy soil are essential for egg laying. Many such areas have been degraded by off-road vehicles. The major nesting site for red-bellies is Gravine Island in Baldwin County. Even in the 1980s, when the species was documented as being in decline, eggs were still taken by humans.

DATA PANEL

Alabama red-bellied turtle

Pseudemys alabamensis

Family: Emydidae

World population: Unknown

Distribution: Streams running into Mobile Delta, Alabama

Habitat: Freshwater streams; rivers with muddy bottoms

Size: Length: females 13 in (33.5 cm); males 11 in (29.5 cm)

Form: Shell with yellow and black ocelli (eye spots) on scutes (shields). Carapace (upper shell) green; plastron (lower shell) orange; colors darken with age. Head and limbs brown with yellow stripes

Diet: Aquatic plants; captive specimens take fish, meat, and earthworms, suggesting that in the wild they also feed on aquatic vertebrates

Breeding: One clutch per year of 3–9 eggs

Related endangered species: Rio Grande cooter (*Pseudemys gorzugi*) LRnt; American red-bellied turtle (*P. rubriventris*) LRnt

Status: IUCN EN; not listed by CITES

See also: Exploitation of Live Animals 1: 49; turtle species 10: 14–25

TURTLE, ALABAMA RED-BELLIED

The adult Alabama red-bellied turtle *has a brownish carapace (upper shell covering the back) and a red plastron (lower shell covering the belly).*

In spite of legal protection, the red-belly is vulnerable to a number of factors. Pollution and pesticides are two potential threats. Lowering water levels and the introduction of plants that choke the waterways cause further habitat destruction.

Collective Guilt

A substantial factor in the decline of the red-bellied turtle has been collecting by hobbyists and others. As is the case with many turtles, the hatchlings are appealing creatures and are often taken as pets. Hatchling red-bellies are particularly attractive, having a green carapace (upper shell) with dark-edged lines and yellow and black ocelli (eye spots) on the scutes (shields). The plastron (lower shell) is red to orange with varying dark markings. The head and limbs are olive to dark brown with yellow stripes. The colors darken with age—the carapace turns brown with reddish-yellow areas. The plastron also often loses the dark markings.

The fate of collected red-bellies has often been death because of ignorance of their requirements or simply neglect when the owner's interest has waned. Turtles need the correct diet, clean water, and sunlight (real or artificial) in order to thrive. Experienced keepers may go on to breed their charges, but all too often turtles that start off with a shell length of about 1 inch (3 cm) gradually outgrow their housing and are dumped in the nearest water.

Commercial traders used to take substantial numbers of red-bellied turtles to sell as pets. No doubt the practice still happens today to some extent. However, under Alabama nongame species regulations it is illegal to take, capture, kill, possess, sell, or trade red-bellies and various other reptiles, amphibians, and other animals without a scientific permit or written permission from the Department of Conservation and Natural Resources. A federal ban on the sale of all turtle species with a shell length of 4 inches (10 cm) or less was introduced in 1975 by the United States Food and Drug Administration. The ban has not been rigidly enforced and is often ignored, nor did it apply to the export of live turtles.

Turtle, Bog

Clemmys muhlenbergii

The bog turtle is one of the smallest turtles in the world. Its colorful markings have made it a popular pet and led to overcollection. The species is also at risk from loss of habitat.

The bog turtle, sometimes referred to as Muhlenberg's turtle, is probably the smallest turtle in the United States and one of the smallest in the world. Bog turtles take between five and seven years to reach maturity, by which time they are about 3 inches (8 cm) long. Eggs are not buried deeply but simply deposited in a small hole scooped out from loose soil or moss at the base of grass tussocks. Although it would seem to have a wide distribution—from Massachusetts down to South Carolina—there are only two major populations (north and south) divided by a substantial gap. Turtle groups in these areas are often widely scattered, and some sites may contain fewer than 20 specimens.

Overcollection

Bog turtles are relatively colorful. They have light patches on the head, forelimbs, and throat, and their scutes (hornlike shields that form the upper shell) have central light-reddish to orange markings that sometimes resemble a "sunburst" pattern. The combined appeal of their small size and attractive appearance has partly been the cause of the bog turtle's decline. They have long been a target for collectors, who keep them as pets or sell them to the pet trade. This has continued even though in some states the species has been protected for over 20 years. However, the laws were seldom enforced, and collection continued unchecked. In 1997 the species was given federal listing as Threatened. Under this legislation anyone convicted of capturing, harming, or even transporting a federally threatened species could be fined up to $50,000 and imprisoned for up to one year. It is unlikely that this will deter all collectors, since the black market price for bog turtles is high.

Although it was decided not to designate Critical Habitat for the species, its protected status meant that construction projects could be stopped or delayed if turtles were found to be present on the site. There were even reports of bog turtles being deliberately planted to prevent work starting.

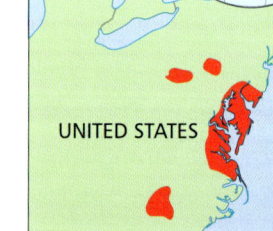

DATA PANEL

Bog turtle

Clemmys muhlenbergii

Family: Emydidae

World population: Unknown

Distribution: Eastern U.S.; scattered locations in New York State, New Jersey, Philadelphia, and the Carolinas

Habitat: Wetlands; slow-moving streams

Size: Length: 3–3.5 in (7.6–8.9 cm)

Form: Shell brown to black; forelimbs and throat spotted or striped; yellow or orange patch on head

Diet: Earthworms, insects, tadpoles, and slugs

Breeding: Usually 2–4 eggs (up to 6 possible)

Related endangered species: Pacific pond turtle *(Clemmys marmorata)* VU; wood turtle *(C. insculpta)* VU; spotted turtle *(C. guttata)* VU

Status: IUCN EN; CITES I

See also: CITES 1: 12; Exploitation of Live Animals 1: 49; turtle species 10: 12–25

Disappearing Habitat

Bog turtles have also declined due to habitat loss and fragmentation. Some of this loss is natural; bogs, ponds, and similar wetland areas are subject to a natural process known as "succession" when dead vegetation accumulates in the water, collecting and binding sediment and eventually becoming land.

However, the majority of the bog turtle's habitat has been destroyed by human activity, particularly the drainage and planting up of wet areas. Succession can be speeded up if plants gain a foothold. Many plant species grow rapidly in marshy ground, soon making turtle movement difficult and blocking the open areas they need for basking. Lowering the water level can also speed up succession. Construction of walls, roads, drainage channels, and other barriers fragments the habitat, preventing turtle movement and isolating them in small groups. The smaller the groups, the greater the adverse effects of inbreeding affecting the long-term survival of the species. Further hazards are water pollution from fertilizers—which also accelerate plant growth—and toxic pesticides.

The number of turtles surviving in the wild is not known. They are secretive, and in their natural habitat they are well camouflaged, making population counts difficult. In some areas their presence went undetected until the 1980s. Several American zoos have captive-breeding groups, and substantial numbers are in private hands. Actual figures of captive bog turtles are impossible to estimate since many private owners keep quiet about their specimens, which may have been acquired illegally.

Future Hopes

Bog turtles will breed in captivity, and clutches of up to six eggs—sometimes more than one clutch per year—have been recorded. In some collections several generations have been bred. Captive breeding may well be the answer to the bog turtle's decline. Provided that existing habitats are preserved or new ones constructed, youngsters could be released back into the wild. However, without this protection the decline of the bog turtle will continue.

The bog turtle's *attractive markings have made the species highly collectable, even though the practice is illegal.*

Turtle, Chinese Three-Striped Box

Cuora trifasciata

About 10 years ago the Chinese three-striped box turtle could be bought in the pet trade for just a few dollars. In the past two or three years its value in Chinese markets has soared to $3,000 for one specimen. Increased demand, both for food and medicinal use, is driving the species toward extinction.

Ever since it was claimed that a medicine made from the Chinese three-striped box turtle could cure cancer, demand for the product has increased, making the turtle the most expensive to be found in China's food markets. Huge sums of money have been made selling the medicine. The turtle—along with a few other *Cuora* species—was once imported into China by the pet trade. Exporters obtained the specimens in the food markets rather than going out to collect them in the wild. Treatment of the turtles prior to reaching the markets resulted in many of them being diseased. Packed tightly into crates, often for journeys of several weeks without food, it is little wonder that many specimens exported to western countries fared poorly when purchased as pets.

Turtles as Food and Medicine

Throughout the Far East turtles and tortoises have featured in various cultures and certain religions. They have also been used for hundreds of years for food and medicine. Traditional Chinese medicine is probably the greatest threat to the three-striped box and to the thousands of other turtles that are imported yearly into China. Turtles are well known for their longevity, which it is thought will be passed on to those eating them. Turtle blood, bones, and shells—particularly the plastron (ventral part of the shell)—are thought to have medicinal properties and be able to cure a number of ailments. Turtle eggs are also used for food and medicine. The medicinal value of the turtles is open to question, and it is possible that the same effects could be produced by herbs. Any beneficial substances from the turtles could also be synthesized chemically, so as to prevent the killing of turtles.

The southern part of China has become more prosperous in recent years, and the demand for turtles has increased dramatically. Turtle dishes

DATA PANEL

Chinese three-striped box turtle

Cuora trifasciata

Family: Emydidae

World population: Unknown

Distribution: Vietnam, China (Guangxi and Hainan), and southeastern Laos

Habitat: Swamps, rice paddies, slow-moving rivers

Size: Length: up to 8 in (20 cm). Weight: 20 oz (575 g)

Form: Carapace (bony shield) is variable shades of brown with 3 raised keels (projections). Head brown to olive with a dark stripe on each side. Plastron (lower shell) is hinged, allowing complete closure

Diet: Insects, mollusks, aquatic vertebrates, and plants

Breeding: One clutch of 2–3 eggs buried in soft soil; incubation period 70–85 days

Related endangered species: South Asian box turtle (*Cuora amboinensis*) VU; yellow-headed box turtle (*C. aurocapitata*) CR; yellow-margined box turtle (*C. flavomarginata*) EN; Indochinese box turtle (*C. galbinifrons*) CR; McCord's box turtle (*C. mccordi*) CR; Pan's box turtle (*C. pani*) CR; Yunnan box turtle (*C. yunnanensis*) EX; Zhou's box turtle (*C. zhoui*) CR

Status: IUCN CR; CITES II

See also: Luxury Products 1: 46; Cultural Differences 1: 94; turtle species 10: 12–25

TURTLE, CHINESE THREE-STRIPED BOX

Chinese three-striped box turtles *can be found in or near water. Their shells are said to have medicinal properties, and demand for their body parts threatens them with extinction.*

are served in restaurants and regarded as an expensive delicacy, even a status symbol.

As turtle supplies in China dwindled, traders started importing the animals from Vietnam. As a result many Vietnamese turtles have now disappeared from their haunts in the wild. To satisfy growing demand, importers have now turned to sources farther afield, including Cambodia, Laos, Nepal, India, Bhutan, and Indonesia.

Since biologists started studying turtles in Chinese food markets, several previously unknown and extremely rare species have been found; some are on Appendix I of CITES. At the present rate of collection such specimens, and even new species not yet discovered, could soon be extinct. The three-striped box turtle is simply one among dozens of other species flooding into China, but its high value makes it a special target for collectors.

Laws and Conservation

Much of the trade in turtles is illegal, but laws protecting wildlife are not always enforced. A shortage of trained staff able to recognize legal and illegal species compounds the problem. Borders are extensive and can be crossed undetected in many places, and authorities sometimes turn a blind eye to wildlife smuggling. Some illegal shipments have been confiscated, but this does not stop the trade.

International concern over trade in turtles has led to conservation moves. The Cuc Phong Conservation Project, set up in 1996 in Vietnam, cares for confiscated turtles and other rare animals, and runs research and education programs. Captive farming in the native countries exists, but species such as the Chinese three-striped box have a low reproductive rate. For the Chinese three-striped box turtle and many other Asian turtles time is fast running out.

Turtle, Hawksbill

Eretmochelys imbricata

For centuries the hawksbill's attractive shell has been the main source of tortoiseshell. Despite international legislation, illegal trade in this commodity continues, and the hawksbill is one of the most seriously threatened sea turtles in the world.

Sea turtles such as the hawksbill have always been exploited by humans for food, oil, and skins. On a local scale a balance can be maintained, but the pressure of human activities over the last 50 years has resulted in all sea turtle species becoming endangered. Although all species are listed on CITES Appendix I, some of the 150 signatory countries flout the ruling. The hawksbill is classed by the IUCN as Critical, making it one of the most severely endangered sea turtles in the world.

For many years the hawksbill's attractively colored shell has been the main source of tortoiseshell, used for glasses frames, combs, ornaments, and jewelry. The scutes (hornlike shields) of the hawksbill shell are exceptionally thick, making them ideal for carving. Japan has been the largest user, importing an average of 30 tons (305 kg) of shell per year between 1970 and 1994. More than half of this was from the Caribbean—particularly Cuba—and Latin America. In the 1980s Japan's stockpile of hawksbill shell represented the death of over 170,000 turtles.

Although a member of CITES, Japan did not ban shell imports until 1993. Proposals by Cuba to allow the exportation of hawksbill shell to Japan by transferring the species from CITES Appendix I to Appendix II were defeated in 1997 and 2000. However, turtle meat and eggs are still consumed and sold in many countries. Illegal shipments of shell are often intercepted, and tourist souvenirs, including whole turtles, stuffed and lacquered, are openly traded in many countries. Bringing any part of a sea turtle back from vacation is illegal, and seizures, sometimes followed by fines, are common.

Hawksbills have been recorded on the coasts of at least 96 different countries, and nesting takes place only on sandy beaches. Suitable sites exist in the Caribbean (particularly Puerto Rico), Central and South America, and Florida. In at least two of their former haunts the species is now thought to be extinct. Often four or more clutches—of up to 140 eggs each—are laid, usually overnight. This process takes up to three hours, during which time the females and their eggs are vulnerable to predators, including people. An interval of two or three years occurs between each breeding. Hawksbills take at least 30 years to mature to breeding age, a factor that badly affects the replenishment of the population.

Human Interference

Although classed as endangered since 1970, the hawksbill's situation has not improved. Estimates of the worldwide population are impossible to arrive at, but observers who monitor breeding females in various countries are convinced that numbers are falling. Even without human interference sea turtles' eggs and hatchlings face severe predation from wild pigs, monitor lizards, crabs, dogs, and seabirds.

Humans multiply the threats. The sandy beaches needed for turtle nesting are encroached on by building, mainly for tourist facilities. Beach leveling and mechanical raking can destroy nests, while offroad vehicles compact the sand, crushing eggs and producing tire tracks that prevent hatchlings reaching the sea. People simply walking on nesting sites, especially at night, deter nesting female turtles and compact the sand. In addition, artificial lighting along

See also: CITES **1:** 12; The Battle for the Beaches **1:** 43; Luxury Products **1:** 46; turtle species **10:** 12–25

TURTLE, HAWKSBILL

DATA PANEL

Hawksbill turtle

Eretmochelys imbricata

Family: Cheloniidae

World population: Unknown

Distribution: Atlantic, Pacific, and Indian Oceans

Habitat: Shallow tropical and subtropical seas; coral reefs; mangrove bays; estuaries

Size: Length: female 24–37 in (62–94 cm); male up to 39 in (99 cm)

Form: Oval shell with serrated (toothed) edge; dark pattern on amber background

Diet: Sponges and mollusks; algae

Breeding: Up to 140 eggs per clutch; 4–5 clutches per season

Related endangered species: All other sea turtles

Status: IUCN CR; CITES I

The hawksbill, *like other sea turtles, is toothless and slow-moving, with a protective shell and paddlelike limbs.*

beaches has increased, and hatchlings that would naturally head toward the light on the horizon at sea instead make for the shore lights and die from either dehydration or predation. Other threats come from fishing nets and lines. Some countries insist on turtle-excluder devices on the nets, but they are not always used. Turtles are often killed or mutilated by boat propellers. Pollution by sewage, pesticides, and other chemicals causes further problems. The hawksbill is gravely endangered by the destruction of coral reefs from silting and excavation for building purposes. Illegal capture of the turtles is also widespread.

Turtle, Pig-Nosed

Carettochelys insculpta

No one knows how many pig-nosed turtles there are in the wild, but its numbers are thought to be declining. Hunting for turtle meat and habitat destruction are the main threats.

The pig-nosed turtle gets its name from its prominent, piglike snout. Its other names—the New Guinea softshell turtle, New Guinea plateless turtle, or the Fly River turtle—come from its first known location: The species was discovered in 1886 in the Strickland River, a tributary of the Fly River in New Guinea. Today its exact distribution is unknown and needs further investigation—it has been recorded in several major rivers around the Fly River. It does not appear to live in estuaries in Australia.

Like sea turtles, the species is totally aquatic, leaving the water only to lay eggs. In keeping with its lifestyle, its limbs are ideally shaped to provide propulsion in water, resembling the flippers of sea turtles. The pig-nosed turtle is omnivorous (feeding on both animal and vegetable substances), although fruit, leaves, and flowers from overhanging riverbank vegetation form the greater part of its diet. The diet varies with the location; in New Guinea mangrove seeds are a main food.

Decline in Numbers

Numbers of pig-nosed turtles in the wild are difficult to estimate, since the reptiles often inhabit remote locations. However, populations have been reported as declining in parts of their range: Australia has put the pig-nosed turtle on the protected species list, and export is banned by law.

The reptile is not protected in New Guinea and is still considered a delicacy by local people in all parts of its range. Controlling the exploitation of the pig-nosed turtle in New Guinea is difficult because of its traditional importance in the diet. In Australia Aboriginal people are allowed to exploit native fauna in accordance with their traditional hunting lifestyle, but the pig-nosed turtle is otherwise protected at state and national levels.

Traditional methods of capturing turtles have changed. Formerly they were speared or grabbed in the water. Nowadays fishing lines are more commonly used. In New Guinea motor boats have made rivers more accessible to hunters, leading to bigger catches.

A closed season has been suggested, during which all hunting of pig-nosed turtles would stop. Such a measure could help turtle populations recover from losses sustained through hunting. However, a nonhunting period would be difficult to implement; legal bans on capturing turtles would no doubt be

---

DATA PANEL

Pig-nosed turtle (New Guinea softshell turtle, Fly River turtle)

Carettochelys insculpta

Family: Carettochelyidae

World population: Unknown

Distribution: Northern Australia, Irian Jaya, and southern New Guinea

Habitat: Rivers, estuaries (not in Australia), lagoons, and swamps

Size: Length: 22 in (56 cm). Weight: 47 lb (22 kg)

Form: Adults have gray to gray-brown carapace (bony shield); creamy-yellow plastron (lower shell). Carapace is smooth, with raised keel (projection) at rear covered with leathery skin. Hatchlings and juveniles have light radiating marks, a pale streak behind each eye, and white along jaws; shell markings fade with age

Diet: Fruit, leaves, flowers, mollusks, crustaceans, and aquatic insects

Breeding: Clutches of up to 40 eggs laid and buried high in river banks during the dry season

Related endangered species: None

Status: IUCN VU; not listed by CITES

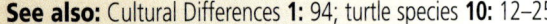

See also: Cultural Differences 1: 94; turtle species 10: 12–25

TURTLE, PIG-NOSED

resisted or ignored. The answer may lie in persuasion; the turtles are valuable to the local people, and conservation lies in sustainable harvesting.

Some places where pig-nosed turtles are found have been turned into wildlife sanctuaries, but regulations are often difficult to police. In addition, habitat destruction is not fully controlled outside national parks. Even inside Kakadu National Park in Australia much of the riverbank was destroyed by water buffalo wallowing in the mud until a control program was started. The turtle is heavily reliant on riverbanks for both food and nesting sites, so anything that destroys the banks threatens the turtle's existence.

Many human activities have also affected pig-nosed turtle habitat. Mangrove clearance, forestry, and mining—particularly where chemical extraction is used—can destroy river banks. There is also the risk that the rivers will become polluted or choked with silt. In addition, increased demand for water from industry can result in a lowering of the water table, making the turtles' haunts too shallow.

The pig-nosed turtle *has a smooth carapace (bony shield). Unlike in many other turtles, the shield is covered with a leathery skin rather than hard plates.*

Mixed Success with Captive Specimens

It is unusual to find pig-nosed turtles in the United States or British pet trade. The turtle's large size and susceptibility to skin diseases may discourage potential keepers. Unless the water in which the turtles are kept is absolutely clean, captive specimens are at risk from infection. The turtles also have a reputation for being aggressive toward each other in confined quarters. However, a recent report claimed that large numbers are taken for the pet trade for sale in Japan and other countries. The shells command high prices for use in traditional Oriental medicine. Several zoos house collections of the pig-nosed turtle, and a few specimens are in the hands of private collectors. Artificial incubation of eggs has been achieved, suggesting that an adequately funded captive-breeding operation should be possible.

Turtle, Western Swamp

Pseudemydura umbrina

The western swamp turtle was first discovered by European settlers in the 19th century, and a scientific description was written in 1901. The turtle then "disappeared" until 1953. Today only a few specimens survive in the wild; investigations have revealed the existence of just two groups in small swamps on the outskirts of Perth in Western Australia.

It is doubtful whether the western swamp turtle ever had a wide distribution, but the specimens surviving now are restricted to a total area of 556 acres (225 ha). Its numbers declined to about 35 until a recovery plan was formulated in 1992. Such scarcity makes it one of the world's rarest reptiles.

The western swamp turtle is the sole surviving member of its genus (group). Fossil records show that it has hardly changed since the early Miocene period, 23 million years ago. Often called the western swamp tortoise, it is one of Australia's smallest chelonian (turtle) species.

Swamp Life

The turtle's habitat has been disrupted by human settlement that reduced the area of the swamp by drainage and land clearance for agriculture, industry, and building. Extraction of water for human use lowered the water table in the region as well. In addition, predation by ravens, foxes, dogs, and cats has taken its toll on young turtles. The two swamps that form its sole habitat in the wild have now been designated as nature reserves. A further 12.4 acres (5 ha) have since been purchased at one of them.

The swamps are wet in winter and spring, but dry out in the hot summers. During the wet period the turtles spend much time in the water foraging for food. Their coloring provides effective camouflage against the sand and clay soils of their habitat. As the swamps start to dry out, they bury themselves and estivate (pass the time in a state of torpor), remaining dormant until the rains return. The summer can be a hazardous time, particularly for hatchlings. The young are highly vulnerable to predators and can easily become desiccated (dried out) in hot weather.

Species Protection

As a result of the rarity of the western swamp turtle the species was listed by CITES in 1975; Australia had already placed a ban on its export some years earlier,

DATA PANEL

Western swamp turtle (western swamp tortoise)

Pseudemydura umbrina

Family: Chelidae

World population: Two hundred in the wild; 190 in captivity

Distribution: Two small reserves near Perth, Western Australia

Habitat: Swamp with clay and sandy soils, wet in winter, dry in summer

Size: Length: 6 in (15 cm). Weight: male 19.5 oz (555 g); female 14 oz (410 g)

Form: Brown to black shell with yellow patches; head and limbs brown. Feet broad and webbed

Diet: Aquatic insects, small mollusks, crustaceans, tadpoles, and worms

Breeding: Lays 3–5 eggs which hatch in the summer. Each hatchling weighs 0.2–0.24 oz (5–6 g). Mature at 10–15 years of age. Life span up to 50 years

Related endangered species: Mary River turtle (*Elusor macrurus*) EN; Dahl's toad-headed turtle (*Phrynops dahli*) CR; Hoge's sideneck turtle (*P. hogei*) EN

Status: IUCN CR; CITES I

See also: CITES 1: 12; The Role of Zoos 1: 86; turtle species 10: 12–25

TURTLE, WESTERN SWAMP

The ancient western swamp turtle *is still at risk, despite a successful recovery plan that includes habitat regeneration and captive-breeding programs.*

and the turtle is also listed under several wildlife-protection plans. However, it takes more than legal protection to save species. The numbers of turtles have to be increased, the habitat improved, and the danger from predators reduced or eliminated. The turtle's low reproductive rate and the 10 to 15 years it takes to reach maturity inevitably hinder its recovery. Given suitable habitat and conditions, however, it can live to about 50 years and ultimately have a long reproductive life.

The swamp turtle rescue operation began in 1988. Led by representatives from various conservation bodies, universities, and Perth Zoo, a recovery plan was formulated. Captive breeding was central to the plan and has continued at Perth Zoo. Groups of turtles in natural enclosures are on view to stimulate public interest. Beginning with only three laying females in 1989, the number increased to 11 by 1998 in a population that totaled 148. Inevitably, some eggs are damaged, some do not hatch, and hatchlings occasionally die. Nonetheless, by 1998 just over 100 young turtles had been released into the two reserves.

Habitat improvement has included the construction of fox-proof fences, the control of ravens and other predators, as well as experimental replanting of the habitat. A "corridor" allowing the turtles access between the two sites has also been planted. Early in 2000 a third possible translocation or release site was identified, and trial releases were carried out. Voluntary groups have been encouraged to assist in protecting the turtle and its habitat.

Future Prospects

The conservation measures implemented for the western swamp turtle may sound like a success story, but the turtle is still listed as Critically Endangered. Its restricted habitat will only support a certain number of individuals. Part of the recovery plan includes finding more suitable sites. Efforts are also being made to establish a second breeding group in another zoo or establishment in case disease should devastate the group at Perth Zoo or those in the wild. The aim of such precautions is to help ensure that the species will never be lost altogether. Considerable amounts of time, effort, and money have gone into saving the western swamp turtle, but its survival remains precarious in its limited range.

Turtle, Yellow-Blotched Sawback Map

Graptemys flavimaculata

Map turtles are sometimes called "sawbacks" because of the toothlike projections down the center of their shell. Like other map turtles, the yellow-blotched sawback increasingly faces threats of pollution in its river habitat.

Of the 12 or so species of map turtle, seven are in decline. The yellow-blotched sawback has the smallest range, living mainly along the Pascagoula River and the Leaf and Chickasawhay Rivers in Mississippi. Exports of map turtles to Britain, Europe, Japan, and Taiwan rose from 325 in 1985 to 84,546 in 1995. It is not known whether the yellow-blotched was among this number, but it has been taken in the past by private and commercial collectors. Many turtles sold in the trade are said to have been farmed, but it is claimed that adults are taken from the wild to replenish breeding stocks.

When the yellow-blotched sawbacks were placed on the IUCN Endangered Species List as Threatened in 1991, many aspects of their behavior and biology were unknown. However, recent studies are providing more information. In the wild females tend to live on mollusks, while males prefer aquatic plants, insects, and larvae. Females become mature when they are about 5 inches (13 cm) long, males when they are about 2.5 inches (6.5 cm) long. In zoo collections females have produced small clutches of between one and five eggs, sometimes laying two or three clutches in a year. The low breeding rate is a problem for a declining species.

Toxic Rivers

Yellow-blotched sawbacks are adapted to living in clean, slow- to moderate-flowing rivers where they use the sandy river banks and sandbars for nesting. They like to bask, making use of rocks or fallen logs for the activity. Most turtle species will only bask in warm, sunny weather, but the yellow-blotched sawbacks will bask even when temperatures are low or when it is raining; This behavior leaves them vulnerable to being killed by thoughtless people who use them as target practice.

However, today, as in the past, the greatest threat is from habitat alteration and destruction. As human settlement spread, trees along the rivers were felled for timber and the land cleared for building. Turtle nesting and basking sites were lost as sandbars and beaches were excavated to improve navigation. Turtle food was swept away during these activities, and some areas of the river became unsuitable for the

---

DATA PANEL

Yellow-blotched sawback map turtle

Graptemys flavimaculata

Family: Emydidae

World population: Unknown

Distribution: The Pascagoula River system in Mississippi

Habitat: Rivers with slow to medium currents and sandy banks for nesting

Size: Males 2.7–4 in (7–11 cm); females 6–7 in (15–17 cm)

Form: Green-brown shell with yellow blotches; yellow and black stripes on head and limbs; yellowish mark behind each eye; ridge of toothlike projections along back

Diet: Plants and insects

Breeding: Between 1 and 5 eggs per clutch; 2–3 clutches per year

Related endangered species: Barbour's map turtle (*Graptemys barbouri*) LRnt; Cagle's map turtle (*G. caglei*) VU; Escambia map turtle (*G. ernsti*) LRnt; Pascagoula map turtle (*G. gibbonsi*) LRnt; ringed map turtle (*G. oculifera*) EN; Texas map turtle (*G. versa*) LRnt

Status: IUCN EN; not listed by CITES

See also: Drainage and Irrigation 1: 40; Saving the Habitats 1: 88; turtle species 10: 12–23

TURTLE, YELLOW-BLOTCHED SAWBACK MAP

turtles because of their greater depth and increased water flow. Industries sprang up along the rivers and began to dump waste products into the water. They killed off food sources, in turn killing off the turtles.

Storm water drains, as well as the construction of dams, levees (embankments to protect against flooding), and flood walls have so altered the riversides that determining the original natural habitat of the yellow-blotched turtle is virtually impossible. In many areas increased recreational use of the rivers and adjacent banks is also obstructing efforts to improve the habitat. Camper vans and offroad vehicles also cause problems for nesting turtles. Some reserves have been established—notably the Pascagoula River Wildlife Management Area, which covers 37,000 acres (15,000 ha) of state-protected land in Mississippi. However, pollution threats from upstream still put the turtles at risk.

The yellow-blotched sawback map turtle *basks on riverbanks, rocks, and logs, a habit that makes it vulnerable to unscrupulous hunters.*

Protective Measures

The turtle's future lies in habitat protection and improvement, especially the reduction of effluent. The species is now protected at both state and federal levels. In some areas of turtle habitat roads are gated and entry prohibited, but signs are ignored by collectors and others. Protection against collecting and deliberate killing requires persuasion and education.

Captive breeding in zoos and private collections has been successful and could help maintain numbers, as long as this goes hand-in-hand with a conservation program for the turtle's river habitat.

Vanga, Helmet

Euryceros prevostii

Unmistakable in appearance, the helmet vanga lives in a restricted area of one of the world's most threatened habitats, the lowland forests of Madagascar. The continuing destruction of tree cover has led to its classification as Vulnerable.

One of many threatened bird species restricted to the island of Madagascar, the helmet vanga has a top-heavy appearance that is as bizarre as it is beautiful, mostly thanks to a massive, misshapen-looking bill. The distinctive bird is found only on the northern half of the island, in the humid evergreen forests along the east coast from Mantadia north to Tsaratanana. It has been recorded only in primary forest, generally below an altitude of 2,600 feet (800 m), although it has been spotted as low as sea level and as high as 3,300 feet (1,000 m). Wherever the bird has been found, it has proved to be scarce, with a decidedly patchy distribution.

Helmet vangas spend most of their lives in the middle layers of the forest in areas with large, mature trees. They often spend long periods perched like statues on horizontal branches at heights of up to about 20 feet (6 m). Their stillness makes the birds difficult to spot and therefore to census accurately.

At other times they are more noticeable, especially when they take to the air; the whirring of their wings is audible up to 80 feet (25 m) away. Powerful fliers, the birds are particularly conspicuous when foraging for prey, which they snatch with their huge bills from trunks, branches, or the ground. Their diet includes large insects such as beetles and crickets, plus the occasional small frog or lizard. Another clue to their presence is their song—a series of tremulous, flutelike whistling notes, descending in pitch and diminishing in volume—that can often be heard before sunrise.

Helmet vangas are seen alone, in pairs, or in small groups. They are frequently encountered searching for food in mixed-species flocks, or flying in company with other birds—mostly other vangas, but occasionally cuckoo shrikes. The vanga family contains a total of 15 species, and all but one are restricted to Madagascar; the blue vanga is also found on the nearby Comoros Islands. The helmet vanga is instantly distinguishable from its relatives by its massive bill.

Disappearing Forests

Most of the helmet vanga's low-altitude forest habitat has disappeared, and what remains is being cleared at an alarming rate, mostly to make way for subsistence farming. The slash-and-burn techniques the settlers employ not only destroy the complex ecosystem of the primary forest, but also progressively degrade secondary regrowth.

A further problem associated with forest loss is that the remaining areas are becoming increasingly fragmented, splitting up populations of the plants and animals they support. The Malagasy fauna includes about 120 endemic bird species, plus a whole range of other unique wildlife.

In addition to the threat from slash-and-burn agriculture, commercial logging also poses a danger in some areas. If destruction continues at the current pace, almost all the remaining lowland forest will be gone within a few decades.

Priorities

For conservationists one urgent priority is to find out how much space a pair of helmet vangas needs in order to survive. Another is to determine whether the birds can disperse across areas where the forest has been cleared, so that the effects of habitat

---

See also: Categories of Threat **1:** 14; Communities and Ecosystems **1:** 22; National Parks **1:** 92; Asity, Yellow-Bellied **2:** 32

VANGA, HELMET

DATA PANEL

Helmet vanga

Euryceros prevostii

Family: Vangidae

World population: More than 10,000 birds

Distribution: Northeastern Madagascar

Habitat: Primary rain forest, mainly in lowlands, but ranging up to an altitude of 3,300 ft (1,000 m)

Size: Length: 11–12 in (28–31 cm)

Form: Highly distinctive. Massive, pale-blue bill with black cutting edges; upperparts reddish-brown; head, neck, and underparts black with pale-brown stripes on flanks and belly; wings reddish-brown with black flight feathers; tail black except for 2 reddish-brown central feathers; sturdy blue-gray legs and feet. Immature birds have duller dark and pale-brown plumage, with pale-brown bill and brown rather than yellow eyes

Diet: Large insects and invertebrates

Breeding: Nest of moss and woven plant fibers built in fork of low tree or at base of tree-fern leaves; female lays 2–3 red-mottled, pinkish-white eggs

Related endangered species: Van Dam's vanga *(Xenopirostris damii)* EN; red-shouldered vanga *(Calicalicus rufocarpalis)* VU; Bernier's vanga *(Oriolia bernieri)* VU

Status: IUCN VU; not listed by CITES

fragmentation can be more precisely understood. On a positive note the species has been recorded in a number of conservation areas, including three national parks as well as three "classified forests," two "special reserves," and two "strict reserves." These areas offer reasonably good protection for the birds.

The helmet vanga *is one of many species unique to Madagascar. Like much of the island's fauna, its fate is closely tied to that of the remaining forest cover.*

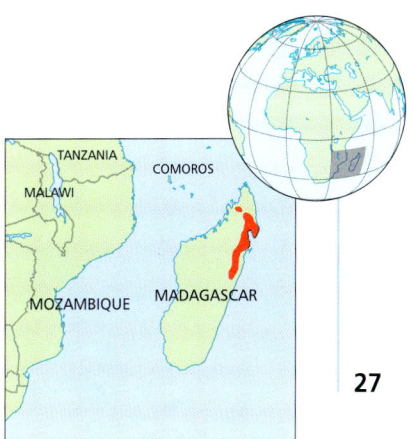

Vicuña

Vicugna vicugna

Prized for centuries for its extremely fine wool, the vicuña has suffered from uncontrolled hunting in recent times. However, its future now seems more secure.

The vicuña lives in small family herds of between five and 10 individuals led by one dominant male. Surplus males may form much larger, loosely organized herds of up to 150 animals. The vicuña is the smallest member of the camel family. Its home is the dry, grassy plains of the high Andean plateau, over 13,000 feet (4,500 m) above sea level.

Vicuñas feed during the day and retreat to a different area to spend the night, using a regular pathway. Unlike other members of the camel family, they need to drink regularly, and they are therefore rarely found far from water. Their territory is marked by communal dung piles, and the animals may range widely over more than 500 acres (200 ha).

Vicuñas are slender animals with a pale-brown coat, reddish-brown coloring on the neck and head, and off-white fur beneath. They are extremely wary and constantly on the lookout for danger. When threatened, they make a loud, high-pitched whistle as a warning call.

Vicuñas can run at speeds of up to 30 miles per hour (50 km/h), despite the high altitude, which would leave most animals breathless. The vicuña is assisted by an exceptionally efficient blood circulatory system. It has a powerful heart, which is larger than in other animals of a similar size, and its blood is capable of absorbing large quantities of oxygen from the air.

A Precious Commodity

Like other mammals that live at altitudes of up to 19,000 feet (5,800 m), the vicuña is exposed to extremely low temperatures, especially at night. As protection it has developed a very long coat of fine wool, which traps a layer of warm air against the skin and reduces the amount of body heat lost.

The vicuña's fine fur has also been highly prized by humans, who use it for making warm clothing. For centuries the native people of the high Andes would round up wild herds of vicuñas and strip them of their wool to spin and weave into a soft cloth that was worn by the nobility. Since the vicuña's wool molted seasonally, it was also possible to drive the herds through dense vegetation and collect the wool scraped off by branches. Such activities rarely resulted in anything more than scaring the animals, so they probably had little effect on the species' abundance.

DATA PANEL

Vicuña

Vicugna vicugna

Family: Camelidae

World population: About 125,000 (in the 1980s)

Distribution: Andes of southern Peru, western Bolivia, northwestern Argentina, and northern Chile above 13,000 ft (4,500 m)

Habitat: Dry, grassy plains at least 13,000 ft (4,500 m) above sea level. Rarely found far from water

Size: Length head/body: 4–6 ft (1.25 m–1.9 m); tail: 6–10 in (15–25 cm); height at shoulder: 2.5–3.5 ft (70–100 cm). Weight: 80–140 lb (35–65 kg)

Form: Slender body and legs. Pale-brown coat; dirty white underneath. Hair forms a long, white mane on the chest

Diet: Almost entirely grass; needs water every day

Breeding: One young per year after 7-month gestation. Life span 15–20 years in the wild

Related endangered species: Wild Bactrian camel (*Camelus bactrianus*)* EN; guanaco (*Lama guanaco*) VU

Status: IUCN LRcd; CITES I

See also: Specialization 1: 28; Luxury Products 1: 46; Camel, Wild Bactiran 3: 24

Originally the total number of vicuñas was probably about 1.5 million; but when the Spaniards invaded Peru in the 16th century, they discovered the luxuriant wool; it soon became fashionable back home in Europe. The Spaniards also brought with them guns, enabling them to shoot vicuñas in large numbers. Skinning the dead animals made it possible to obtain much more of the precious wool in a shorter time. When Spanish rule ended in 1825, the vicuña was made a protected animal. Enforcement of the law was difficult, however, because the value of the wool remained high. Large numbers of vicuña continued to be killed.

The huge demand for vicuña wool continued during the 19th and 20th centuries, and was often satisfied by shooting the animals. Killing tens of thousands of vicuñas every year ensured that they became steadily rarer, and by 1960 there were only about 6,000 left.

The vicuña is a member of the camel family that resembles a llama. The fine wool coat of the animal was evolved as protection against conditions of extreme cold high in the Andes Mountains.

Protection

Although the vicuña population has increased steadily since the 1960s, the animal has disappeared from large parts of its former range, and the remaining herds are widely scattered. About half the vicuña population now lives in the Pampas Galeras National Park in Peru.

Today the vicuña is fully protected, and international trade in its wool is strictly controlled. Only wool shorn from living animals that can then be released can be legally sold. Such measures should ensure that further losses do not occur and that the animal will not become extinct.

Viper, Milos

Macrovipera schweizeri

The Milos viper has been endangered for 14 years, but practically nothing has been done to protect it or its habitat. However, the causes of its decline are well known, and proposals for conservation measures have been made.

The Milos viper occurs only on the islands of Milos, Kimolos, Polyaigos, and Siphnos in the western Cyclades, Greece. Milos, the largest island with an area of 100 square miles (160 sq. km), has the biggest viper population, but suitable habitat has been deteriorating for more than 15 years. The viper's preferred habitat is rocky hillsides with small trees and bushes interspersed with open areas. Much of Kimolos is used for agriculture; it is arid and has little suitable habitat. Polyaigos contains some good areas of habitat since it is not disturbed by people. Siphnos is also used for agriculture. Its viper population has not yet been fully surveyed.

Adult Milos vipers feed mainly on birds, and their young feed on lizards; both avoid areas of dense vegetation, as do their prey. The islands are staging posts for many migratory birds in spring and fall, and some stay there to breed. The vipers are frequent visitors to the watercourses where the birds gather to drink. Although mainly a terrestrial species, the viper is often seen in bushes sheltering from the sun and waiting to ambush birds. Its activity patterns are dictated by the weather. In hot weather it is active mainly at night; in cooler weather it is active during the day. Winter is spent in hibernation, but on mild days the vipers come out to bask.

One unusual feature of the Milos viper is that it lays eggs; other European vipers are livebearers (give birth to live young). Female vipers lay eggs only every other year; breeding may not take place at all if the spring has been cold and they have not fed well. In captivity clutches of up to 10 eggs have been recorded. Eggs and young are eaten by predators such as rats and feral (wild) cats or destroyed by human activity. The cats also kill adult vipers.

Balancing Act

Milos has a population of fewer than 5,000 people concentrated mostly in the eastern corner of the island. The vipers live on the sparsely populated, more mountainous west. Other islands have fewer people. The current viper population on Milos is estimated at 2,500; Polyaigos and Kimolos each have between 600 and 900. This may sound a lot, but unless they can maintain a balance between births and deaths, they will become extinct. Habitat destruction has been ongoing on Milos for several years. Quarrying for minerals and cement production has laid waste much of the suitable viper

DATA PANEL

Milos viper (Cyclades blunt-nosed viper)

Macrovipera schweizeri

Family: Viperidae

World population: About 4,300

Distribution: Western Cyclades islands, Greece

Habitat: Mostly rocky areas with open spaces between bushes

Size: Length: 30 in (75 cm)

Form: Heavy-bodied snake; 2 hollow fangs on short maxilla (upper jaw); red-brown blotches on lighter background

Diet: Birds and lizards

Breeding: Between 8 and 10 eggs laid every other year

Related endangered species: Several species of viper in Europe and Asia, including Latifi's viper *(Vipera latifi)* VU of Iran and mountain viper *(V. albizona)* EN of Turkey

Status: IUCN CR; not listed by CITES

See also: Tourism 1: 42; Research 1: 84; Snake, Leopard 9: 12

The Milos viper's *venom is quite strong, but few people are bitten, and no fatalities have been recorded.*

habitat in the west. The mineral industry on Milos is vital to the national economy, and expansion of the business is planned. Traffic supports the industry, and road kills are becoming more common, particularly at night in summer. Wildlife was not moved before the quarrying began, and spoiled areas have not been restored. Natural restoration takes several years, even if the new growth is not grazed; overgrazing by sheep and goats is an additional problem in some areas.

Until recently Milos has not been badly affected by tourism, but now tourist numbers have increased, and a second airport is planned. House building and land clearance for agriculture are also changing the viper's habitat. Tourism may prove a mixed blessing, possibly slowing down industrial expansion, but it might also destroy more habitat and increase disturbance. Vipers found near tourist areas might be deliberately eradicated so that they do not deter visitors. Recent surveys have found that vipers have been deliberately killed. Until 1977 trappers could claim 10 drachmas (then about 15 U.S. cents) from the authorities for each viper caught, but in 1981 a presidential decree on wildlife protection outlawed the collection or killing of all wildlife. A cause of decline had been collection by hobbyists and by people intending to sell the vipers. Substantial numbers were taken in the 1980s, but collecting has been reduced in recent years.

In 1985 creation of a biogenetic reserve was recommended after a report by the Societas Europaea Herpetologica (SEH). Another report by the SEH in 1986 proposed greater control of quarrying, the employment of game wardens, and education programs to inform the public and so protect the species. A survey between 1993 and 1997 examined the viper's ecology, population, and threats to its habitat. Recommendations were made, but no action taken. Since then the need for conservation has been pressed at annual meetings, but to no effect. The government seems reluctant to aid the conservation of endangered species. Most of the areas considered for conservation are of archaeological importance and do not contain any viper habitats. However, habitat protection is vital for the future of the Milos viper.

Vireo, Black-Capped

Vireo atricapillus

Adapted to breeding in the sun-scorched territory around the Texas–Mexico border, where regular wildfires once maintained dense, shrubby undergrowth, the black-capped vireo has been dealt a double blow by successful fire prevention and scrub clearance for grazing land and building.

Many wild landscapes are in a permanent state of change. Lowland lakes silt up to become first marshes, then damp woodlands. Mud flats become saltmarsh; sand dunes turn into grassy hills; and dry grassland is colonized by scrub, which protects saplings in a young forest. Such "succession" is relentless, but it can be stopped or even started again from scratch. Storms can strip a dune or wipe out a forest; grazing animals can destroy the scrub. Or the area can be swept by fire.

In some regions fire is such a common event that certain plants have adapted to it, sprouting and taking over when other plants are killed. In northern Mexico and the central southern United States, summer wildfires have traditionally kept the natural juniper woodland in check, stopping the succession to forest and allowing fire-adapted, multistemmed oak and sumac to form low, dense scrub. Rich in insect life and secure nest sites, the scrub is an ideal habitat for many small songbirds, including the black-capped vireo.

Each spring black-capped vireos seek places where the scrub has reached the right density. They nest and breed, feeding their young on caterpillars, other insects, and spiders. At the end of summer they fly to spend the winter in southwestern Mexico, and in spring they return to look for new nesting sites. Unfortunately, in recent years this has become increasingly difficult.

Extinguished

Efficient fire fighting has made wild brushfires much less common throughout the region, and as a result, large areas of the vireo's former range in west-central Oklahoma and north-central and central Texas are now overrun by juniper woodland. In other places, such as the Edwards Plateau west of Austin, Texas,

---

DATA PANEL

Black-capped vireo
Vireo atricapillus

Family: Vireonidae

World population: About 6,000–10,000 birds

Distribution: Breeding range restricted to sites in Oklahoma, Texas, and north-central Mexico. Winters on Pacific coast of Mexico

Habitat: Breeds in low, irregular, dense scrub in the transition zone between grassland and forest. Winters in dry, deciduous scrub and bushy thickets

Size: Length: 5 in (12 cm). Weight: 0.3–0.4 oz (8–10 g)

Form: Small, active songbird with short, moderately stout bill and red eyes. Male has black head with white "spectacles," olive upperparts and flanks, blackish wings with olive edges, and 2 pale-yellow wing bars. Female slightly duller with gray head. Juveniles brown

Diet: In summer gleans insects and spiders from foliage. In winter takes what animals it can find, plus seeds

Breeding: Between April and August clutch of 3–4 eggs laid in a cup nest of grass, leaves, bark, and spider silk built in a low bush; eggs are incubated by both parents and hatch in 13–17 days. Nestlings fed by both parents; fledge at 9–12 days. Both males and females often start second clutches with new mates

Related endangered species: St. Andrew (San Andrés) vireo *(Vireo caribaeus)* CR; Chocó vireo *(V. masteri)* EN

Status: IUCN VU; not listed by CITES

See also: Categories of Threat 1: 14; Natural Disasters 1: 57; Bellbird, Three-Wattled 2: 82; Warbler, Kirtland's 10: 38

goats and other grazing animals have eaten out the scrub and reduced much of the region to dry grassland. Added to this, many areas of apparently unproductive scrub have been plowed. Others have been built over, particularly around Austin. The change of habitat has encouraged the spread of cowbirds, which lay their eggs in the vireo nests (like some cuckoos), often destroying the vireo's young at the same time. In recent years nearly all the black-capped vireo nests on the Edwards Plateau have been taken over in this way, so young vireos have not fledged.

The overall result has been a dramatic decline in vireo habitat and numbers. In the United States they have been reduced to small, scattered populations, and each year more birds disappear, mainly through the destruction of scrub habitat. However, numbers are stable in the far southern part of their historic breeding range, and the birds seem to be safe on their Mexican wintering grounds, so all is not lost.

Saving the Black-Capped Vireo

In 1991 the black-capped vireo was classified in United States law under the Endangered Species Act (1991) as Endangered. In an attempt to improve the bird's status, the United States Fish and Wildlife Service devised a detailed recovery plan. A number of measures were recommended, including protecting existing populations, ensuring at least six populations of 500 to 1,000 pairs in Oklahoma, Texas, and Mexico, and safeguarding the bird's winter habitat.

A new wildlife reserve—the Balcones Canyonlands National Wildlife Refuge—was created near Austin, and it now protects a key population. Other refuges are in the Fort Hood Reserve north of Austin and the Wichita Mountains in Oklahoma. Cowbird-trapping programs are in operation in these reserves.

Conservation of the black-capped vireo is already showing results. An action plan over the species' entire range should stem the declines and ensure the black-capped vireo a future.

Black-capped vireo *numbers are increasing in reserves after a cowbird-trapping program that has reduced the takeover of vireo nests.*

Vulture, Cape Griffon

Gyps coprotheres

Despite increased awareness of the situation and some initiatives aimed at reducing losses, numbers of the magnificent Cape griffon vulture continue to decline.

The Cape griffon vulture is a large, heavy billed bird, well adapted for feeding on carcasses of large animals. The adaptations include a grooved, toothed tongue to aid quick eating, a long, powerful neck for rummaging deep in a carcass, a sparse layer of down covering the head and neck, a large crop (pouch for storing food), and a ruff of dense feathers at the base of the neck for warmth when flying at high altitudes.

Cape griffon vultures are gregarious birds, feeding, bathing, roosting, and breeding together. Unlike most other vultures of southern Africa, they nest and roost on cliffs, a habit that restricts their range. They prefer cliffs made of rock such as sandstone or quartzite. Good sites with many ledges that are inaccessible to predators tend to be scarce, and many have been used by generations of birds. Large colonies contain 500 to 900 breeding pairs, although most are smaller.

Breeding pairs get together to display, rebuild their nests, and mate in March. As a result of the egg's long incubation and the dependence of their young, adults stay within 6 to 60 miles (10 to 100 km) foraging distance of their colonies from March almost to the start of the next breeding cycle. The young take four to six years to reach maturity, wandering as much as 750 miles (1,200 km) from their birthplaces.

Dangers in the Modern World

Although there are still more than 80 colonies of Cape griffons, the species has suffered a decline over the past three generations. There were an estimated 4,000 pairs in 1999, but colonies have disappeared on the edges of the species' range, and the bird is now extinct as a breeder in Swaziland, Zimbabwe, and Namibia. Even in its strongholds of Transvaal (South Africa), Botswana, Lesotho, and neighboring parts of South Africa there are declines at many colonies. The reasons are varied, but all are to do with people.

DATA PANEL

Cape griffon vulture (Cape griffon vulture)

Gyps coprotheres

Family: Accipitridae

World population: About 8,000 birds

Distribution: South Africa, Lesotho, Botswana, and Mozambique; a few nonbreeders in Zimbabwe and Namibia; extinct in Swaziland

Habitat: Savanna and grassland, usually near mountains

Size: Length: 3.3–3.8 ft (1–1.2 m); wingspan: 8.4 ft (2.6 m). Weight: 15.4–24 lb (7–11 kg)

Form: Very large vulture. Dark-brown spots along trailing edges of wing-coverts (feathers covering flight feathers) and dark-brown flight feathers contrast with creamy-buff plumage; head and neck almost naked with bluish skin, apart from ruff of downy white feathers at base of neck; black bill and straw-colored eyes; juvenile has brown eyes and pink neck

Diet: Carcasses of large mammals, both wild and domesticated

Breeding: Breeds in colonies on cliff faces; builds nest platform of sticks lined with grass on open ledges; 1 off-white egg incubated by both parents for about 8 weeks; chick covered in white down; cared for by both parents, fledging in about 5 months

Related endangered species: White-rumped vulture (*Gyps bengalensis*) CR; lappet-faced vulture (*Torgos tracheliotus*) VU; long-billed vulture (*G. indicus*) CR; Eurasian black or cinereous vulture (*Aegypius monachus*) LRnt; red-headed vulture (*Sarcogyps calvus*) LRnt

Status: IUCN VU; CITES II

See also: Superstition 1: 47; Education 1: 94; eagle species 4: 52–57; Kite, Red 6: 6

VULTURE, CAPE GRIFFON

Before people settled in Africa, Cape griffons got a steady supply of food from the corpses of dead grazing mammals left by predators such as lions. A reduction in numbers of both prey and predators has led the vultures to depend on carcasses of domestic livestock, resulting in a unique problem. Carcasses left by predators are torn apart and their bones crushed, leaving small pieces of bone that the parent vultures eat and regurgitate for their nestlings. Livestock carcasses do not contain the small pieces of bone, and the resulting lack of calcium-rich bone in the Cape griffon chick's diet leads to bone abnormalities and may reduce survival rates.

Food supplies are restricted further by farmers who burn or bury livestock carcasses to reduce the risk of disease. There has also been direct persecution by farmers who believe the vultures pose a threat to their livestock, and some birds have drowned after falling into deep water tanks or reservoirs, unable to get out. Vultures also die after feeding on carcasses laced with poison intended for predators such as jackals and dogs. In addition, Cape griffons are, along with other species, hunted for their use in traditional medicine and magic rituals.

Cape griffon vultures are vulnerable when trying to land on electricity poles and they are prone to colliding with power cables. The increasing number of vehicles on the roads also poses threats. Disturbance at their breeding and roosting colonies is caused by hikers, rock-climbers, hang gliders, low-flying aircraft, and even researchers studying them.

Conservation

Conservationists have done much to educate communities about the need to protect and preserve the Cape griffon vulture. A priority is still to increase protection for breeding colonies, eliminate the threat of hunting, and reduce deaths from poisoning and electrocution. Providing carcasses with broken-up bones helps remedy problems with chick-feeding.

Cape griffon vultures, *despite their size and ungainly appearance on the ground, are elegant in the air, gliding in the updraft from cliffs or on thermals for hours.*

Warbler, Aquatic

Acrocephalus paludicola

There is much uncertainty about the status of the aquatic warbler, but there is evidence of considerable declines in its key breeding areas in central and eastern Europe.

The aquatic warbler breeds and winters in marshy habitats, especially sedge-fen mires and on rich floodplains. Its preference for areas that are covered with water makes it a difficult bird to census, the more so since the species is elusive even within such habitats. The only effective way of estimating the size of populations is to count the singing males in spring. Such technicalities may seem unimportant, but they do at least suggest the significant problems that confront conservationists in attempting to answer even the most basic questions about the status of the bird.

Counting the Birds

As a result of the difficulties associated with counting the birds, the European population has been grossly underestimated until the last few years. In 1994 numbers of singing males were thought to be as low as 5,700, but by 1999 a revised estimate suggested that there were between 13,500 and 21,000 singing males. What changed between those years was that extensive surveys found significant new populations. In Belarus, for example, the aquatic warbler was considered possibly extinct in 1994, but recently discovered populations are now estimated at between 7,300 and 13,000 singing males. The story is similar in Ukraine, where only 500 males were estimated in 1997, but surveys in 1998 revealed between 2,400 and 3,400 males. Since so much of the population has been discovered from 1995 onward, information on population trends is naturally limited, making the task of assessing global trends in numbers difficult.

Surveying problems are particularly acute in Russia, where the status of the aquatic warbler is particularly unclear. There are currently a mere 100 to 500 singing males estimated for European Russia, but historical records suggest that there may also be as many as 11,000 in western Siberia. Further information on the birds is urgently needed, but recent searches have failed to track down any birds at all. Without some reliable estimate of the numbers in Siberia and of the threats confronting the birds there, it is difficult to judge the relative importance of other populations in relation to a global total or to assess overall trends for the species as a whole.

DATA PANEL

Aquatic warbler

Acrocephalus paludicola

Family: Sylviidae

World population: Estimated at 27,000–42,000

Distribution: Breeds in Hungary, Poland, Belarus, Ukraine, and Russia, with smaller populations in Germany and Lithuania. Birds regularly occur on passage throughout western Europe and northwestern Africa, apparently wintering in Senegal, Mali, and Ghana

Habitat: During the breeding season and in winter inhabits sedge-fen mires and similar marshy habitats. On migration prefers low stands of sedge and reed near open water

Size: Length: 5 in (13 cm); wingspan: 6.5–7.5 in (16.5–19.5 cm). Weight: 0.5 oz (14 g)

Form: Small, brown warbler with distinctive patterning; snipe-type stripes on head, with broad, yellow-buff supercilium (eyebrow) and crown stripe; black-brown stripes on mantle bordered by 2 broad, yellow-white stripes; otherwise upperparts brown with dark streaking. Pale breast; adults show some streaking on flanks

Diet: Large insects, especially dragonflies, caterpillars, and spiders

Breeding: Nests are built on the ground under dry sedges. Female alone cares for young; mating system varies between promiscuity (mating indiscriminately) and polygyny (the male mating with several females)

Related endangered species: Fifteen *Acrocephalus* warblers are listed, including the streaked reed warbler (*A. sorghophilus*) VU; Manchurian reed warbler (*A. tangorum*) VU; and millerbird (*A. familiaris*) CR

Status: IUCN VU; not listed by CITES

See also: Populations 1: 20; Drainage and Irrigation 1: 40; Warbler, Kirtland's 10: 38

A final problem stems from the fact that there is considerable uncertainty about exactly where the birds winter. The migration route through western Europe and northwestern Africa is fairly well established, but the only wintering records are from Senegal, Mali, and Ghana in western Africa, which can hardly account for the entire population. The scarcity of such records is probably explained by the fact that the birds do not sing in winter, which in view of their general elusiveness and relatively low observer coverage makes them hard to record. The combination of factors means that conservationists have little idea of the threats facing aquatic warblers and their habitats for almost half of each year.

A Story of Decline

Despite all the uncertainty, some facts are known for sure. It is not disputed that there have been large declines in Europe throughout the 20th century. In the last hundred years the aquatic warbler has become extinct as a breeding bird in France, Belgium, the Netherlands, the former West Germany, and what used to be Czechoslovakia and Yugoslavia, as well as in Austria, Italy, and probably Latvia.

We also know that the European populations are continuing to decline because of habitat loss. Since 1970 between 80 and 90 percent of suitable habitat has been destroyed in the three river systems that hold 75 percent of the European population. The decline is mostly the result of drainage for agriculture or for peat extraction, although the damming of floodplains, unfavorable water-management practices, and the canalization of rivers have also played a part.

Four key countries (Belarus, Germany, Hungary, and Poland) protect the warbler in law by actively managing habitat and through systems of nature reserves. The challenge is now to extend such measures to other countries and, most importantly, to find out more about the distribution and numbers of the birds. A true understanding of the species' status can only come about with clearer knowledge of the real figures.

The aquatic warbler
inhabits marshes and fens during the breeding season. It can be surprisingly difficult to spot; in fact, the bird is heard far more often than it is seen.

Warbler, Kirtland's

Dendroica kirtlandii

Kirtland's warbler is one of the rarest birds in North America, and it has been the subject of conservation action for many years. However, new evidence suggests that the answer to the species' problems may lie in the Bahamas rather than, as was thought, its breeding area in Michigan.

Kirtland's warbler breeds mostly in a very small area of Michigan. In 1994 the breeding range was estimated at a mere 7 square miles (18 sq. km), and in 1999 there were only 903 singing males. The status of the bird may appear to be critical, but for Kirtland's warbler this represents a comparatively healthy situation. There were major declines in the breeding population between 1900 and 1920 and between 1961 and 1971. Even after 1971 the population dwindled to all-time lows of 167 singing males in 1974 and 1987. However, since 1987 the population has recovered steadily, reaching 903 singing males in 1999 and then falling slightly to 890 in 2000. The last two figures represented the highest totals ever recorded since surveys began in 1951.

Action in Michigan

The recovery was initially attributed to intensive conservation action on the breeding grounds. Threats to the species' survival have been typically explained as the suppression of forest fires and widespread brood parasitism (takeover of the nest) by brown-headed cowbirds. The warbler's preferred habitat—stands of jack pines at heights of 6.6 to 13 feet (2 to 4 m)—occurs naturally only after extensive fires. The suppression of such fires in Michigan has led to suitable breeding habitat declining by 33 percent since the 1960s. The threat from brown-headed cowbirds is apparent from the fact that 70 percent of Kirtland's warbler nests were parasitized in 1972.

Conservation measures have had some success in addressing these threats. Forest management to replicate the effects of natural fires and create suitable young tree habitat for the warbler has been carried out in several areas, covering 200 square miles (520 sq. km). A trapping program has reduced nest parasitism by brown-headed cowbirds from 70 percent to 3 percent. The species has also been the focus of environmental education and

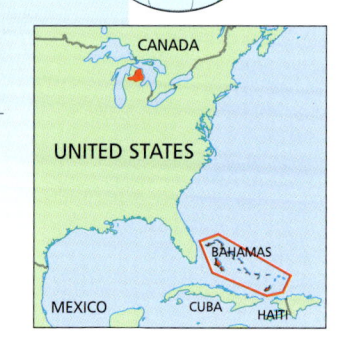

DATA PANEL

Kirtland's warbler

Dendroica kirtlandii

Family: Parulidae

World population: About 890 singing males were counted in 2000, equating to 1,780 birds

Distribution: Breeds in Michigan. Singing males have also been recorded in northern Wisconsin and in Ontario and Quebec, Canada. Winters in the Bahama Islands and the Turks and Caicos Islands

Habitat: Breeds in homogeneous stands of jack pines *Pinus banksiana*. Winters either in Caribbean pine forests or natural and secondary scrub habitats

Size: Length: 6 in (15 cm); wingspan: 8 in (20 cm). Weight: 0.4–0.5 oz (12–16 g)

Form: Large gray-and-yellow warbler. Male blue-gray above with diffuse black streaking on upper back and scapulars ("shoulder" feathers). Black lores (surface of head between eyes and base of the bill) and split white eye-ring. Yellow underparts with black streaking on flanks. Female similar but paler, with brown tinge to mantle and no black lores. Immatures have grayish streaking and spots on throat

Diet: On breeding grounds insects, including sawflies, grasshopper nymphs, moths, and flies. Adults also feed on pine sap and blueberries. In the Bahamas insects and small fruit

Breeding: Nest cup made on ground; 3–6 brown-spotted whitish eggs (usually 4) laid May–June; incubated by female alone for 13–15 days. Fledging in 9 days or more

Related endangered species: Golden-cheeked warbler (*Dendroica chrysoparia*) EN; elfin-woods warbler (*D. angelae*) VU; vitelline warbler (*D. vitellina*) LRnt

Status: IUCN VU; not listed by CITES

See also: Biomes 1: 18; Research 1: 84; Vireo, Black-Capped 10: 32; Warbler, Aquatic 10: 36

ecotourism initiatives in the region—including the now annual Kirtland's Warbler Festival—that draw attention to the plight of the bird and its habitat.

Where Do They Winter?

Although the initiatives have had some success, the species still fails to occupy all the suitable breeding habitat, which suggests that other factors may be holding back population growth. It is well known that the warbler winters in the Bahamas and the Turks and Caicos Islands, but there is debate about which habitat the birds occupy. There have been two studies reviewing the records from these islands, but they have reached different conclusions.

One study shows that the species uses mainly Caribbean pine woods, the other that it occupies natural and secondary scrub. If the species prefers scrub, there is much available habitat within the Bahamas, and threats must be concentrated on its breeding grounds. But if it inhabits Caribbean pine, the threat could be habitat destruction of its wintering grounds.

There is some evidence to support this: The degradation and recovery of the fire-dependent pine ecosystem in the northern Bahamas matches trends in the Kirtland's warbler population over the 20th century. If true, this association is worrying. The current breeding range is about nine times larger than the total area of pine woods, yet virtually all conservation efforts are focused in Michigan. Conservationists urgently need an answer to where the birds winter. Only then can the long-term future of the Kirtland's warbler be guaranteed.

Kirtland's warbler *is a small, active insect eater. It builds its nest on the ground, hidden among tangled vegetation.*

Whale, Blue

Balaenoptera musculus

It took fewer than 50 years of intensive whaling to bring the largest animal the world has ever known to the brink of extinction. Whether the remaining blue whale population is large enough to make a recovery remains to be seen.

Humans have hunted whales for well over a thousand years, but it was not until the 1860s that new technology allowed whalers to hunt the largest species of all. Whaling in the late 19th century was difficult and dangerous; but by targeting the largest of the great whales, the whalers could reap enormous profits. Hunting for blue whales began in the North Atlantic; but as the populations there declined, attention turned to other oceans. In the early 1900s 90 percent of the world's quarter of a million blue whales lived in the Southern Hemisphere. When these rich hunting grounds were discovered, whaling stations were established on small islands in the Southern Ocean. At first whalers had to operate close to coastal factories and could not fully exploit the whales that remained far from land. However, with the arrival of the first factory ships in the mid-1920s, they could process their kills on the open ocean, and consequently the death toll soared.

By 1960 it became obvious that the blue whale was heading for extinction, but it was still several years before an international ban on commercial whaling was agreed. The intervening years cost the species several thousand more lives, bringing the total death toll to 350,000 in fewer than 70 years.

After the killing stopped there were high hopes that the blue whales would recover. By the mid-1980s there was evidence of a slight increase in numbers, and surveys showed that pregnancy rates had doubled, from about 25 percent in 1930 to over

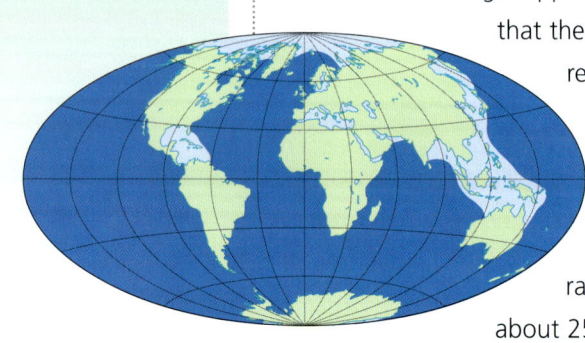

DATA PANEL

Blue whale (great northern rorqual, sulphur-bottom)

Balaenoptera musculus

Family: Balaenidae

World population: About 3,500

Distribution: Three separate populations: in the North Atlantic, North Pacific, and Southern Ocean respectively; the whales migrate annually between polar and tropical waters

Habitat: Deep oceans

Size: Length: 79–89 ft (24–27 m); occasionally up to 110 ft (33 m); females larger than males. Weight: 110–132 tons (100–120 tonnes); occasionally up to 209 tons (190 tonnes)

Form: Vast, streamlined body; bluish-gray skin with pale markings and white to yellow underside. Rounded snout; deep throat furrows; 2 blowholes with large splashguard; small dorsal fin set well back on body

Diet: Krill (planktonic shrimps) and other crustaceans

Breeding: Single young born after gestation of 10–12 months; weaned at 7–8 months; mature at 10 years. May live up to 110 years

Related endangered species: Fin whale (*Balaenoptera physalus*)* EN; sei whale (*B. borealis*)* EN; minke whale (*B. acutorostrata*)* LRnt

Status: IUCN EN, though some populations listed as VU or LRcd; CITES I

See also: Hunting 1: 42; Populations 1: 20; whale species 10: 42–59

Blue whales *dive for about 10 to 20 minutes at a time before surfacing to take a dozen or so breaths, sending a spout of spray as high as 30 feet (9 m) into the air with each exhalation.*

50 percent. The total world population was estimated at the time at about 12,000 individuals.

However, the early optimism proved premature. Estimates vary as to how many blue whales there now are, but recent statistics put the world population as low as 3,500. It is doubtful whether so few whales represent a viable population.

Impoverished Oceans

The main reason why the whales' numbers have not recovered is simply because their habitat has altered for the worse. The annual catch of krill (planktonic shrimps) taken by the world's fisheries rose from practically nothing in the early 20th century to over 500,000 tons (455,000 tonnes) in 1986. An average blue whale needs about 7,700 pounds (3,500 kg) of krill a day to sustain its great bulk. Now that krill is fished on such a huge scale, there may simply not be enough food to meet the whales' requirements.

The seas are also more polluted now, and not just with chemicals. Toxins and biologically active substances that have been shown to damage other marine wildlife almost certainly affect large whales. In addition, whales are affected by noise pollution and alterations in local currents brought about by coastal developments. Large inland projects can also result in thousands of tons of silt being dumped at sea, making the water unsuitable for both whales and their food.

Whale, Fin

Balaenoptera physalus

Decades of overhunting decimated populations of the world's second-largest whale. Although protected now, the species is not recovering as well as predicted.

The fin whale is a near relative of the blue whale and comes a close second to its cousin in length, although it is not nearly as heavy as the blue. In other respects the two species are remarkably similar; hybrid fin-blue whales have even been identified by DNA analysis, much to the surprise of scientists. It may be that the two species have started interbreeding because of the scarcity of mates of the same species.

Fin whales are generally creatures of the open ocean and are rarely seen close to shore. They are also among the fastest-swimming whales and as a result were not widely hunted until the invention of steam-powered ships in the 1860s. The first commercial fin whale hunters were Norwegians, who began hunting in the North Atlantic. In 1868 the invention of the exploding harpoon made it much easier and less dangerous to kill large whales. Even so, the rate of killing in the North Atlantic was relatively low—at least by later standards—since each whale that was caught had to be tied to the side of the ship before it could be brought back to shore to be butchered.

Fatal Discovery

The real decline of the fin whale began after the discovery of vast herds of large whales that gathered each summer in the Southern Ocean. At the start of the 20th century the herds included up to a quarter of a million blue whales and well over half a million fin whales—about four-fifths of the world population. In the 1920s the invention of factory ships with ramps for loading whale carcasses on board meant that it was no longer necessary to bring every whale ashore. The ships stayed at sea for weeks or months on end, processing the meat, oil, bones, and baleen of whale after whale. To begin with, the fin whale was not the target of choice for most whalers; but as the population of blue whales dwindled in the 1930s, more fin whales were taken. Apart from a brief respite during World War II, the catch increased steadily, reaching a peak of about 30,000 a year between 1952 and 1962.

By 1960 the southern population had fallen to just over 100,000. Despite the dramatic decline it was not until the late 1960s that the International Whaling Commission (IWC) succeeded in significantly reducing the kill. Eventually, in 1986 the IWC established a complete ban on the killing of fin whales for commercial purposes. By that time, however, there were fewer than 15,000 individuals remaining in the whole of the Southern Hemisphere.

Although a few countries persist in killing a number of fin whales each year for "scientific purposes," the species is now fairly well protected.

See also: Life Strategies 1: 24; Hunting 1: 42; whale species 10: 40–59

However, in the 30 years since the decline of the fin whaling industry, the southern population of fin whales has not recovered as well as had been hoped. The main problem is that the teeming swarms of krill on which the whales feed are themselves being depleted by humans and by animals such as squid, seals, penguins, and various seabirds. These species increased in number as the whales declined, and now the ocean simply cannot support the number of whales it once did.

The fin whale faces other problems, too. Chemical contamination, noise pollution, and global warming are altering the nature of its habitat. The fortunes of the fin whale, as of other species, are inextricably linked to the health of the oceans as a whole.

Fin whales are migratory; both northern and southern populations spend their summers feeding in cold temperate and polar waters and migrate to warmer latitudes to breed in the winter. Yet individuals from the two populations never meet because the seasons in the different hemispheres are at opposite times of the year.

DATA PANEL

Fin whale (finback, finner, herring whale, common rorqual, razorback)

Balaenoptera physalus

Family: Balaenidae

World population: About 78,000

Distribution: Three populations: in the North Atlantic, North Pacific, and Southern Ocean respectively

Habitat: Deep temperate and polar oceans

Size: Length: 59–73 ft (18–22 m), occasionally up to 86 ft (27 m); females about 10% bigger than males. Weight: 33–88 tons (30–80 tonnes)

Form: Long, slim-bodied whale with pointed snout; skin smooth and gray-black; right side of head white, left side dark; prominent dorsal fin placed well back on body

Diet: Fish, krill, and other crustaceans

Breeding: Up to 6 fetuses develop at once but only 1 young is successfully reared; born after gestation of 11–11.5 months; weaned at 6–7 months; mature at 6–11 years. May live more than 100 years

Related endangered species: Blue whale *(Balaenoptera musculus)** EN; sei whale *(B. borealis)** EN; minke whale *(B. acutorostrata)** LRnt

Status: IUCN EN; CITES I

Whale, Gray

Eschrichtius robustus

One of the most charismatic and best known of all cetaceans (whales and dolphins), the gray whale was one of the first of its kind to receive real protection from whalers. Today the species faces other problems, namely, increasing coastal disturbance and pollution.

Gray whales may have done more to raise the profile of whales than any other large species. This is mainly because of their coastal habitat; they feed, breed, and migrate in shallow water, and so can be watched from the shore. There is much for spectators to admire, for grays are one of the most active whale species, regularly indulging in antics such as breaching (leaping out of the water), lobtailing (smacking the water's surface noisily with the tail), and spy-hopping (bobbing upright with the head out of the water to look around). The whales seem to relish playing in the surf off gently sloping coasts and frequently beach for hours, only to refloat on the next tide, to the relief of concerned onlookers. Grays are widely recognized as among the friendliest whales as well as the easiest to watch. They are curious and approach boatloads of whale-watchers so readily that at times it is hard to know who is watching whom!

However, relations between people and gray whales have not always been so good. In whaling circles the gray earned the nickname of "devilfish" because mothers would often charge at whaling boats in desperate attempts to protect their calves. The gray whale was in fact one of the first large whales to be targeted by human hunters, since its liking for shallow inshore waters meant that it could be easily trapped and killed. There is evidence that aboriginal peoples on both sides of the North Pacific were successfully hunting them as early as 2,000 years ago.

Slow Swimmers

The gray whale also has the disadvantage of being a slow swimmer, which meant that in the 17th and 18th centuries it could be hunted from sailing ships. Whalers from Norway, Britain, and the United States hunted the gray whales of the North Atlantic to extinction toward the end of the 18th century. A century later the breeding populations on both sides of the Pacific seemed to have disappeared as well.

DATA PANEL

Gray whale (California gray whale, devilfish, scrag whale)

Eschrichtius robustus

Family: Eschrichtidae

World population: About 27,000

Distribution: Eastern and western regions of the North Pacific

Habitat: Shallow coastal waters

Size: Length: 40–50 ft (12–15 m); females larger than males. Weight: 17–39 tons (15–35 tonnes)

Form: Robust-bodied animal with relatively small, narrow head; skin mottled dark gray, often with extensive patches of encrusting barnacles and algae. There is no dorsal fin, but a row of bumpy "knuckles" extends from the hump to the large tail fluke; throat has just 2 or 3 furrows

Diet: Bottom-dwelling organisms, especially crustaceans

Breeding: Single young born in warm waters in winter after 13-month gestation; weaned at 7 months; mature at about 8 years. May live up to 70 years

Related endangered species: No close relatives, but many other whales are threatened

Status: IUCN LRcd; CITES I

See also: Populations 1: 20; CITES 1: 12; whale species 10: 40–59

By the time deep-sea whaling got underway in the late 19th century, the gray whale had already become rare, and attention had shifted to the more lucrative blue and fin whales. Fewer than 1,200 gray whales were caught between 1921 and 1947, at which time an international ban on commercial hunting of this species was put in place. Thanks largely to the ban, the eastern Pacific population of gray whales now numbers some 26,000 individuals, and their recovery has been complete enough to allow the resumption of small-scale whaling by such aboriginal peoples as the Inuit and the Makah tribe of Washington State.

Modern Threats

So-called "traditional" hunts are still controversial, but probably less damaging than other more modern threats to the gray whale population. For example, many whales die every year after becoming entangled in fishing nets, and grays are also affected by chemical pollution, coastal development, and noise. The busy shipping lanes of the West Coast of the United States

Gray whales *can reach a length of 50 feet (15 m). Their skin is mottled and heavily parasitized; barnacles and whale lice live on it. Young grays are smooth in comparison to the elders, as this picture of a mother and her calf shows.*

mean that on migration most gray whales now choose to travel up to 40 miles (65 km) offshore, while in earlier times the whole population often used to pass within 2 miles (3 km) of the coast.

On the other side of the Pacific there has been no such recovery, and a gray whale sighting close to Japanese shores is rare enough to be newsworthy. The remaining western Pacific population probably numbers only a few hundred individuals. As a whole, the species retains its IUCN Endangered status, even though the eastern Pacific population is now considered secure but Conservation Dependent.

Whale, Humpback

Megaptera novaeangliae

Having faced extinction in the 1960s, the humpback whale has responded well to protection. As long as the ban on whaling stays in place, it is set to become one of the world's best conservation success stories.

Over the past two or three decades the humpback whale has become something of a wildlife celebrity. It is one of the most widely recognized large whales, and its acrobatic displays, inquisitive personality, and intricate and varied songs have earned it a place in the affections of humans.

But the story has not always been a positive one. Prior to the worldwide ban on whaling in the mid-1980s the humpback had been one of the most widely hunted species and came within a whisker of extinction. A relatively slow-swimming animal, the humpback made an easy target, especially when large herds gathered in shallow coastal waters to breed. They were easy to approach, often coming close to whaling boats out of curiosity and discovering the danger too late. Commercial hunting of humpbacks dates back over 300 years, and before that many aboriginal peoples killed humpbacks for subsistence using simple hand-made weapons. These traditional hunts are still permitted, but the quotas are very low and are reviewed from year to year.

A Booming Industry

Now the killing has all but ceased, but there is still money to be made from humpbacks. Many former whaling communities have developed into ecotourism resorts specializing in whalewatching. There is little doubt that the profits from this rapidly expanding industry have reduced the pressure to resume hunting and played a significant part in the species' recovery. Nevertheless, it is important that the whales are not disturbed by excessive pressure from boatloads of excited tourists, especially during the breeding season.

Humpback Behavior

Humpbacks are among the most vocal of whales and their long, complex songs, hauntingly beautiful to the human ear, feature in popular music, classical compositions, and relaxation therapies. The songs, which last anything up to half an hour, vary slightly from place to place—a bit like human dialects—and they change gradually over time as whales pick up variations from each other. Like birdsong, these sounds are generally used by solitary males and are thought to attract females and let other whales know who is around.

Other fascinating aspects of humpback behavior include their feeding techniques. They generally filter feed in a similar manner to other baleen whales, but have also developed some rather special techniques of their own. One of the most impressive is bubble-netting, whereby one or more whales swims in an upward spiral around a shoal of fish, releasing a steady stream of bubbles that form a dense curtain through which the fish will not swim. The fish bunch closer together and move upward to escape the circling whales; but once they reach the surface, they are trapped, and the whales move in, swallowing huge mouthfuls of fish and water. The furrows in the whale's throat allow it to expand so that it can gulp in hundreds of densely shoaling fish at a time.

The nets used by fishing crews are curtains of death for whales as well as fish. Once entangled in the mesh, a humpback is usually doomed. Along with disturbance from boats, these nets are one of the major threats to humpback whales today.

See also: Organizations 1: 10; Hunting 1: 42; What Is a Mammal? 1: 60; whale species 10: 40–59

WHALE, HUMPBACK

The humpback whale *is one of the most popular species for whale-watchers; it is large, curious about boats, and often apparently full of high spirits. For an ever-increasing number of people an encounter with whales is the highlight of a vacation if not the experience a lifetime.*

DATA PANEL

Humpback whale (humpwhale, hunchbacked whale)

Megaptera novaeangliae

Family: Balaenopteridae

World population: 30,000

Distribution: Global

Habitat: Mostly deep ocean but ventures into shallower waters to breed

Size: Length head/body: 36–46 ft (11–14 m); occasionally up to 50 ft (15 m); female slightly larger than male. Weight: 33 tons (30 tonnes)

Form: Large dark-gray to black baleen whale with tapering, knobby head; pectoral fins very long (one-third body length) and patterned with irregular and unique white markings; tail flukes (lobes) also large and often marked with white

Diet: Small shoaling fish and crustaceans

Breeding: Single young born in tropics during temperate winter after 11-month gestation, usually every other year; weaned at 11 months; mature at 4–6 years. May live up to 77 years

Related endangered species: Blue whale *(Balaenoptera musculus)** EN; fin whale *(B. physalus)** EN; sei whale *(B. borealis)** EN; minke whale *(B. acutorostrata)** LRnt

Status: IUCN VU; CITES I

Whale, Killer

Orcinus orca

Killer whales—or orcas as they are less emotively known—are not man-eaters by nature. In the vast majority of encounters with humans it has been the people that have done the killing.

Killer whales are the world's largest predators of mammals and birds. They are known to hunt seabirds, seals, sea lions, and also other whales and dolphins, including large baleen whales. The bulk of their food, however, is made up of fish and squid.

Killer whales have never been a principal catch for whalers, but whaling crews whose main target was the larger baleen whales would also take orcas if they happened to come across them. Hunting reached a peak during the winter of 1979 to 1980, when whalers from the Soviet Union alone killed over 900 orcas in the Southern Ocean.

Killer whales and fishermen have always competed for similar fish, such as salmon and cod. At times humans have benefited from the whales' efforts: Fishermen would sometimes drop nets to scoop up the dense shoals of fish rounded up by killer whales. More frequently, however, the rewards have gone the other way. Orcas have been known to leap in and out of purse seine nets (large nets used to enclose a school of fish) to steal the contents. They can also swim alongside drift nets (nets supported by floats or a drifter), biting off the body of every trapped fish and leaving irate fishermen to haul up nets full of heads. A killer whale eats between 2.5 and 5 percent of its body weight each day, a quantity of fish that some fisheries are simply not willing to give up. As a result, orcas have sometimes been killed in order to protect fish stocks. One controversial incident took place in

DATA PANEL

Killer whale (orca)

Orcinus orca

Family: Delphinidae

World population: At least 100,000

Distribution: Worldwide

Habitat: Seas and oceans; generally in deep water, but most often seen close to shore

Size: Length: 18–33 ft (5.5–10 m); males can be almost twice as long as females. Weight: 3–10 tons (2.5–9 tonnes)

Form: Robust, jet-black body, with bright white chin, belly, and eye patch; gray saddle; dorsal fin tall, especially in males; pectoral fins large and paddle shaped

Diet: Fish, squid, seals, sea lions, turtles, and seabirds; also small whales and dolphins

Breeding: Single young born at any time of year after 17-month gestation; weaned at 14–18 months; mature at 12–16 years. Males may live up to 60 years, females to 90 years

Related endangered species: Hector's dolphin (*Cephalorhynchus hectori*) VU; short-finned pilot whale (*Globicephala macrorhynchus*) LRcd; pantropical spotted dolphin (*Stenella attenuata*) LRcd; striped dolphin (*S. coeruleoalba*) LRcd

Status: IUCN LRcd; CITES II

See also: Exploitation of Live Animals 1: 49; Pesticides 1: 51; whale species 10: 40–59

the mid-1950s, when the United States Navy, acting at the request of the Icelandic government, allegedly used machine guns to wipe out killer whales from selected fishing areas.

Orcas on Display

Several hundred killer whales have been captured alive and taken to marine parks and dolphinaria, where they are trained to perform a variety of tricks. Unpopular though the exploitation of captive whales is now, there is little doubt that such exhibitions have worked wonders for the killer whale's image, revealing its unexpectedly playful nature. The species has grown in public affection, causing many people to question the morality of hunting orcas or indeed of keeping them in captivity.

One whale, a male called Keiko, has come to symbolize the whole issue of cetaceans in captivity.

A starring role in the feature film *Free Willy* made Keiko world-famous; and when news of his poor treatment in captivity reached the media, there were widespread calls for his rehabilitation and release. The process has been a lengthy one, but Keiko is now back in his native Icelandic waters, living in a large sea pen and awaiting the day when he will be allowed to rejoin his relatives in the wild.

Even when not subjected to direct persecution, killer whales are at risk. Being at the top of the marine food chain means that they are exposed to heavy accumulations of chemical contaminants in the flesh of their prey. Pesticides, fertilizers, sewage, and industrial effluents contain potentially harmful compounds, although no one yet knows just how damaging they might be.

Killer whales *can be individually recognized from differences in the shape and markings of the dorsal fin and back.*

Whale, Minke

Balaenoptera acutorostrata

Saved by a worldwide ban on whaling in the 1980s, the minke whale is more numerous than its larger cousins. However, if some nations were to resume commercial whaling, the minke would be top of their list to hunt.

Despite being the smallest of the rorqual (filter-feeding whalebone) whales, the average minke weighs in at 9 tons (8 tonnes). A large proportion of its bulk is meat and blubber, products for which it has been hunted on a small scale for hundreds of years. Until relatively recently minkes had escaped the wholesale slaughter that nearly wiped out their larger cousins. For several decades the overexploitation of blue and fin whales in the Southern Ocean actually benefited the minke, because it reduced the amount of competition for food.

The minke whale has a thick layer of blubber that enables it to venture farther into the icy waters of the Arctic and Antarctic than any of its close relatives. Minkes eat enough during the summer to last them through the winter, when they migrate to warmer waters and do not feed.

In large whales the time at which an individual reaches sexual maturity is determined more by size than age. When food is plentiful—as it was for southern minkes between the 1950s and 1970s—young whales grow much faster and mature more quickly. In 1944 an average minke first bred at about 13 years of age. By the early 1980s most minkes were sexually mature after only six years. Not surprisingly, the population boomed, increasing by 800 percent in the period from 1930 to 1979.

Commercial Whaling

By the early 1970s factory whaling ships had all but wiped out the largest species of rorqual whale and had begun to hunt minkes. Although much smaller than blue and fin whales, and so less valuable, minkes were by that time far more numerous and much easier to catch. Minkes are more curious than other large whales and readily approach ships. Many paid dearly for their curiosity: The minke death toll peaked at over 12,000 a year by 1977. At this time the scale of the slaughter prompted growing public outrage. The

---

DATA PANEL

Minke whale

Balaenoptera acutorostrata

Family: Balaenopteridae

World population: 825,000

Distribution: Global

Habitat: Deep water, but seldom more than 100 miles (160 km) from land

Size: Length: 26–36 ft (8–11 m); female slightly larger than male. Weight: 7–11 tons (6–10 tonnes)

Form: Slim whale with markedly triangular head; skin dark gray above, fading to almost white on belly; often has pale chevron-shaped patch around pectoral fin

Diet: Antarctic populations eat mostly krill (planktonic shrimps); northern minkes also consume squid and small fish

Breeding: Single calf born after gestation of 10–11 months; weaned at 5 months; mature at 6 years. Life span up to 60 years

Related endangered species: Blue whale *(Balaenoptera musculus)** EN; fin whale *(B. physalus)** EN; sei whale *(B. borealis)** EN; humpback whale *(Megaptera novaeangliae)** VU

Status: IUCN LRnt; CITES I

See also: What Is a Species? **1:** 26; Hunting **1:** 42; whale species **10:** 40–59

minkes were saved by the international ban on whaling that was put in place in 1985. To begin with, Japan and Norway ignored the ban, protesting that minkes were not endangered. However, the fact that minke whales were protected before the species reached crisis point is the main reason that they are relatively secure today.

About 1,000 minke whales are still killed each year; some as part of legal traditional hunts by indigenous peoples, others for "scientific" purposes. International regulations allow a number of whales to be killed each year for research, a loophole that has been exploited by some whaling nations, principally Japan. There is no doubt that the market for whale parts is alive and well, and meat from the "scientific" quota of minke whales often ends up on sale to the Japanese public. The northwestern Pacific population of minke whales is already the smallest, with just 25,000 individuals. There is little doubt in the minds of most conservationists that if commercial whaling were allowed to begin again, it would get out of hand, since it is difficult to enforce quotas.

Mini Minkes

Whaling is not the only subject of minke whale debate. For many years scientists have recognized the existence of a different type of minke living in the Southern Hemisphere. Known as dwarf minkes, the whales rarely grow longer than 23 feet (7 m) and have a distinctive white patch extending from the base of the pectoral fins onto the flank. Some scientists recognize the southern form as a separate species, but it may only be a local variety, and a full comparative study has yet to be made.

Whale, Northern Right

Eubalaena glacialis

Even after 60 years of international protection, the northern right whale is battling against extinction. Intensive conservation is needed to halt the damage inflicted by 1,000 years of unregulated hunting.

Northern right whales are the most endangered of all the large whales, and the species' name describes the main reason: For centuries the animal was known to whalers as the "right whale" to hunt. It lived close to the shore, fed near the surface, was easy to approach by boat, and floated when it was dead. Furthermore, a single carcass could yield several hundred barrels of oil—even more than the blue whale—and its long, thin baleen (whalebone) plates were considered to be of the finest quality.

European right whales were hunted to virtual extinction by the early 18th century. By then the American whaling industry was well established and had already depleted the western Atlantic stocks. In the mid-19th century American whalers could make $10,000 profit on a single carcass—equivalent to a third of a million dollars in today's terms. With such vast fortunes to be made, the whalers turned their attention to the right whales of the eastern North Pacific. In the space of about 10 years these had become as rare as their Atlantic counterparts.

Death by Misadventure

Although the northern right whale has been protected by international agreement since 1937, the population has barely increased, and many whales still die needlessly. Since 1970 there have been 16 confirmed right whale fatalities as a result of boats accidentally plowing into whales feeding in busy shipping lanes. The actual figure is likely to be higher, since shipping accidents frequently involve collisions with "unidentified submerged objects," and a wounded whale may travel some distance before dying alone and unrecorded. Whales are also often killed or injured in accidents involving fishing nets and tackle.

End of the Line

The average birthrate of right whales in the northeastern Atlantic has dropped from one young born per female every three years in the 1980s to one birth every

---

DATA PANEL

Northern right whale

Eubalaena glacialis

Family: Balaenidae

World population: About 320

Distribution: Coastal regions of North Atlantic. North Pacific right whales may be a different species

Habitat: Temperate ocean

Size: Length: 40–55 ft (13.6–18 m); females slightly larger than males. Weight: 22–112 tons (20–102 tonnes)

Form: Large black whale with long, tapering body; no dorsal fin; huge mouth with arched upper jaw; head with barnacle-encrusted skin callouses

Diet: Planktonic crustaceans

Breeding: Single calf born every 2–5 years after 13-month gestation; season of birth varies with regions; weaned at 7 months; mature at 9 years. Life span unknown but probably comparable with other large whales—at least 30 years

Related endangered species: Southern right whale *(Eubalaena australis)* LRcd

Status: IUCN EN; CITES I

See also: Hunting 1: 42; Inbreeding and Interbreeding 1: 56; whale species 10: 40–59

The northern right whale *lacks a dorsal (back) fin and has barnacle-encrusted skin callouses on its head.*

five years a decade later. Pollution may be one reason: Coastal waters are hotspots for this, and the chemicals in industrial effluent are known to build up in the body tissues of whales, causing illness or death.

The decline in birth rate may be partly due to pollutants called endocrine disrupters, which interfere with normal bodily functions by blocking or mimicking the actions of hormones. Another explanation may be inbreeding due to the small size of the remaining populations, a theory borne out by the increased number of miscarriages and genetic abnormalities.

In recent years changing weather patterns in the North Atlantic have led to a decrease in the abundance of marine plankton, the whales' main food source. This may be temporary, but even if conditions revert to normal, it may be too late to save the species. There is evidence that competition between right whales and sei whales, which are also endangered, is increasing as the two species are forced to occupy similar niches and compete for a diminishing quantity of plankton.

At the current rate of decline the last northern right whale will probably die in about 190 years. The estimate is this long only because the whales are long-lived. The point of no return, when the remaining northern right whales no longer constitute a viable breeding population, may be reached much sooner.

Whale, Sei

Balaenoptera borealis

A close relative of the blue and fin whales, the sei whale is also a species under threat. Its habit of feeding on the surface has led to severe exploitation, and it faces an uncertain future.

The sei is perhaps the fastest of the great whales, capable of swimming at over 30 miles an hour (50 km/h). The whale's speed and relatively small size meant that sei populations survived the early years of Antarctic whaling relatively unscathed, while blue and fin whales were driven to the brink of extinction. Before 1950 only about 1,000 sei whales were killed each year from a population of about 300,000—a harvest that may well have been sustainable. By the 1960s, however, the larger whales were becoming harder to find, and sei whales became the target of choice for commercial whalers. As a result, the population plummeted.

With hindsight it is difficult to understand how whaling on such a scale was allowed to continue as long as it did. By the time the whaling fleets turned their attention to the sei, the consequences of large-scale hunting were already evident. The blue whale population had been decimated in the 1920s and the fin whale's in the 1930s. World War II had provided a brief respite; but once it was over, the hunting resumed with the sei whales—the next largest after the blue and fin whales, and so the next most profitable. Sei whaling peaked between 1963 and 1964, when, according to International Whaling Commission (IWC) figures, 25,454 whales were slaughtered. The species could not withstand such exploitation for long. By 1979 sei whales had become so rare that the annual catch had dropped to 150. In that year the IWC set a quota of 100 whales as the maximum that could be taken. In 1986 sei whaling was finally banned altogether.

Unstable Existence

Like other large rorquals (whales of the genus *Balaenoptera*), sei whales have populations in both the Northern and Southern Hemispheres, and migrate from subpolar feeding grounds to winter breeding areas nearer the tropics. A recent estimate put the world population at 30,000, of which 12,000 live in the North Atlantic, 9,100 in the North Pacific, and only 8,300 in the Southern Hemisphere, the species' former stronghold.

DATA PANEL

Sei whale (pollack whale, coalfish whale, sardine whale, Japan finner, Rudolphi's whale)

Balaenoptera borealis

Family: Balaenidae

World population: About 30,000

Distribution: Worldwide; populations in Northern and Southern Hemispheres do not meet due to opposite migration patterns

Habitat: Mostly deep oceans

Size: Length: 43–69 ft (13–21 m). Weight: 22–33 tons (20–30 tonnes)

Form: Streamlined whale with dark-gray skin and variable pale markings on underside; dorsal fin sickle shaped; single ridge runs along top of head from snout to blowhole

Diet: Fish, squid, krill, and other crustaceans; takes smaller food items than other rorquals

Breeding: Single young born after gestation of 10–12 months; weaned at 6–7 months; mature at 7–10 years. May live up to 74 years

Related endangered species: Fin whale *(Balaenoptera physalus)** EN; blue whale *(B. musculus)** EN; minke whale *(B. acutorostrata)** LRnt

Status: IUCN EN; CITES I

See also: Populations **1:** 20; Life Strategies **1:** 24; whale species **10:** 40–59

As with other rorquals, sei whales feed by swallowing huge mouthfuls of water and straining out small food items on their hairy baleen plates as the mouth closes, forcing the water out. In addition, the sei has perfected the art of "skimming." The method involves straining food out of the water with the help of the baleen, but instead of processing single mouthfuls at a time, the whale swims slowly along the ocean's surface with its mouth open, allowing water to flow through it continuously. At intervals the sei pauses to gulp down the food that has collected on the baleen. Such a method involves less effort than swallowing and straining, and allows the whale to collect a wider range of prey, including much smaller particles than those normally taken by other whale species. In survival terms, however, the technique has one major disadvantage. It leads sei whales to spend more time on the surface than other great whales, since most small prey is concentrated at the top of the water column. The surface is also where the whales are most likely to be affected by noise and disturbance from human activities. In some parts of their range the habit also places them in competition with another endangered species, the gray whale.

Sei whales *are surface feeders and are often seen swimming on their sides. Their dives are shorter and shallower than those of other large whales.*

Whale, Sperm

Physeter macrocephalus

The extraordinary-looking sperm whale is something of a mystery. It has been hunted on and off for 300 years for its oil, but is now protected. The true extent of the damage done to the world's sperm whale population by hunting may never be known.

The sperm whale is a record breaker in more ways than one. Not only is it the world's largest living carnivorous animal, it also has the largest brain of any creature and is the deepest diving mammal. Thanks largely to the American author Herman Melville's novel *Moby Dick* (1851), it is also one of the best-known whales.

Sperm whales were first hunted in the early 18th century. What is striking about the original hunt is that, despite the huge danger and expense of hunting whales, so much of the animal was wasted. The meat, skin, and most of the bones were considered virtually worthless.

Valuable Products

One of the most valuable sperm whale products was ambergris, a gray, waxy substance that lines the whale's intestines. Its function may be to protect the animal from the bites of squid and other prey. Ambergris was widely used by the perfume industry as a fixative that helped perfumes retain their scent. Ironically, it is not necessary to kill the whales to get the ambergris, since lumps of it can be found floating in the sea or washed ashore, having been coughed up or excreted by the whales. Today many perfume makers use artificial fixatives, so this strange substance is worth much less.

Carved or decorated sperm whale teeth called scrimshaw can fetch a high price, but their value is more related to the quality of craftsmanship than the ivory itself. The true value of a dead sperm whale was always its oil. Gallons of oil could be extracted by melting down the sperm whale's blubber. In large individuals the blubber sometimes forms a layer under

DATA PANEL

Sperm whale (spermaceti whale, cachalot)

Physeter macrocephalus

Family: Physeteridae

World population: Estimates vary from 200,000 to 1.5 million

Distribution: Global; in all the world's oceans and many adjoining seas

Habitat: Mostly deep ocean

Size: Length: 36–60 ft (11–19 m). Weight: 17–55 tons (15–50 tonnes); males larger and up to 3 times heavier than females

Form: Large whale with vast, boxlike head up to one third of total length. Single S-shaped blowhole on left-hand-side of snout; skin dark bluish-gray, fading with age; often wrinkled and covered in scars; white markings around mouth. Body tapers from head to tail. Teeth only in lower jaw

Diet: Mostly squid; some octopus and fish, including sharks

Breeding: Single young born in fall after gestation of 14–16 months; weaned at 2 years; female first breeds at 8–13 years, male at 25–27 years due to social hierarchy. Life span up to 77 years

Related endangered species: No close relatives, but various dolphins and other toothed whales are threatened, including vaquita porpoise (*Phocoena sinus*) CR

Status: IUCN VU; CITES I

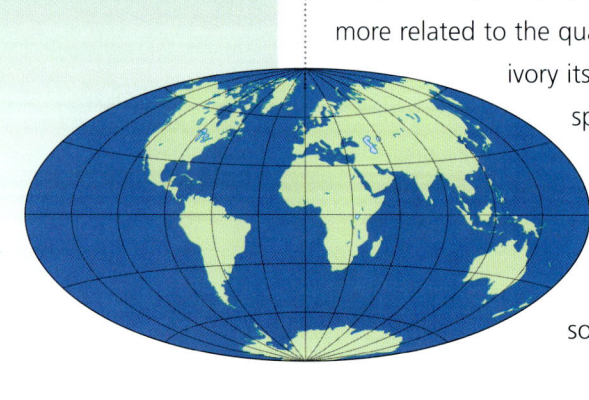

See also: Luxury Products **1:** 46; Inbreeding and Interbreeding **1:** 56; whale species **10:** 40–59

The sperm whale *gets its name from the oil-filled organ in its head—the spermaceti. No one is sure what the spermaceti does, but it may be used in the control of buoyancy or the production of sound.*

the skin up to 12 inches (30 cm) thick. The oil was used as a lubricant and in ointments and cosmetics. An additional 500 gallons (1,900 liters) of oil could be harvested from the spermaceti organ in a single whale's huge head. This was especially valuable since it was fine enough to be used to lubricate delicate machinery. It could also be turned into wax for making high-quality candles that burned cleanly with little soot. Spermaceti candles were popular in the late 18th and early 19th centuries, but were eventually replaced by kerosene lamps.

A Change in Hunting Practice

The sperm-whaling industry eventually declined. For almost a century the whales were not disturbed, and the world population stabilized. If hunting had not resumed in about 1930, it is estimated that there could be more than 3 million sperm whales in the world today.

The modern method of hunting is far more intensive. It peaked in the 1960s and 1970s, when 20,000 to 30,000 whales were slaughtered each year, five times as many as in the early 19th century. Although hunting is now banned, scientists still argue about the damage it actually did. Estimates of the current sperm whale population vary enormously, from just 200,000 to over one and a half million. One effect of hunting has been a shift in the sex ratio. Being much bigger, male sperm whales have always been targeted more than females. By the 1980s, when whaling ceased, there were more than twice as many females as males. It is feared that the imbalance may have led to increased inbreeding, which will damage the gene pool.

Whale, White

Delphinapterus leucas

The white whale, or beluga, exhibits a diverse array of unusual and engaging characteristics. Sadly, however, its numbers have declined because of a long history of exploitation.

Belugas are among the most vocal whales. Many of their more musical calls can be heard above the ocean's surface, earning the species the nickname "sea canaries." Below the waves, however, the clicks, trills, moos, whistles, squeaks, and twitters produced by a herd of beluga has been likened to the noise of a busy farmyard! Although some of these sounds are undoubtedly used for communication, many are involved in echolocation; the whales have a distinctive bulge—known as the melon—on their foreheads, which they use for focusing pulses of sound on underwater obstacles or prey.

Belugas can survive in extremely shallow water, an ability they put to good use when hunting. Herds of belugas have been known to drive schools of fish into shallow bays or up sloping beaches until they have nowhere to escape. Their taste for fish, which sometimes takes them hundreds of miles up rivers, brings them into competition with fishermen, and at one time the whales were killed to preserve fish stocks. Today less drastic methods may be used to scare the animals away, such as playing them recordings of predatory killer whales.

White whale meat is used for both human and animal consumption, especially by aboriginal peoples of the Arctic and subarctic regions. The whale's oily blubber, which can be up to 8 inches (20 cm) thick, serves to make soap, margarine, and various lubricants; the oil extracted from the head is considered to be of especially fine quality. Beluga bones are ground up for fertilizer, and the hide is tanned to make soft leather. Commercial hunting is now restricted by the International Whaling Commission, but natives of Greenland and North America are

DATA PANEL

White whale (beluga)

Delphinapterus leucas

Family: Monodontidae

World population: Between 40,000 and 70,000

Distribution: Arctic Ocean and some adjoining seas

Habitat: Fjords, estuaries, and other shallow coastal waters of Arctic and cold temperate seas

Size: Length: 10–15 ft (3–4.6 m); males larger than females. Weight: 1,100–3,300 lb (500–1,500 kg)

Form: Chubby, dolphinlike animal; large, bulging forehead, small eyes, expressive face; distinct, flexible neck; no dorsal fin; adults have unmistakable white skin

Diet: Fish, including cod, salmon, and herring; also octopus, squid, crabs, and various bottom-dwelling crustaceans, mollusks, and worms

Breeding: Single young born every 2–3 years in April–September after 14-month gestation; weaned at 18–24 months; females mature at 4–7 years, males at 8–9 years. May live up to 35 years

Related endangered species: Narwhal *(Monodon monoceros)* DD

Status: IUCN VU; CITES II

See also: Populations 1: 20; Hunting 1: 42; whale species 10: 40–57

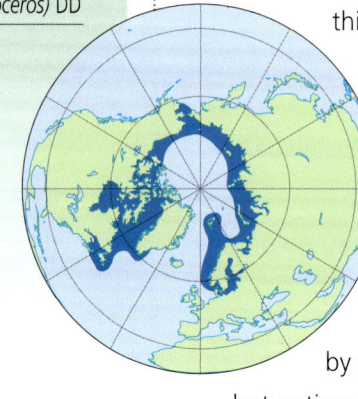

Belugas *are born with dark-brown or black skin that gradually fades to white as the whale matures.*

still permitted to kill over 2,000 animals per year. Hunting white whales is easy because they come so close to shore.

The Threat from Hunting and Pollution

Some of the more accessible beluga populations have already been hunted to extinction, and others have declined severely. For example, the resident population in Canada's Gulf of St. Lawrence, which once numbered over 20,000 animals, was reduced by the 1970s to just 300. For a long while it seemed that even with legal protection the population would never recover, since the waters of the gulf had become so polluted that the belugas often failed to breed. Of the few calves that were born, many had serious deformities that made them unable to swim. At one time levels of pollutant in white whale tissue were so high that the corpses of whales were themselves disposed of as toxic waste. It seems, however, that the story may have a happy ending. Strict hunting and pollution controls have begun to take effect, and the population is starting to recover; by 1998 there were once more almost 1,000 white whales in the St. Lawrence River.

Whiptail, St. Lucia

Cnemidophorus vanzoi

The St. Lucia whiptail inhabits three islands off the Caribbean island of St. Lucia. In the face of threats from introduced predators the species represents a modest conservation success story.

In spite of its name, the St. Lucia whiptail has only been found on the Maria Islands (Major and Minor), which are situated just over half a mile (1 km) off the southeastern coast of St. Lucia, a volcanic island in the Caribbean. The Maria Islands are home to seven other reptile species, including a rare snake: the St. Lucia racer. The whiptail and the racer are found nowhere else in the world. In an effort to increase numbers, a population of whiptails has also been introduced to Praslin Island, also off St. Lucia.

The whiptail might have inhabited St. Lucia itself, but there are no records of its existence there. If it ever lived on St. Lucia, the cultivation of bananas and coconuts, together with the introduction of predators, probably destroyed its habitat.

Keeping Predators at Bay

As with many species now living in the region, rats arrived with settlers and bred rapidly, soon becoming a pest. In an attempt to control the rats, the Indian mongoose was introduced. Between them the mongoose and rats had a severe effect on wildlife on many of the islands.

Fortunately, the uninhabited Maria Islands are free of both the mongoose and rats, in spite of their proximity to St. Lucia. Since 1982 the islands have been nature reserves under the control of the St. Lucia National Trust and the Department of Forests and Fisheries. A warden controls access to the islands and makes sure that predators, such as rats, do not come ashore from other places. The local people are proud of the St. Lucia whiptails and support their conservation, and the lizard's colors match those of the St. Lucia national flag.

The whiptails on Maria Minor are smaller and less colorful than their counterparts on Maria Major. Genetic studies have been carried out to assess the differences between the two populations. Such information is needed before crossbreeding of the two races can be considered.

Because of the rarity of the lizards it was decided to set up a captive-breeding program, first at the San Diego Zoo in 1984, and then later at the Jersey Wildlife Preservation Trust in the Channel Islands in 1988. The aim was to establish a stock of whiptails that could be reintroduced into the wild at some future date. Although other whiptail species do not take well to captivity, the program was successful for a few years. When disease broke out, the project was abandoned. Praslin Island—only 250 yards (80 m) from the mainland of St. Lucia—was then surveyed to assess the possibility of introducing the St. Lucia whiptail there. The island has an area of just over 2.5 acres (1 ha). It was infested with rats that had to be cleared if the lizards were to survive.

A team using rat poison successfully eradicated the rat population in eight days. The poison apparently did not harm other creatures. Although hermit crabs were known to eat it, they were not killed; the poison affects the blood chemistry of rats, but not that of invertebrates.

A year later it was found that the eradication of the rats—which feed on plant seeds—had allowed the vegetation on Praslin Island to regenerate. Goats that had formerly lived on the island had been removed. Praslin was now considered suitable for relocating whiptails since the vegetation and other conditions were similar to those on Maria Major. Two other types

See also: Introductions **1:** 54; The Role of Zoos **1:** 86; Lizard, Ibiza Wall **6:** 40; Tuatara **10:** 6

of lizard had managed to survive there, and the food supply was adequate. Fifty-four whiptails were collected from Maria Major in 1995 and translocated to Praslin. Since then they have adapted well and have been breeding regularly. The Praslin population is now thought to number about 100. Further studies have been carried out to learn more about the whiptail and to assess the possibility of establishing colonies on other small islands.

Finding New Island Homes

Finding new locations for the whiptails is considered advisable, since the three islands presently holding populations are small and vulnerable to natural disasters such as fires or hurricanes. In addition, Praslin Island is near enough to St. Lucia for predators to get across by swimming or rafting on floating vegetation.

To date the whiptail is a modest success story. The eradication of rats has led to the improvement of the whole ecology of Praslin Island. Ground-nesting birds have returned, and the two other lizard species are also benefiting from the restored habitat. Even so, where such small populations of lizards live in such a limited area, they will always be vulnerable.

The male St. Lucia whiptail *is a striking lizard, having spotted sides and an orange-yellow underbelly.*

DATA PANEL

St. Lucia whiptail (racerunner)

Cnemidophorus vanzoi

Family: Teiidae

World population: About 2,000

Distribution: The Maria Islands and Praslin Island off St. Lucia in the Windward Islands, Lesser Antilles, the Caribbean

Habitat: Open woodland; scrub vegetation with open areas

Size: Length: male 18 in (45 cm); female 14 in (35 cm)

Form: Long, whiplike tail that is about 60% of total body length. Males have black head and body with white stripes on back and white spots on side; yellow underside; turquoise tail. Females and immature males are brown with cream stripes and spots

Diet: Insects

Breeding: Between 6 and 8 eggs buried in loose substrate, but some predators can still find them

Related endangered species: Orange-throated whiptail *(Cnemidophorus hyperythrus)* DD

Status: IUCN VU; not listed by CITES

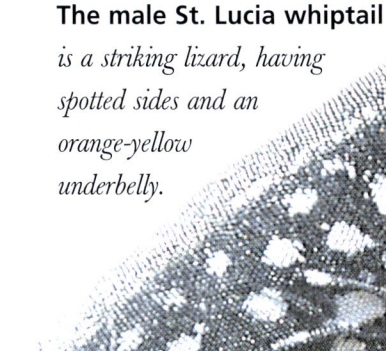

Wildcat

Felis silvestris

Like many predators, the wildcat has suffered extensive persecution. Today the major threat to its survival is genetic dilution of the species as it increasingly interbreeds with domestic cats.

The wildcat is a solitary and secretive animal found mainly in forested areas across continental Europe and in Scotland. Its range also extends east to the Caspian Sea, an inland salt lake that lies between Europe and Asia. Its major prey is small mammals and birds: mostly mice, voles, rabbits, and other wild species. However, wildcats have been unpopular with humans, who suspect them of being a threat to domestic stock such as lambs and chickens and a danger to children. Although these fears are greatly exaggerated, the wildcat has been trapped, shot, and poisoned widely. Moreover, in the past its skin was prized for its warmth, and its fur became a luxury fashion item for trimming clothing.

Habitat Loss

The wildcat is not seriously endangered. However, the expansion of cities and intensification of farming have resulted in habitat loss. Although some wildcats manage to live close to farms and on the edges of European towns, where they may even visit garbage dumps to feed, they have become more scarce. There are now large areas of Europe where they are extinct, and the remaining populations are widely separated.

See also: Populations **1:** 20; Inbreeding and Interbreeding **1:** 56; Cat, Iriomote **3:** 30; Lynx, Iberian **6:** 52

WILDCAT

DATA PANEL

Wildcat

Felis silvestris

Family: Felidae

World population: More than 50,000, but in widely separated subpopulations

Distribution: Europe, east to the Caspian Sea

Habitat: Forested areas

Size: Length head/body: 22–30 in (50–75 cm); tail: 12 in (30 cm); height at shoulder: 16 in (40 cm). Weight: 10–30 lb (4.5–13.5 kg)

Form: Resembles a domestic tabby cat, but is larger and has 7–11 bold stripes on its flanks. The tail is banded with several clear rings and the tip is blunt, not pointed as in domestic cats

Diet: Small mammals and young rabbits; birds; also frogs and insects

Breeding: One litter per year, up to 8 kittens (normally 3–4), born May–August. Life span up to 10 years

Related endangered species: Iberian lynx *(Lynx pardinus)** EN; Iriomote cat *(Mayailurus iriomotensis)** EN; various big cats

Status: Not listed by IUCN; not listed by CITES

The wildcat looks like a domestic tabby, but is larger and has more distinct body stripes and a blunt end to the tail.

Interbreeding Problems

The biggest threat by far to wildcats is "genetic pollution" through interbreeding with domestic cats. The wildcats of Europe are so similar to the African wildcat (from which the domestic form is thought to originate) that some zoologists think the two species are actually the same. They are certainly closely related, which is why they interbreed so easily. As a result, the natural wildcat population has begun to include crossbred animals (hybrids). This genetic dilution undermines the purity of the species. Ironically, as the wildcat's habitat has shrunk, the animal has been forced into new areas where it encounters domestic cats more often. This has led to more interbreeding and further genetic dilution. Thus the greater the wildcat's breeding success, the more uncertain its future. At the very least, hybridization will result in a confused picture, with some areas having true wildcats, and others having hybrids. In addition, interbreeding makes the species difficult to monitor.

The Berne Convention, the European Union Habitats Directive, and the national legislation of many countries recognize the wildcat's rarity and have given the animal legal protection. Yet these laws are unable to prevent the main threat of interbreeding. Moreover, since hybrids are not legally protected, the legislation is weakened because anyone killing a wildcat can claim that they thought the animal was a hybrid. Such an assertion cannot be easily disproved. If wildcats and domestic cats really are the same species then it seems impractical to give the animal legal protection, since there are millions of house cats all over the world!

Wolf, Ethiopian

Canis simensis

Confined to the cool uplands of Ethiopia, the Ethiopian wolf has been driven out of most of its former range. Only a few remain outside the Bale Mountains, and the animal has become the world's rarest member of the dog family.

Ethiopian, or Simien, wolves live on the bleak moorlands of the high Ethiopian mountains, normally at altitudes of at least 10,000 feet (3,500 m). The African-alpine habitat is very fragile, but is home to a wide range of special animals. The Simien wolf is named after the Simien Mountains in which it occurs.

Ethiopian wolves live in small social groups, consisting of closely related family members, often with several adult males. Only the dominant pair breed, producing cubs in a burrow, or lair among the rocks. Although they are highly sociable creatures, the wolves hunt alone, moving slowly across the moors and listening for small mammals moving under cover of the dense grass and heather thickets. The wolf pauses long enough to locate any likely prey, then pounces, stabbing its feet down into the dense vegetation to pin the victim to the ground, from where it can be retrieved using the teeth. It is then eaten or carried back to the den to feed the cubs.

Changes to Habits and Habitats

The wolves are usually active during the day, but in many places there is now so much daytime disturbance from people and cattle that they have been forced to be nocturnal. This causes several problems. At high altitudes the open mountain habitats get exceedingly cold at night, with temperatures dropping to well below freezing. Many small mammals are forced to retreat into their burrows deep underground, making them less accessible to the wolves that prey on them. However, the mice and mole-rats on which the wolves feed are abundant in the moorland areas; in places there may be over 7.5 tons of

DATA PANEL

Ethiopian wolf (Simien fox or Simien jackal)

Canis simensis

Family: Canidae

World population: Fewer than 400 (1998 estimate)

Distribution: Arussi, Bale, and Simien Mountains of Ethiopia, Africa

Habitat: Bleak mountain moorland at altitudes of at least 10,000 ft (3,500 m)

Size: Length head/body: 36–42 in (90–100 cm); tail: 12 in (30 cm); height at shoulder: 24 in (60 cm). Weight: 24–33 lb (11–15 kg); male up to 39 lb (18 kg)

Form: Tall, foxlike animal with reddish-brown fur. Contrasting white underside and "socks." Thick tail has black tip and is often white at the base

Diet: Small mammals, particularly mole-rats; occasionally carrion

Breeding: Only dominant animals breed, producing families of 3–5 cubs after gestation of about 9 weeks. Life span unknown, but probably 5–10 years

Related endangered species: Red wolf *(Canis rufus)* * CR; African wild dog *(Lycaon pictus)* * EN

Status: IUCN CR; not listed by CITES

See also: Disease 1: 55; Dog, African Wild 4: 22; Wolf, Red 10: 72

WOLF, ETHIOPIAN

rodents per square mile (2.6 tonnes per sq. km), so there should be no food shortage.

There was little to fear from people until recently; there were few settlements at such high altitudes, and no domestic animals were kept there. Occasionally, wolves would stray to lower altitudes and were shot in the mistaken belief that they posed a threat to domestic sheep and cattle. (In fact, wolves rarely prey on anything larger than a hare.) Past misuse of the land at lower altitudes, however, has caused soil erosion, and this has forced more people to try to live on the mountains, bringing them into more frequent contact with the wolves.

Another problem has been contact with domestic dogs. The dogs carry several diseases (including rabies, hepatitis, and distemper) that can kill the wolves. The dogs may also attempt to mate with the wolves, creating hybrids that are neither dog nor wolf, and destroy the genetic purity of the population.

The new settlers in the mountains have systematically removed the sparse, woody vegetation for fuel, depriving wolves of cover. Good feeding areas have been plowed up to grow crops. Grazing by livestock has also contributed to habitat destruction, reducing prey availability.

As a result of such pressures, the Ethiopian wolf is now almost extinct in the Simien Mountains, with perhaps only 50 individuals remaining and fewer in other parts of the range. The northern population is likely to become extinct soon. The other wolf stronghold is in the Bale Mountains in southeast Ethiopia, where a national park should protect the main part of the population. A captive-breeding population may be established to provide animals to add to wild groups. However, in recent years Ethiopia has suffered greatly from wars and famine. Wolf conservation is not a high priority and cannot easily be achieved without a lot of international, economic, and scientific assistance.

The Ethiopian wolf *looks like a large fox. As in most Canis species, one litter is born each year. The young start to take solid food when they are between two and six weeks of age.*

Wolf, Falkland Island

Dusicyon australis

The Falkland Island wolf was the only land carnivore on the remote Falkland Islands, seen occasionally by seamen who sheltered there from storms. It was hunted to extinction in the 1800s.

The Falkland Islands lie some 250 miles (400 km) off the Argentinean mainland, surrounded by cold stormy seas. It is a mystery how the native wolf got there at all. Some people have suggested that it drifted there on pack ice; others thought that it might have been taken there as a domestic animal, then left to its own devices so that eventually a wild population was established. However, only a few thousand years ago the islands were linked to the mainland. There are fossils of a similar wolf found in Chile, so it is likely that the animals lived on the Falklands all along. They then developed into a separate species after they were isolated by the rising sea levels that cut off the islands from the mainland.

The Falkland Island wolf was first described by a British naval officer who went to the islands in 1690. He wrote that it looked like a fox, but that it was twice as big as the foxes he knew of in England. This impression could have been created by the wolves' thick fur, grown as protection against the winds that sweep across the island's open moorlands. A young wolf was kept as a pet on board the officer's ship, but jumped into the sea during a battle.

In 1741 a shipwrecked crew was stranded on the Falkland Islands and lived in fear of the wolves, which (they said) waded into the sea to attack them.

Fearless Creatures

For centuries the wolf was the only land mammal present on the Falkland islands (apart from the mouse) and rarely encountered people. It had no reason to fear them—many of the local birds are unusually tame for the same reason. Later, visiting sailors commented on how the wolves showed little fear of people. Such a trait might easily be mistaken for being bold and dangerous, leading earlier visitors to fear the animals. In fact, the wolves were probably attracted to people out of curiosity and because they frequently left food around. The wolves often raided camps and even entered tents to steal food from the sleeping seamen. Apparently, the wolves barked occasionally, but only quietly. Otherwise they behaved more like foxes in that

DATA PANEL

Falkland Island wolf (South American fox, Antarctic wolf)

Dusicyon australis

Family: Canidae

World population: 0 (Extinct)

Distribution: Formerly found on the Falkland Islands in the South Atlantic

Habitat: Open moorland and rocky shores

Size: Length head/body: about 3 ft (1 m); tail: 11–16 in (28–40 cm); height at shoulder: about 24 in (60 cm)

Form: Wolf that resembles a fox. Brown body speckled with white; short, brown legs; white belly. Ears black behind. Tail thick and white tipped, like that of a fox

Diet: Seabirds and eggs scavenged along the shore

Breeding: Unknown

Related endangered species: Red wolf *(Canis rufus)** CR; Ethiopian wolf *(C. simensis)** CR; African wild dog *(Lycaon pictus)** EN; bush dog *(Speothos venaticus)** VU; dhole *(Cuon alpinus)** VU

Status: IUCN EX; not listed by CITES

See also: Hunting 1: 42; Dog, Bush 4: 24; wolf species 10: 64–73

they lived in burrows and scavenged widely in search of eggs laid by the numerous wild geese and cormorants. They also ate seabirds such as penguins, of which there are five species, all abundant and quite tame, on the Falkland Islands.

In 1833 Charles Darwin arrived for a brief visit to the islands during his famous voyage around the world aboard the ship the *Beagle*. He too commented on how tame the wolves were. By then the Falklands had been settled by ranchers who kept cattle there and considered the wolves to be a threat to their animals. They told how it was possible to kill a wolf by attracting it to a piece of meat held in one hand, while using the other to slit its throat with a knife. Already the wolves had been exterminated in the eastern part of East Falkland around the main settlement of Port Stanley, and Darwin predicted their complete extinction unless the farmers could be persuaded to tolerate them.

The colonial government of the Falkland Islands ignored this warning and instead offered payments to anyone who killed the animals. Their aim was to help the newly arrived Scottish sheep farmers establish their flocks on the islands without the threat of the wolves.

The Falkland Island wolf, also known as the South American fox, was like a fox in appearance and habits, but was in fact closely related to other extinct dogs from the South American mainland.

Hunted to Extinction

The bounty payments paid for dead wolves and the activities of American fur dealers collecting wolf skins combined to wipe out most of the animals by about 1860. The London Zoo received a specimen in 1868, one of the few survivors of a batch of wildlife sent from South America by a dealer. Meanwhile, local shepherds insisted that the wolves killed sheep to suck their blood, and the government increased its bounty payments. Naturally, local farmers would have exaggerated such claims because the bounties were a useful additional source of income. The last wolf was killed at Hill Cove in 1876. Today only 11 stuffed specimens are known to exist, including the three that Darwin collected during his visit. Darwin's specimens were eventually taken to the Natural History Museum in London and are still there.

Wolf, Gray

Canis lupus spp.

Although still common in Alaska and some other areas, the gray wolf is now extinct or critically endangered in many parts of its former range.

The gray wolf is the largest member of the dog family. At one time it had the widest distribution of almost any land mammal, being found nearly everywhere in the Northern Hemisphere. Throughout this range wolves have inspired considerable fear over the centuries, and this has been reinforced by spine-chilling stories; they are the subject of much folklore. As people and their domestic animals have spread and increased in number, conflict with wolves has escalated, resulting in extermination of wolves in many parts of their range.

Today about 2,000 gray wolves still survive in Spain, and a few hundred more in Italy and Greece. There are about 50 left in Sweden, and there are occasional reports of strays turning up in Norway (where unfortunately they stand a good chance of being shot by farmers). Between 1991 and 1992 wolves spread from Italy as far as the French Alps, but at least six were shot soon afterward.

Today wolves are still unwelcome residents across much of their European range. In Romania about 700 (from a population of fewer than 3,000) are shot each year. In Greece wolves face a shortage of suitable large mammal prey, and people are actively encouraged to kill them. In Italy, however, where farmers are paid compensation for sheep killed by wolves, local wolf populations seem to have stabilized or even increased a little, to about 200.

Fortunately, the wolf remains fairly abundant in northern territories particularly Alaska, Canada, and the former Soviet Union. There have also been attempts to reintroduce the animals to areas in which they had previously been eradicated. In 1995 wolves were released back into Yellowstone National Park in the United States, a move that was highly controversial. The fear of wolves runs deep, and there are concerns for the safety of

DATA PANEL

Gray wolf (timber wolf)

***Canis lupus* spp.**

Family: Canidae

World population: Many thousands, (50,000 plus in former Soviet Union and adjacent countries, for example); rare or extinct in many parts of former range

Distribution: Canada and Alaska; also northern Asia and into Eastern Europe. Remnant populations in Spain, Portugal, Sweden, and Arabia

Habitat: Open woodland (especially coniferous forest), mountains, tundra, and bogs

Size: Length head/body: 39–51 in (100–130 cm); tail: 14–20 in (35–52 cm); height at shoulder: 26–28 in (65–70 cm). Weight: male 66–175 lb (30–80 kg); female 50–120 lb (23–55 kg)

Form: Large dog, almost white in northern latitudes; dark gray to nearly black farther south. Tail held high when running

Diet: Birds and small- to medium-sized animals; packs cooperate to kill larger species such as deer

Breeding: Between 3 and 7 cubs born per year in single litter after 9-week gestation; mature at 2 years (but often longer before they actually breed). Life span up to 20 years in captivity; probably 10–15 in wild

Related endangered species: Red wolf *(Canis rufus)** CR; Ethiopian wolf *(C. simensis)** CR; African wild dog *(Lycaon pictus)** EN; maned wolf *(Chrysocyon brachyurus)** LRnt

Status: IUCN VU; CITES II (some races Appendix 1)

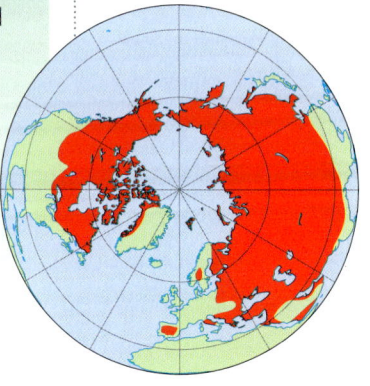

See also: National Parks **1:** 92; Wolf, Maned **10:** 70; Wolf, Red **10:** 72

cattle and sheep in the vicinity. Such projects can only succeed with public support; otherwise the animals are exterminated before a new population has time to establish itself.

A Shortage of Suitable Prey

A serious problem for wolves in Europe and in the more densely inhabited parts of North America is that the expansion of farming has reduced the numbers of deer and other suitable prey. Without sufficient food to support them, wolf populations have fragmented. Wolves have then been forced to attack sheep and to scavenge around garbage dumps, bringing them into more frequent contact with people and increasing the risk of crossbreeding with domestic dogs.

In Spain a recent increase in the deer population was followed by a reduction in the number of sheep killed by wolves. Since the wolves were preying on the deer, they did not need to kill the sheep. This small victory is a reminder that conservation initiatives need to look at the health of the environment as a whole as well as the fate of individual species.

Perhaps there is also encouragement to be gained from Canada, where wolf-watching trips are becoming popular activities in national parks. Growing familiarity may help reduce some of the fear that people have for the wild ancestor of the domestic dog, helping make the gray wolf's long-term future a little more secure.

Gray wolves *do not attack humans, despite the legends. People are at greater risk of dying from domestic dog attacks than from wolf attacks. Wolves do attack coyotes, however, and may help keep coyote numbers in check.*

Wolf, Maned

Chrysocyon brachyurus

A concerted effort to save the maned wolf began in the 1970s; the species would not have survived into the 21st century without it. Today the future looks brighter, but the animal is still at risk.

South American folklore suggests that the maned wolf can kill a chicken simply by staring at it. With such a reputation it is not surprising that the species has been persecuted nearly to extinction.

The maned wolf looks and behaves like a fox, but the similarities are misleading. The species is not closely related to any other member of the dog family. It is unique and deserves the effort that has already been invested in securing its future.

The main threats to the maned wolf are habitat destruction, persecution by ranchers, and illegal hunting. Maned wolves need plenty of space. Mated pairs of males and females share a territory of up to 12 square miles (31 sq. km). For much of the year they spend little time together, but in the breeding season the male is much more attentive. He will help groom any cubs and provide regurgitated food for them. The wolves live at low population densities, since the male will not tolerate another male in his territory. Wolves also need substantial distances between them and the nearest human activity. Consequently, many areas of otherwise excellent habitat are unoccupied by the wolf. Conserving the maned wolf requires large tracts of protected land to be set aside. This is not popular with ranchers and farmers.

The conflict between farmers and wolves is ancient and ongoing. The maned wolf's reputation is not really deserved: It is a myth that they kill cattle and horses. They are not strong enough and do not have the shearing teeth and powerful jaws that true wolves use to rip up large prey. The jaws of the maned wolf are designed for snapping up smaller creatures. The teeth are pointed and peglike, good for gripping slippery or wriggly prey, but not much use for tearing up larger meals. The only domestic animals in real danger from the maned wolf are chickens and the occasional weak lamb.

Captive Breeding

Maned wolves breed only once a year, and the females are only fertile for one or two days. In a small population, failure to mate or the loss of a litter can dramatically slow down growth in numbers. Captive-breeding programs form an important part of the efforts to save the maned wolf. Zoos worldwide are cooperating to boost numbers and maintain genetic diversity. Initially the stress of living in captivity made many females kill their own young. To prevent the killing, new litters were hand-reared by keepers—never an ideal situation, especially when cubs should be learning how to survive in the wild. There were doubts about whether a hand-reared cub would know how to raise its own young. Many of the problems are being overcome with time, and the number of litters being successfully reared by captive pairs is rising.

A healthy captive population does not guarantee the success of a reintroduction program, however. Unless the problems that caused the decline in the wild are dealt with, any released animals will meet a similar fate. Reintroductions will only work if the way is prepared by strict legislation and vigorous enforcement of protection. A major effort will have to be made to improve the public image of the maned wolf if its future is to be made secure.

The maned wolf's *most striking feature is its long legs. Thought to have evolved to help it see over long grass, they have earned the species the nickname "fox on stilts."*

See also: Captive Breeding **1:** 87; Reintroduction **1:** 92; Wolf, Red **10:** 72

WOLF, MANED

DATA PANEL

Maned wolf

Chrysocyon brachyurus

Family: Canidae

World population: 1,500–2,500

Distribution: Formerly northern Argentina; also Bolivia, southern Brazil, Paraguay, and Peru

Habitat: Scrubby forest and grassland; swampy areas

Size: Length: 4–4.3 ft (1.2–1.3 m); height at shoulder: 34 in (87 cm). Weight: 44–51 lb (20–23 kg)

Form: Long-legged dog with long, red fur, darkening to black on legs and nape. Long hair on nape forms rough mane. White on the bushy tail; head looks small and has large, erect ears

Diet: Small mammals, including rabbits and armadillos; also birds, fish, reptiles, amphibians, mollusks, and insects; large amounts of seasonal fruit

Breeding: In the wild 1–5 pups born October–December after 9-week gestation; weaned at 3 months; mature at 1 year. Life span up to 15 years

Related endangered species: Other wolves, for example, red wolf (*Canis rufus*)* CR; Ethiopian wolf (*C. simensis*)* CR; African wild dog (*Lycaon pictus*)* EN; dhole (*Cuon alpinus*)* VU

Status: IUCN LRnt; CITES II

Wolf, Red

Canis rufus

It has taken an immense conservation effort to save the red wolf from extinction; and while a small number have been successfully returned to the wild, the fight to preserve the species is by no means over.

When Europeans first colonized North America, the red wolf was abundant from Texas to Pennsylvania in the north and to Florida in the south. For the settlers the wolves embodied all that was wild and frightening about the New World. Worried about dangers to their livestock and to themselves, people shot, snared, trapped, and poisoned the wolves without mercy.

At the same time, the wolves' wilderness habitat was tamed. Forests were cleared and prairies turned into pasture or plowed. The changes in the landscape brought a further threat to the wolves from their close relative the coyote. Coyotes are less well suited to forested landscapes and prior to interference by settlers had remained well to the west of the red wolf's habitat. However, as the forests disappeared, the coyotes moved in. The wolf and coyote were able to interbreed, so even in areas where persecution was minimal, purebred red wolves began to disappear, although hybrids remained.

By the 1960s the purebred red wolves were restricted to a small area of swampy coastal prairie on the Gulf coast of Texas and Louisiana. It was a poor-quality habitat, and the wolves struggled to survive. Over half the pups died from hookworm infections, and virtually every adult was afflicted with heartworm and mange. In 1975 the situation reached a crisis point. Conservationists working for the recently established Red Wolf Recovery Team believed that the only way to save the species was to bring the entire surviving population into captivity.

For a decade there was not a single red wolf left in the wild. Fourteen of the healthiest wolves were selected to breed in captivity. By the time the last of the wild-caught wolves died in 1989, small populations of captive-bred descendants had been

---

DATA PANEL

Red wolf

Canis rufus

Family: Canidae

World population: About 290 (1995 estimate)

Distribution: Most in captivity; small reintroduced populations on islands off Florida coast, Mississippi, and South Carolina; also on mainland in North Carolina

Habitat: Forest, swampland, and prairie

Size: Length head/body: up to 4.3 ft (1.3 m); tail: up to 17 in (42 cm); male larger than female. Weight: 40–88 lb (18–40 kg)

Form: Narrow-bodied, long-legged wolf with large ears. Coat varies from tawny to gray or black, tinged with red

Diet: Rodents, rabbits, deer, hogs, crayfish, insects, and carrion

Breeding: Up to 12 young (usually 3–7) born in late spring after 9-week gestation; weaned at 8–10 weeks; mature at 22–46 months. Life span up to 14 years

Related endangered species: Gray wolf *(Canis lupus)** VU

Status: IUCN CR; not listed by CITES

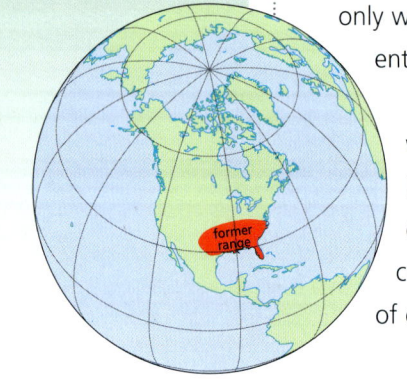

See also: Captive Breeding **1:** 87; Wolf, Gray **10:** 68; Wolf, Maned **10:** 70

WOLF, RED

reintroduced to several small island refuges in Florida and South Carolina, and to one mainland site, the Alligator River Wildlife Refuge in North Carolina. In 1996 there were 60 red wolves living wild, with over 200 in captivity.

An Uncertain Future

Wolves divide public opinion, and the red wolf has its enemies as well as its fans. The antiwolf lobby claims that the reintroductions put livestock and people at risk. In 1996 much was made of scientific research that indicated that the red wolf was in fact a hybrid

The red wolf *appears to be thriving where it has been reintroduced. Its ability to hunt and breed successfully does not seem to have been affected by a captive upbringing.*

between the gray wolf and the coyote. The implication was that only true species should be entitled to protection. It is possible that prior to the changes that put red wolves and coyotes in the same habitat, the red wolf was on its way to becoming a true species. Conservationists believe that losing a species in the making is as bad as losing one that is established; their battle for the red wolf will continue.

Wolverine

Gulo gulo

The wolverine used to roam over much of Europe and North America. Today it is widely hunted for its fur and is increasingly rare. Its reputation as a bloodthirsty predator has also led to widespread persecution of the species.

Although it will eat all manner of things, the wolverine is a carnivore. It preys on small mammals, but often eats larger animals—such as deer—in the form of carrion. The decline of wolves and other large predators has reduced the availability of leftovers on which wolverines can feed. Human hunters deprive wolverines of even the scantiest scraps by removing their kills completely.

Under Pressure

Living at the edge of the Arctic, where food is scarce, a wolverine will kill in excess of its immediate need and store the surplus food for later. This apparent greed has given rise to its other common name: "glutton." Its lifestyle and skulking appearance have made the animal unpopular, and there are many folk tales among Arctic peoples about its cunning and bloodthirstiness. Reindeer herdsmen, for instance, fear that the wolverine will attack their animals, and trappers complain that wolverines steal bait and captured animals from their traps; the wolverine has many enemies eager to kill it on sight.

Wolverines have also been hunted for their fur. The long hairs tend not to freeze together in the intense cold of the Arctic, so the pelts are prized by native people for trimming the hoods of winter coats. The fur provides protection from the wind and does not become encrusted with ice from the wearer's frozen breath. Wolverines have been shot and trapped extensively across their northern range in Europe, North America, and Russia.

They used to be found much farther south than at present, even as far down as Germany in Europe and Arizona and New Mexico in the United States. Now they are extinct east of Montana; they had disappeared from the Midwest by the early 20th century. A few remain in California and Idaho. They are still widespread in Canada, although rare or extinct in the eastern provinces. British Columbia is a stronghold, with perhaps 4,000 to 5,000 animals. Little is known about numbers of wolverines in Russia and Siberia (where they occur east to Kamchatka), but they are believed to be still relatively numerous there. In northern Scandinavia wolverines have become rare, and most now occur in the remote mountains of Norway and Sweden. It is thought that there are only 40 left in Finland.

Naturally Scarce

Part of the problem lies in the fact that the wolverine is a naturally scarce animal. It ranges over vast areas and lives at low population densities. Often there is only one per 200 square miles (500 sq. km). This means that the animals rarely come across each other to breed. Fragmented populations become vulnerable to piecemeal

See also: What Is an Endangered Species? **1:** 8; Marten, Pine **6:** 74

WOLVERINE

extinction, dying out in one place after another with little chance of natural recolonization. Even a relatively low mortality rate can leave large gaps in the population. Mortality rates increase during periods of severe weather and food shortage.

Although wolverines have full legal protection in Scandinavia, they are still widely killed. Permits are even available to trap or kill the animals if they are believed to endanger domestic beasts such as reindeer.

Despite their reputation, wolverines are sensitive creatures and wary of humans. They are easily disturbed, and the isolated areas to which they have been driven are becoming increasingly accessible to motor vehicles. Road construction, tree-felling, and the building of cabins and houses threaten to invade the privacy of the few remaining wolverines.

The wolverine *resembles a small bear, but is actually the largest member of the weasel family. It is found in North America and northern Europe.*

DATA PANEL

Wolverine (glutton)

Gulo gulo

Family: Mustelidae

World population: Unknown, but low thousands

Distribution: Found widely across northern Canada and the U.S., northern Europe, and Russia

Habitat: Arctic and subarctic tundra and taiga

Size: Length head/body: 26–36 in (65–90 cm); tail: 5–10 in (13–25 cm); height at shoulder: 14–18 in (36–45 cm); females at least 10% smaller than males. Weight: 20–65 lb (9–30 kg)

Form: Largest member of weasel family; looks like a small bear. A low, thickset animal with short legs and large paws; tail thick and bushy; coat dark brown but paler on face, flanks, and base of tail. Sometimes pale all over

Diet: Mostly rodents (sometimes larger mammals); also fruit, berries, carrion, birds, and eggs; occasionally invertebrates

Breeding: Mates in summer, but development delayed until midwinter. Up to 4 young born (February–March), 1 litter per year. Life span up to 11 years in wild, 18 in captivity

Related endangered species: European mink *(Mustela lutreola)** EN; giant otter *(Pteronura brasiliensis)** EN; European otter *(Lutra lutra)** VU

Status: IUCN VU; not listed by CITES

Wombat, Northern Hairy-Nosed

Lasiorhinus krefftii

The northern hairy-nosed wombat survives the harsh climate and scanty food supplies of its dry grassland home by conserving energy. Its burrowing habit— which is part of its energy-saving lifestyle—is unpopular with farmers, who once treated it as a pest. Numbers are now extremely low.

The northern hairy-nosed wombat was first discovered and properly described from a fossil skull found in New South Wales, southeastern Australia, in 1869. In many ways this original, long-dead specimen has turned out to be a grim omen for the future. By the time a living animal was officially described and named, the species was already in decline. In fact, most populations were extinct by the beginning of the 20th century, and by 1982 it was estimated that there were only 20 northern hairy-nosed wombats left alive in the wild. This tiny group was confined to a small area of Epping Forest National Park, in east central Queensland, Australia.

Even before the arrival of European settlers in Australia, life was tough for the hairy-nosed wombat. The climate was harsh and unforgiving, and prolonged periods of drought meant that only tough grasses and scrub could grow. The wombat survived by means of its specially adapted lifestyle; it is able to compensate for a poor food source by eating less and adopting a very low-energy lifestyle. It basks in the morning and evening sun so it does not have to expend energy to warm its body. During the day, however, it conserves water by staying underground in an extensive burrow system. Another survival strategy is the wombat's slow breeding. Each female wombat gives birth to just one young in a year, and only then if there is a reasonable crop of grasses with which to feed the newcomer. In drought years the wombats simply do not breed.

Decline

As European settlers began to farm the land, new problems emerged for the hairy-nosed wombat. One cause of the animal's decline is thought to have been competition for food from introduced herbivores, such as sheep and cattle. The wombats feed on two main species of grass: bunch spear grass and three-awned grass, both of which are also favored by sheep and cattle.

Another reason for the reduction in numbers is persecution by farmers. Wombats are excellent diggers and their warrens of interconnected burrows can destabilize the ground on which cattle and sheep graze. It is their enthusiastic burrowing habits that have made the

DATA PANEL

Northern hairy-nosed wombat (Queensland hairy-nosed wombat, soft-furred wombat, yamion)

Lasiorhinus krefftii

Family: Vombatidae

World population: About 70

Distribution: Epping Forest National Park in east central Queensland, Australia

Habitat: Dry, sandy grassland with patches of dense scrub

Size: Length: 39–43.5 in (97–110 cm); females slightly larger than males. Weight: 55–82 lb (25–37 kg)

Form: Stout-bodied animal with short, powerful legs and long claws; fur brown and silky; head large with squared-off muzzle, small eyes and ears, and long whiskers; female's pouch opens to the rear to prevent filling with sand when burrowing

Diet: Grasses

Breeding: Single young born during wet season (November–April); stays in pouch for 6–7 months; weaned at 8–9 months; fully independent at 12 months. Life span not known

Related endangered species: No close relatives except the common wombat (*Vombatus ursinus*), which is widespread and relatively numerous

Status: IUCN CR; CITES I

See also: Inbreeding and Interbreeding 1: 56; National Parks 1: 92; Koala 6: 10

species so unpopular. By tunneling under fences that had been put in place to keep rabbits out, the wombats became unwitting accomplices to the farmers' worst enemy; little grazing was left after the rabbits had moved in. Inevitably, the ranchers acted to protect their livestock, eradicating the wombats at every opportunity.

Prospects for the Future

In the years since the critical status of the northern hairy-nosed wombat was realized, there has been a concerted effort to save the species. Attempts to keep the animals in captivity have been unsuccessful, so their future depends entirely on the survival of the one wild population. The Epping Forest wombats are closely monitored, and cattle and other herbivores are kept well away. In the last 15 years the animal has benefited from its protected status and numbers have shown a slow but steady increase. The population now consists mostly of young animals, and the prospects for continued growth are good.

However, there is by no means a guaranteed future for the northern hairy-nosed wombat. There are signs that the Epping Forest population is dangerously inbred, which is not surprising considering that they are all descended from the same small number of animals. The wombats have only 41 percent of the genetic variation that was shown by a now extinct population from another part of Australia. Since the remaining wombats are genetically similar to each other, they are likely to share common weaknesses to diseases and other conditions.

The northern hairy-nosed wombat *is one of the world's largest burrowing animals. Many of its burrows are over 100 feet (30 m) long and usually form part of a complex underground network.*

Woodpecker, Ivory-Billed

Campephilus principalis

The magnificent ivory-billed woodpecker is now extinct in the southeastern United States. Although new evidence suggests that it hangs on in what is probably its last refuge—a small area of mountain forest in Cuba—it is probably on the brink of extinction.

The ivory-billed woodpecker is the world's second largest woodpecker. The largest is its close relative, the imperial woodpecker of Mexico, which is only slightly bigger than the ivory-billed woodpecker and is extinct or almost extinct.

At one time the northern race (*principalis*) of the ivory-billed woodpecker could be found throughout the southeastern United States. Despite its relatively wide range, the bird was restricted mainly to mature swampy forests with many dead trees bordering rivers. The forests were gloomy and almost impenetrable, with dense canopies of giant, moss-covered cypress trees, tangles of creeping plants, and massive trunks of fallen trees. The ivory-billed woodpeckers also favored mature pine forests with plenty of dead trees.

For centuries the woodpeckers were safe in their wilderness. A few were killed by Native Americans for their bills, which were used as decorations. Although such harvesting may have had a local effect on numbers, it is unlikely to have had a major effect on the population. However, things soon changed after the settlement of North America by Europeans.

Drop in Numbers

Despite the difficulty of traveling into them, the forests proved an irresistible attraction to logging companies. As the timber industry expanded to fuel industrial growth toward the end of the 19th century and into the early 20th century, the number of ivory-bills plummeted. Researchers have estimated that each pair of ivory-billed woodpeckers needs at least 6 square miles (16 sq. km) of prime, undisturbed forest. At such low densities the species would never have been common; but with much of its habitat invaded by the loggers, it was soon in trouble.

By 1900 deforestation and the attendant disturbance, together with direct persecution from commercial bird collectors eager to secure specimens of the increasingly rare bird, had eliminated the ivory-bill from all but the southernmost parts of its United States range. By 1939 the species was down to an estimated two dozen breeding birds in the

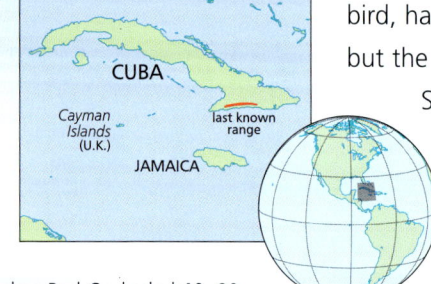

DATA PANEL

Ivory-billed woodpecker

Campephilus principalis

Family: Picidae

World population: Unknown

Distribution: Once occurred throughout southeastern U.S., but now extinct there; almost extinct in Cuba, but recent evidence suggests it occurs in the mountain forests of the Sierra Maestra in southeastern Cuba

Habitat: U.S.: occurred in swampy bottomland, broadleaf, and cypress forests. Cuba: lowland and montane pine, mixed and broadleaf forests; now only found in montane pine forests

Size: Length: 19–21 in (48–53 cm). Weight: 16–20 oz (450–570 g)

Form: Large woodpecker; plumage black, with large white patch on each wing; pair of white "braces" on back; pair of white stripes extend from upper back (mantle) onto head; males have large area of red on crest, females have all-black crests; juveniles browner, with shorter black crest; bill ivory-colored to cream; legs and feet gray; eyes white, brown in juveniles

Diet: Mainly larvae of wood-boring beetles; also fruit, berries, and nuts

Breeding: January–April in U.S., March–June in Cuba; excavates nest-hole in large, dead or dying tree; females lay 2–4 (usually 3 or 4) white eggs; incubated by both parents for about 20 days; young cared for by both parents; fledge in about 7 weeks

Related endangered species: Ten species, including imperial woodpecker (*Campephilus imperialis*) CR and Okinawa woodpecker (*Sapheopipo noguchii*) VU

Status: IUCN CR; not listed by CITES

See also: Speciation 1: 26; Habitat Loss 1: 38; Woodpecker, Red-Cockaded 10: 80

WOODPECKER, IVORY-BILLED

United States, and by 1968 a total of only six stray individuals were reported from swamp-forests in parts of Texas and Louisiana. Today the United States race is likely to be extinct.

Cause for Hope

Hope was kindled that a tiny remnant population of the ivory-bill—the last of the species in the world—still survived in Cuba. The Cuban birds belonged to the race *bairdii* that is similar to the race *principalis*, apart from having a shorter and narrower bill and a longer white neck stripe. As with the United States birds, it was human impact that had caused the demise of the Cuban ivory-bills. Loggers moved in, and crops replaced the native forests.

Ivory-bills are shy and difficult to find; in one Cuban survey researchers saw birds on only eight occasions after 750 hours of searching. During the late 1980s, however, sightings of ivory-bills were reported from remaining native pine forests in eastern Cuba, but by the mid-1990s the species was considered extinct when intensive searches failed to find more evidence of remaining birds. However, fresh evidence was obtained in 1998, this time in the highest reaches of the Sierra Maestra, an area of mountain forest in southeastern Cuba where the species had never before been recorded.

There is an urgent need to confirm the ivory-billed woodpecker's existence and to determine how many are left. If a population is found, it is likely to be tiny. Consequently, great determination will be needed to save the species by protecting its habitat effectively. On the other hand, numbers may have fallen to such a low level that recovery is impossible.

The ivory-billed woodpecker *is the world's second largest woodpecker. It uses its ivory-colored beak to extract the larvae of wood-boring beetles from dead tree trunks.*

Woodpecker, Red-Cockaded

Picoides borealis

Once found over a large area of the southeastern United States, the red-cockaded woodpecker is now reduced to a fraction of its former numbers. Populations have been fragmented by predation, competition from other animals for nest sites, logging, and natural disasters.

In 1839 the great American bird artist John James Audubon observed that the red-cockaded woodpecker was a common bird of the pine forests of southeastern United States, with a range that extended from New Jersey south to Florida and as far west as Texas and Oklahoma. As woodlands were cleared or degraded, the species suffered a relentless decline, which went relatively unnoticed until the 1970s. Then researchers discovered to their alarm that numbers were much reduced, occupying a mere one percent of the species' original range, and that the small woodpecker would soon face extinction unless something was done.

Compared with the other woodpeckers of North American woodlands, red-cockaded woodpeckers have very special habitat requirements. They need open woodland with mature trees of a few southern species of pine—mainly longleaf, shortleaf, and slash pine, but also loblolly pine and some other species. They excavate their neat, round nest holes not in dead trees, like most other woodpeckers, but in mature living pines (averaging between 70 and 120 years old) and infected with red heart, a fungal disease that causes the heartwood to become soft and thus somewhat easier for the birds to drill into. Even so, it may take a group of woodpeckers anything from a year to three years to complete the task.

Hopeful Interlopers

The woodpeckers live in extended family groups called clans. Each clan typically consists of a breeding pair, their young, and sons of the breeding male. The whole clan unites to defend a territory, and all members share the duties of incubating the eggs and

DATA PANEL

Red-cockaded woodpecker

Picoides borealis

Family: Picidae

World population: About 11,000 birds

Distribution: Patchily distributed in southeastern U.S.

Habitat: Open, mature pine and pine-oak woodland

Size: Length: 8–8.5 in (20–22 cm); wingspan: 15 in (38 cm). Weight: 1.5–2 oz (40–55 g)

Form: Small bird with pied (having markings of 2 or more colors) plumage; black "cap" and white cheek patches; back with intricate "ladder" pattern of black-and-white bars. Tiny patches of red feathers (cockades) on rear cheeks of male rarely visible. Juveniles sometimes have small red patch on crown

Diet: Chiefly insects, especially wood-boring beetles and their grubs; also bark beetles, ants, moths, caterpillars, woodland cockroaches, spiders, and millipedes; plant food includes pine seeds, pecan nuts, berries, and fruit

Breeding: Nests in holes in mature pine trees; 3–4 white eggs in clutch, laid late April to early June; incubation period 10–11 days; nestlings fledge after 26–29 days

Related endangered species: Sulu woodpecker *(Picoides ramsayi)* VU; Arabian woodpecker *(Dendrocopus dorae)* VU; ivory-billed woodpecker *(Campephilus principalis)** CR

Status: IUCN VU; not listed by CITES

See also: Communities and Ecosystems **1:** 22; Natural Disasters **1:** 57; Woodpecker, Ivory-Billed **10:** 78

feeding the young. A typical clan needs a territory of about 200 acres (80 ha) to supply its nesting and feeding needs, but small clans in prime habitat can make do with as little as 60 acres (24 ha), and large clans in less ideal areas may need more than 600 acres (240 ha). The territory contains many nest holes—up to five in one tree and about 50 in total—and they may be used by generations of woodpeckers.

Red-cockaded woodpeckers, and especially their eggs and young, fall victim to certain predators, including various small mammals such as flying squirrels and rat snakes. The nest holes are much sought after by other creatures. Hopeful interlopers include red-headed woodpeckers, other birds such as bluebirds, and flying squirrels. Red-cockaded woodpeckers are also vulnerable to human disturbance from loggers, hunters, or tourists.

Natural Friends and Enemies

The open, mature pine woodland habitat of the woodpecker has been sustained for centuries by natural fires started by lightning; such fires deter the growth of hardwoods. Modern forestry, however, has resulted in the wholesale logging of large areas for timber. Areas have also been cleared to make way for farmland, and fire-prevention programs have been introduced. As a result, hardwood trees have invaded and largely replaced the pines, making the area unsuitable for nesting. The key threat is fragmentation of habitat, which isolates clans and puts them at risk.

As well as constant, long-term hazards, there is also the threat of devastation from the hurricanes that periodically occur in parts of the woodpecker's range. For instance, in 1989 Hurricane Hugo destroyed 100,000 acres (40,500 ha) of South Carolina's Francis Marion National Forest. The protected area contained about a quarter of the world population of red-cockaded woodpeckers.

There are now fewer than 30 isolated populations of red-cockaded woodpeckers, containing some 4,700

The red-cockaded woodpecker *chisels into pine trees infected and softened by a fungal disease.*

clans. Conservation is an urgent task, not just for the woodpeckers themselves, but also because they play a crucial role in the intricate web of life in a special habitat. Abandoned nest holes become home to a whole range of creatures, including reptiles, ants, wasps, and other woodpeckers. Pileated woodpeckers enlarge the holes, which may then be used by wood ducks, screech owls, or raccoons, and pine beetles kill nest trees.

Conservation programs focus on translocating females to clans lacking them, providing artificial nest holes, and deterring pileated woodpeckers with protective plates. Other measures include prohibiting clearance of the forest, removing invading hardwoods, and deterring predators.

Worm, Palolo

Eunice viridis

One of nature's best timekeepers, the palolo worm lives on the rocky seabed of coral reefs in the South Pacific, including Fiji and Samoa. A marine bristle worm, it has a reproductive cycle that is governed by the seasons and phases of the moon. The predictability of its spawning means that the species is easily and effectively harvested.

Part of the family of segmented marine worms, the bristle worms are so called because their bodies have obvious bristles, known as chaetae. The palolo worm belongs to this group, and as such it is a relative of the familiar lugworms and ragworms that are widely used by sea anglers as bait. Palolo worms live mainly in the tropical seas. They are found especially in the southwestern Pacific around the islands of Fiji and Samoa.

The palolo worm is particularly famous for its precise reproductive timetable that is exactly controlled by season, tides, and phases of the moon. For much of the year the young worms live in burrows formed in crevices in coral limestone. They line the burrows with mucus for protection. Their heads lie near the burrow openings; but because they are photonegative (they avoid light by moving away from it), they only come out to search for food at night. Their food—small marine animals—is caught with head tentacles and manipulated into the mouth by the jaws.

Body Changes at Maturity

As the worms mature, the number of body segments increases and may reach 1,000. The body form alters at the rear, and the segments of the posterior region lengthen and develop additional eyes. The two paddlelike limbs on each segment carry bristles that become more flaplike as an adaptation for better swimming. When the tail is modified, the worm is known as an epitoke. It changes its behavior at this time because its hind parts become photopositive (attracted to light). The worms appear to reverse their position in their burrows, with the photopositive tail sticking out of the burrow entrance and the photonegative head in the base of the burrow. In mature worms the segments of the epitoke have most of their normal internal structures reduced and become packed with either sperm or eggs.

If such preparation for breeding were not remarkable in itself, the culmination of the breeding process is truly amazing. On (usually) the seventh night following the first full moon after the fall equinox the epitoke separates from the rest of the worm. The intensity and duration of this

DATA PANEL

Palolo worm

Eunice viridis

Family: Eunicidae

World population: Unknown

Distribution: Southwestern Pacific Ocean, around Fiji and Samoa

Habitat: Crevices in coral reefs and coral limestone in shallow water

Size: Length: 15.6 in (40 cm)

Form: Marine bristle worm; segmented body divided into distinct regions when mature. Paddlelike limbs on each segment (parapodia) have bristles (chaetae) that aid swimming. In preparation for reproduction posterior segments lengthen and develop eyes. Modified worm is known as an epitoke

Diet: Small marine animals

Breeding: Separate sexes. Reproductive cycle governed by tidal patterns, lunar periodicity, and seasons. Epitoke detaches from main body, swims to surface, and releases contents (either egg or sperm) at surface in response to light intensity

Related endangered species: No other Eunicidae species listed by IUCN, but some land-based segmented worms are considered at risk, such as Washington giant earthworm (*Driloleirus americanus*) VU

Status: IUCN DD; not listed by CITES

See also: Life Strategies 1: 24; Luxury Products 1: 46; Nemertine, Rodrigues 7: 8

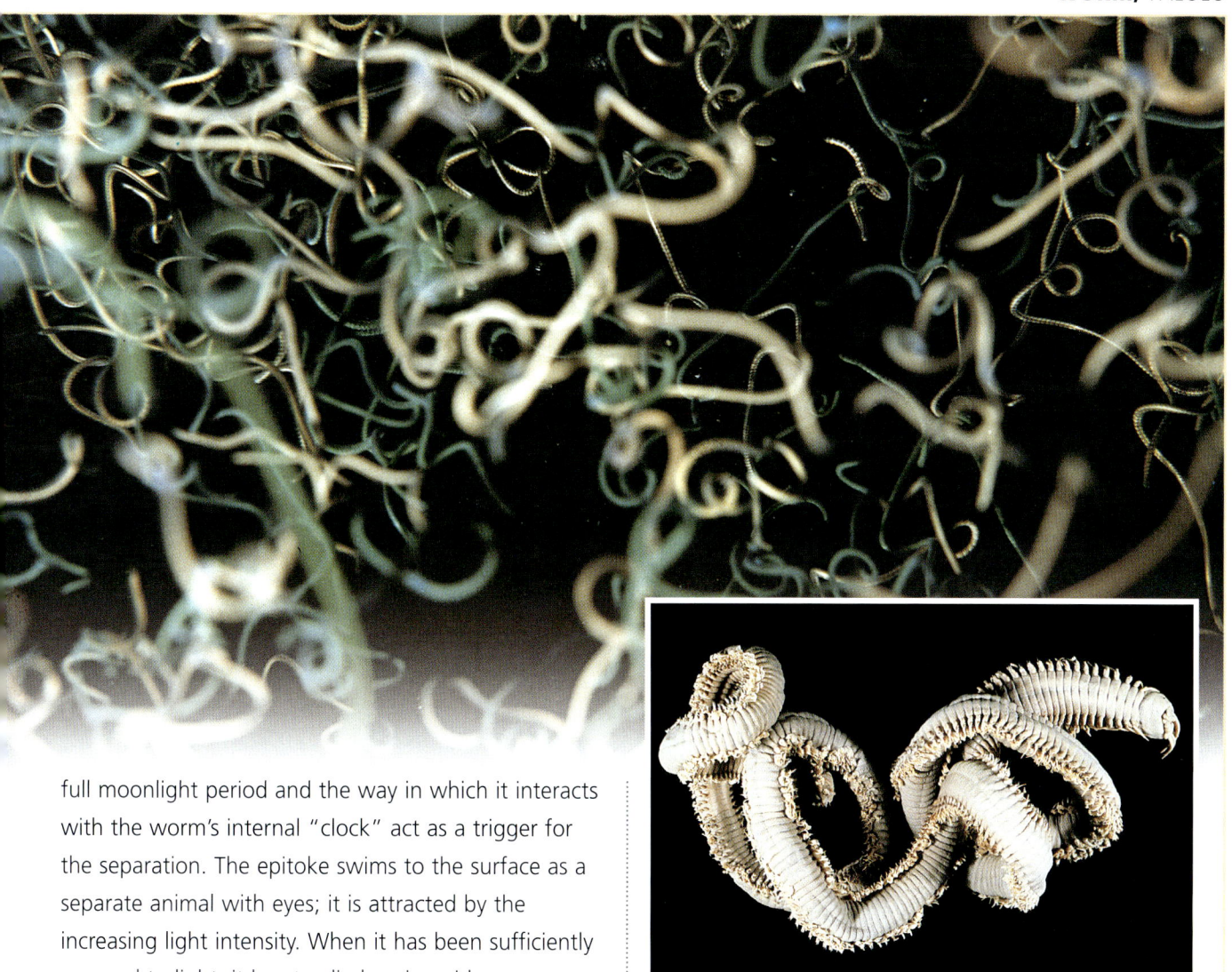

full moonlight period and the way in which it interacts with the worm's internal "clock" act as a trigger for the separation. The epitoke swims to the surface as a separate animal with eyes; it is attracted by the increasing light intensity. When it has been sufficiently exposed to light, it bursts, discharging either sperm or eggs. Fertilization occurs in the surrounding water, and swimming larvae are formed. They settle on the seabed and repeat the cycle.

How the worms know that the moment to spawn has arrived is still unclear. It is unlikely that they watch the moon from their burrows, but changes in light intensity and duration are apparent under the surface. It is possible that once the first few epitokes have broken free, chemicals released by them may trigger the release of others. This is called a synchrony device (one that occurs simultaneously).

Harvesting

The highly predictable habits of the palolo worm have almost certainly evolved to increase fertilization success and population growth. Ironically, the regularity of the worm's internal "clock" has also

Palolo worms *(above) can have as many as 1,000 segments (inset). They develop a modified tail, which detaches itself and paddles to the surface to spawn.*

made it highly vulnerable. Its behavior patterns with the seasons, light levels, and prevailing tidal patterns mean that it is easy for local people to accurately predict the palolo harvest time. The harvesting process can remove the reproductive stages from the worm's life cycle, thus depleting populations.

At the time when the palolo epitokes rise, large crowds of Fijians and Samoans gather to scoop up the surfacing animal. (In pre-Christian Samoa the event marked the start of the New Year.) The worm pieces are eaten either raw or lightly fried and are regarded as a great delicacy.

Worm, Velvet

Peripatus spp.

Some scientists have regarded the velvet worms as "missing links" in the evolutionary chain of the animal kingdom. Their habitat—in the litter of the forest floor in moist areas—makes them vulnerable to human activities such as logging and forest clearance.

Velvet worms are terrestrial invertebrates that are placed in their own phylum: Onychophora (meaning claw-bearers). As a result of their widely scattered distribution and nocturnal habits, velvet worms are poorly known; few scientists have had the opportunity to observe live examples. The best known genus in the phylum is *Peripatus*, of which there are about 20 species. Velvet worms look like large caterpillars. They are covered in dry, velvety skin, and they have about 20 pairs of short legs.

Missing Links

Scientists have considered velvet worms as "missing links," lying somewhere in the evolutionary progression between annelids (earthworms and their allies) and arthropods (crustaceans, insects, and spiders). For example, velvet worms have antennae and clawlike mandibles (mouth parts) like arthropods, but their eyes are similar in structure to those of annelids, and they have a thin, flexible body wall (like annelids) rather than an exoskeleton. They move by contracting sheets of muscle (and with little assistance from their soft, unjointed legs), like worms.

Fossil evidence suggests that velvet worms existed 500 million years ago. There are about 70 species of Onychophora in widely separated parts of the world, indicating that the Onychophora are an animal group that evolved before the ancient land masses separated. However, whether velvet worms are forerunners of today's centipedes and millipedes (arthropods) is debatable. Recent research suggests that velvet worms may indeed be closer to modern-day arthropods than annelids and that they should perhaps be classified as such. In due course the exact classification of velvet worms will be worked out on the basis of molecular investigations.

Slime Attack

The body of the velvet worm is divided into between 14 and 44 segments (depending on the species). Each segment has a pair of short legs with curved claws on the feet. Since they have no skeleton, the worms can squeeze through small holes. They hunt at night, feeding on small insects and cutting up prey with their strong jaws.

On either side of the intestine are glands that produce a sticky slime, which is squirted from a pair of papillae or fingerlike projections on both sides of the mouth. On contact with air the slime solidifies into sticky threads. Small animals readily become entangled in the threads, although the mechanism is thought to be more for defense than to subdue prey.

Moisture Dependent

Velvet worms live in leaf litter on the forest floor, under stones or logs, or in the soil. Their skin has pits that are connected to thin breathing tubes (tracheae). Since there

See also: The Animal Kingdom **1:** 58; Habitat Loss **1:** 38; Worm, Palolo **10:** 82

are so many openings and because they cannot be closed, water vapor is constantly lost from the body. (Arthropods have fewer such openings, and theirs can be closed.) In the velvet worm's moist habitat, however, water loss is compensated for: The worms take up water through minute pouches situated near the base of their legs. They fill the pouches by pressing up against damp surfaces. Water is also replaced by drinking the body fluids of insect prey.

Velvet worms are vulnerable to many aspects of human activity. Clearing of the forests by logging, the development of farmland, and the construction of highways all seriously damage the moist forest habitat on which the worms depend. The velvet worms are also at a disadvantage: Unlike many other animals, they cannot move rapidly enough over short periods to redistribute themselves into new habitats.

One of the *Peripatus* species, Macroperipatus insularis *of Jamaica, giving birth*.

DATA PANEL

Velvet worm

***Peripatus* spp. (about 20 species)**

Family: Peripatidae

World population: Unknown

Distribution: West Indies, Central America, and northern regions of South America

Habitat: Southern temperate and tropical forests, among leaf litter and under bark

Size: Length: females up to 5.9 in (15 cm) long; males shorter

Form: Cylindrical body; conspicuous antennae on head; clawlike mandible; thin body wall; 14–43 pairs of short, soft unjointed legs

Diet: Plant material; also insects and other worms

Breeding: Sexes separate; male places capsule of sperm on skin of female. Her white blood cells digest skin under capsule, allowing sperm to enter blood stream; when sperm have found their way to the ovary, they migrate through the ovarian wall and fertilize eggs. Eggs develop and are nourished in uterus. Live young born after a gestation period of about 13 months

Related endangered species: About 70 species of velvet worm; 20 species of the genus *Peripatus*. All are probably vulnerable to destruction of moist forest habitats by logging and development

Status: IUCN EN; not listed by CITES

Wren, Zapata

Ferminia cerverai

Restricted to a single region of swampland on the island of Cuba, the Zapata wren has been lucky to survive near-extinction in the 1960s and 1970s, when parts of its isolated habitat were drained and repeatedly burned by local farmers. It could happen again; with nowhere to go, the wren could vanish virtually overnight.

The Zapata Swamp of western Cuba extends over much of the 80-mile- (135-km-) long Zapata Peninsula, which lies on the south side of the island, near Havana. It is a region of marshland, ponds, and lakes, mixed with wild grassland, scrub, and forest: a near-wilderness that has become a refuge for many of Cuba's rarer birds. Driven from many parts of the island by deforestation for timber and agriculture, the birds feed and nest alongside a species that is endemic to western Cuba (found nowhere else in the world): the Zapata wren.

The small, brown, dark-barred Zapata wren is remarkable for having extremely short wings, making it almost flightless. It travels almost entirely on foot, slipping through low vegetation to snap up spiders, snails, small insects and lizards, and berries. It nests in the tall tussocks of sawgrass that grow on the wet grasslands, claiming its territory with a loud, musical warble. The sound of a rival's song will often attract a male Zapata wren to the spot.

Threats

Within its small range—some 363 square miles (940 sq. km)—the Zapata wren enjoys a relatively quiet existence. Yet since it was first scientifically described in 1926 the species has become increasingly rare. It has suffered from a range of human activities, including attempts to drain parts of the swamp for use as agricultural land. In addition, during the dry season local farmers burn off the sawgrass to improve the grazing for their animals. The burning destroys wrens' habitat and may even kill the wrens. Since the birds are reluctant to

DATA PANEL

Zapata wren (Fermina wren)

Ferminia cerverai

Family: Troglodytidae

World population: About 1,000–2,400 birds

Distribution: Zapata Swamp, western Cuba

Habitat: Freshwater marsh and grassland with scattered bushes and low trees

Size: Length: 6.3 in (16 cm)

Form: Small songbird with unusually short wings and a long tail, long legs, and a long bill. Upperparts grayish brown, with black spots on head and black bars on back and wings. Underparts pale gray

Diet: Insects, spiders, small snails, small lizards, and berries

Breeding: Breeds January–July, nesting in sawgrass tussocks; lays up to 6 white eggs

Related endangered species: Six species of wren are threatened, including Apolinar's wren *(Cistothorus apolinari)* EN and Niceforo's wren *(Thryothorus nicefori)* CR

Status: IUCN EN; CITES II

See also: Categories of Threat 1: 14; Introductions 1: 54; Finch, Mangrove 4: 76; Fody, Mauritius 4: 88

fly, they are also easy prey for alien predators such as the small Indian mongoose—introduced to Cuba in the 1870s to control the hordes of rats living on the island's sugarcane plantations. The rats themselves probably also kill adult wrens and their young.

As a result of these problems, the wren population dwindled throughout the 1960s and early 1970s. By 1974 the species seemed to have reached the point of near-extinction and was classified as Critically Endangered. It survived, and a survey in 1998 revealed that it was more numerous than had been feared; but the bird remains extremely rare and seems to be still declining. The remaining wren population is fragmented and scattered, yet limited to such a small area in the northern and central parts of the Zapata Swamp that a local catastrophe—either natural or man-made—could easily wipe out the whole lot.

The Zapata wren, *like many other species of wren, reveals its whereabouts with a loud, warbling song.*

The Future

The Zapata wren does enjoy a certain amount of protection. Most of the Zapata Peninsula lies within the Zapata National Park, and parts of the swamp form the Santo Tomás Faunal Refuge, covering an area of 5.7 square miles (14.8 sq. km). Unfortunately, the regulations protecting wildlife within the swamp are not often enforced. Cuba's political isolation within the Caribbean does not help the situation. Fuel and other supplies are difficult to obtain, and many Cubans have no choice but to exploit the natural resources available to them.

If the Zapata wren is to survive, its wetland habitat must be better protected, with stricter enforcement of the conservation rules. There is also an urgent need for further research into the bird's range and population numbers, as well as the factors that are currently threatening its survival. Only when such information has been gathered will it be possible to improve and protect the Zapata wren's habitat, reduce mortality rates, and reverse the bird's apparently relentless decline.

Xenopoecilus

Xenopoecilus saranisorum

Xenopoecilus is a fish that has a limited range and an unusual reproductive strategy. Its restricted distribution—just one lake in Sulawesi, Indonesia—makes it extremely vulnerable to habitat changes. The introduction of nonnative species, along with the deterioration of water quality, have combined to endanger xenopoecilus's status in the wild.

No matter how a fish is classified in taxonomic terms, it will generally fall within one of two groups with regard to reproductive strategy. It will be either oviparous (an egglayer) or viviparous (a bearer of live young). Most of the time this demarcation works well. While there are several examples of fish that bear live young after internal fertilization (many sharks, for example), in the majority of fish species egg fertilization and development occur outside the body. External fertilization is achieved in a multitude of ways, ranging from straightforward egg-and-sperm scattering in open water with no subsequent parental involvement to egg deposition on a prepared surface and intense brood care by one or both parents, or even incubation in the mouth of the eggs by one or other of the parents.

Halfway House

Xenopoecilus—along with a few other species as diverse as some sharks and rays, two killifish, and a characin—does not fit neatly into either the egglaying or livebearing categories. Instead, it employs internal fertilization (as livebearers do); then the females expel the eggs—but only partially. The eggs are not released entirely into the surrounding water. Several hours after mating (once the eggs have been fertilized internally) the female produces a small number of eggs (often fewer than 20), each bearing a thread or filament by which it stays attached to the female's vent.

At this point the female tucks her pelvic (hip) fins in, pulling them back in such a way that they partially cover the bunch of eggs, giving them some protection. The eggs are then carried around by the female for the two weeks that it takes the embryos to complete development.

Apparently, this carrying around is important for the survival of the young. If the thread attaching an egg to the female breaks, and the egg drops off several days before embryonic development has been completed, it will usually fail to survive. However, if it

DATA PANEL

Xenopoecilus (Sarasin's minnow)

Xenopoecilus saranisorum

Family: Adrianichthyidae

World population: Unknown; believed to be low

Distribution: Lake Lindu Sulawesi, Indonesia

Habitat: Top layers of the water column; prefers vegetated areas

Size: Length: about 3.2 in (8 cm)

Form: Body elongated and compressed with a pointed snout and large mouth and eyes. Dorsal (back) fin is set well back. In the male the side of the body is adorned by a row of dark spots that are less prominent or barely visible in the female. Males have larger dorsal and anal (belly) fins than females; females have longer pelvic (hip) fins

Diet: Largely insects, aquatic invertebrates, and small fish

Breeding: Males display with extended fins that darken at this time, as does the body. During mating, which often occurs in the morning, the male wraps his dorsal and anal fins around the female. Several hours later the female produces a small cluster of eggs that remain attached to her vent by thin filaments. The female protects the cluster by folding the pelvic fins back and covering the eggs. Hatching takes place after about 2 weeks

Related endangered species: Egg-carrying buntingi *(Xenopoecilus oophorus)* EN; Popta's buntingi *(X. poptae)* CR; duck-billed buntingi *(Adrianichthyis kruyti)* CR

Status: IUCN EN; not listed by CITES

See also: Introductions 1: 54; Captive Breeding 1: 87; Shark, Silver 8: 84

drops off just before hatching, its chances of survival to full term are good; that is, if it manages to avoid the attention of the female, which is an avid egg eater.

Threatened Family

There are three species in the genus *Xenopoecilus*: *X. oophorus*, *X. poptae,* and *X. saranisorum*. All are under some threat in the wild, along with the other member of the subfamily, the duck-billed buntingi. This small subfamily of just four species belongs to the family Adrianichthyidae, which includes the ricefish or medakas that are popular among aquarists. A majority of them also exhibit the unusual trait of internal fertilization with delayed or partial release of eggs, making them of interest to scientists as well as aquarium keepers.

The species *Xenopoecilus saranisorum,* known as xenopoecilus, or Sarasin's minnow (a misleading name) has been kept and bred in aquaria for several years. Much of what we know about the species has therefore been gleaned by dedicated hobbyists and scientists who maintain captive-bred stocks.

As long as captive-bred stocks are sustained, the species will continue to survive, if only in captivity.

Xenopoecilus is a surface swimmer that appreciates plant cover. In the wild it has been affected by competition with introduced species and changing water quality as a result of deforestation.

Indeed, aquarium-bred xenopoecilus may be the only representatives of the species that will be left if conditions in the wild do not improve in the near future. This is a precarious situation, but perhaps less so than that in Lake Lindu in Sulawesi, the natural home of xenopoecilus.

From the little that has been published on Lake Lindu it appears that pollution is not a major threat. However, deforestation in the region may be causing alterations to water quality, while nonnative species that have been introduced primarily for food and angling purposes may pose the greatest threat of all. Experiences elsewhere indicate that some exotic species can prove impossible to eradicate and can wipe out indigenous species within an alarmingly short period of time. When the distribution of the indigenous species is restricted—as is the case with xenopoecilus—the risks of extinction escalate.

Yak, Wild

Bos grunniens

The ultimate "survival machine," the sturdy yak is in its element even in the harshest Himalayan winter conditions. However, it is not adapted to deal with the threats of hunting, habitat disturbance, and competition from its domesticated relatives.

Yaks are the eastern equivalent of the American bison, and they are among the hardiest mammals on earth. Between 2,000 and 3,000 years ago the yak's ancestors were successfully domesticated and used for milk, beef, and wool production. Domestic yaks were also used as pack and draft animals, and their dried dung served as fuel on the Tibetan plateau, which has no trees. Today the world population of domestic yaks is probably over 12 million. By contrast, wild yaks are now extremely rare: Recent estimates have put the population at just a few hundred animals.

An immensely hardy animal, the yak survives seemingly without difficulty on the hostile, high plateaus of the Himalayas, enduring winter conditions among the harshest on earth. Temperatures in this area can fall to as low as -15°F (-26°C). The yak uses heat generated by plant material fermenting in its intestines to help keep warm; adult yaks are also covered in thick, woolly hair. However, with such adaptations to the extreme cold yaks are not so tolerant of warm temperatures. Herds that move to lower pastures to bear young in spring retreat as summer arrives, returning to altitudes of about 15,000 feet (4,550 m), where there is snow all year round.

Yaks are social animals, and most individuals will spend their lives as part of a herd. The largest herds are made up of females and young, with bachelor males forming smaller bands. There are obvious advantages to living in a group; formidable as fully grown yaks are, they still have at least one serious natural predator, namely, the Tibetan wolf.

Sure-Footed Climbers

The scarcity of good food in its habitat forces the yak to wander widely in search of grasses, lichens, and other low-growing alpine plants. Deep snow is hard to walk through, but the yaks save

DATA PANEL

Wild yak

Bos grunniens

Family: Bovidae

World population: Fewer than 1,000

Distribution: Tibetan plateau (northern Tibet); Kansu in northwestern China; eastern Kashmir in India

Habitat: Alpine tundra and steppe; spends summer above snow line

Size: Length: up to 10.6 ft (3.3 m); height at shoulder: up to 6.5 ft (2 m); females about 60% smaller than males. Weight: males 670–2,200 lb (300–1,000 kg); females lighter than males

Form: Massive ox with dense, brown-black woolly hair. High humped shoulders; low-slung head. Both sexes have curved horns

Diet: Grasses, herbs, and lichens

Breeding: Adults mate in winter; a single calf is born in the following fall. Life span up to 25 years

Related endangered species: American bison (Bison bison)* LRcd

Status: IUCN VU; not listed by CITES

See also: Inbreeding and Interbreeding 1: 56; Anoa, Mountain 2: 20; Gaur 5: 18; Kouprey 6: 14; Takin 9: 50

energy by walking in single file, stepping into the footprints of the animal in front. Each large cloven hoof is augmented with an enlarged dewclaw (a partly developed extra hoof), which gives a strong grip. Despite their bulk, the yaks are sure-footed climbers, able to hop from rock to rock to avoid the deepest snowdrifts. Only in the worst storms and blizzards do they come to a halt to wait out the weather, standing in small groups with their heads turned away from the driving wind and icy snow.

On the Brink of Extinction

The wild yak should surely be thriving in a habitat where no other species can match its power and suitability for the environment. It suffers from only moderate predation and has very little natural competition. However, as is so often the case, this magnificent example of natural design is being pushed to the brink of extinction by the actions of humans. Wild herds are hunted throughout much of their range; and as human settlements have expanded, yaks are finding themselves outcompeted by domestic herds or in some cases simply assimilated into them.

Wild and domestic yaks often interbreed. Consequently, the genetic purity of the wild type has been diluted, and the offspring are less able to cope with life in the wild.

The yak is a massive, powerful creature with a voice to suit its stature. Its deep, grunting call has earned it a scientific name that translates literally as "grunting ox."

Zebra, Grevy's

Equus grevyi

Disappearing faster than any other large African mammal, Grevy's zebra is now found only in parts of northern Kenya and southern Ethiopia.

Grevy's is the largest of the three species of zebra. Its distinctive narrow stripes made it attractive to hunters, who sold the hides for use in making decorative objects. Large numbers of Grevy's zebra were hunted even as late as the 1970s. The threat has now receded because Grevy's zebra is listed in Appendix I of the CITES agreement, so export and international trade in the animal are prohibited.

The main threats to Grevy's zebra populations are now the effects of habitat loss, pressure of competition from domestic animals, and the exclusion of the zebras from the areas they have traditionally occupied, male Grevy's being strongly attached to territories. The zebra populations have also been hit hard by droughts in recent years.

Slow Breeders

Grevy's zebra breeds very slowly. The animals take six years to reach maturity, and their exceptionally long gestation (13 months) means that mares cannot give birth every year. Only one foal is born each time, which then takes at least six months to rear. Slow breeding is common among larger animals, especially those living in challenging semidesert areas, where it can be an adaptation to the limited ability of the habitat to support offspring. It also protects the animals, especially the females, in areas of limited supplies; there is no point in producing or trying to rear more offspring if they and their mother then die as a result of stress and food shortage. Formerly, natural predators killed relatively few zebras, so the populations were not badly affected. However, once hunting by humans became more common, zebra populations started to decline. At that point their slow breeding rate meant that the animals could not maintain their numbers in the face of heavy losses.

DATA PANEL

Grevy's zebra

Equus grevyi

Family: Equidae

World population: About 4,000; probably fewer

Distribution: A few areas of Ethiopia and Kenya. Recently extinct in Somalia, Sudan, Djibouti, and Eritrea

Habitat: Prefers dry grasslands where fire or elephants have destroyed many trees, leaving open areas. Many used to congregate in the wet season on flooded grasslands

Size: Length head/body: 8–10 ft (2.4–3 m); tail: 16–30 in (40–75 cm); height at shoulder: 4.5–5.2 ft (1.4–1.6 m). Weight: mares 850 lb (350–400 kg); stallions 950 lb (380–450 kg)

Form: Horselike animal with many narrow stripes, a white belly, and large, white-tipped ears

Diet: Grasses, particularly the tough species that other grazers cannot manage

Breeding: One foal born after 13-month gestation; births occur every 2–3 years. Foals take at least 6 months to become independent and may remain with their mother for 3 years. Life span at least 18 years in the wild, 24 in captivity

Related endangered species: Quagga (*Equus quagga*)* EX; mountain zebra (*E. zebra*)* EN; African wild ass (*E. africanus*)* CR; Asiatic wild ass (*E. hemionus*)* VU

Status: IUCN EN; CITES I

See also: CITES **1:** 12; Ass, African Wild **2:** 34; Quagga **8:** 8; Zebra, Mountain **10:** 94

Grevy's zebra *is distinguished from other species of zebra by its narrow, closely spaced stripes and white ear tips.*

Dwindling Numbers

Grevy's zebra used to be found all over the Horn of Africa, throughout much of Ethiopia and Somalia, and in northern Kenya. However, by the 1970s their distribution had shrunk alarmingly. There were estimated to be about 13,700 animals left in Kenya in 1977, this number plummeting to 4,276 by 1988; a decline of 70 percent in a decade. The rate of disappearance was the fastest of any large mammal in Africa. Today Grevy's zebra is extinct in Somalia, and the remaining animals are now mostly confined to protected reserves in Kenya, where they still nevertheless suffer disturbance from tourists. There are about 550 in captivity in zoos around the world.

The decline is continuing. The wetter areas where the Grevy's zebras graze have increasingly been taken over for farming and grazing of livestock, so the shy animals are kept away from drinking places and fenced out of the best grazing areas. Humans also take water from the higher parts of rivers to irrigate crops, which results in less being available in the lowlands where zebras feed and drink.

Boreholes have been created to bring water to the surface for people and livestock, but this removes water from underground, vital for replenishing springs, causing moist green feeding areas to dry up. Domestic sheep and goats eagerly seek any remaining vegetation that might have fed zebras.

Zebra, Mountain

Equus zebra

Mountain zebras live in small, isolated groups and so are vulnerable to piecemeal extinction. Hunting has also been a significant threat.

The mountain zebra occurs as two populations of separate subspecies living in different highland areas. Hartmann's mountain zebra is widely distributed in southwestern Africa, and several hundred may remain in the wild. The Cape mountain zebra is a smaller animal, confined to higher altitudes in Cape Province and the Karoo in South Africa.

Mountain zebras live in small harem groups, generally numbering fewer than 10 animals and dominated by a single stallion. These breeding groups may remain stable for several years, while bachelors and nonbreeding mares gather in temporary groups or live alone. Occasionally, loose herds of up to 30 animals may form. Unlike other zebras, mountain zebras do not tend to form mixed herds with other mammals such as gazelles, antelopes, and wildebeest.

Harsh Conditions

Mountain zebras live on semidesert mountain slopes in southern Africa, near enough to the coast to benefit from the moist air coming off the sea. As the sea air rises up the slopes, it cools and forms mist and dew, especially at night. The moisture supports relatively lush vegetation and also supplies small springs where animals can drink in an otherwise waterless landscape. In some instances the zebras can remain in the same small area, perhaps of only 1 to 2 square miles (3 to 5 sq. km), for much of the year. But in places like the Karoo, where there are summer droughts, they may need to undertake seasonal migrations of 70 miles (120 km) or more between winter and summer feeding grounds.

Animals with isolated populations, particularly mountain species like the mountain zebra, tend to experience piecemeal extinction as a result of small populations being "picked off" by natural disasters or being reduced to such small numbers that they die out through lack of breeding success.

Hunted to the Brink

Mountain zebras were hunted for their meat and especially for their boldly marked skins. They were easy to shoot with rifles, and too many were killed for their natural rate of

---

DATA PANEL

Mountain zebra (Cape mountain zebra, Hartmann's zebra)

Equus zebra, Equus zebra zebra, Equus zebra hartmannii

Family: Equidae

World population: About 2,000–3,000 animals

Distribution: Southwestern Angola and Namibia to the Cape and Karoo in South Africa

Habitat: Shrubby grassland at higher altitudes where daytime heat and dryness are offset by mist and dew at night

Size: Length head/body: 7.3–8.5 ft (2.2–2.6 m); tail: 16–22 in (40–55 cm); height at shoulder: 4–5 ft (1.2–1.5 m). Weight: male 600–850 lb (275–386 kg); female smaller

Form: Horselike animal with black-and-white stripes on shoulders and neck; only 3 or 4 broad stripes on haunches; thin stripes on face, mane, and legs

Diet: Almost exclusively grass

Breeding: One foal born after a year-long gestation. May stay with its mother for up to 2 years. Takes 4–5 years to reach maturity. Life span at least 25 years

Related endangered species: Quagga (*Equus quagga*)* EX; Grevy's zebra (*E. grevyi*)* EN; African wild ass (*E. africanus*)* CR; Asiatic wild ass (*E. hemionus*)* VU

Status: IUCN EN; CITES I (Cape) and II (Hartmann's)

See also: Populations 1: 20; Quagga 8: 8; Zebra, Grevy's 10: 92

reproduction to replace, leading to dwindling numbers. The Cape mountain zebra populations were already in decline in the 18th century, and the animal was given legal protection as early as 1742. However, the animals continued to be hunted until each small population was wiped out. The subspecies was only saved from total extinction by a single farmer, Henry Lombard, who kept 11 animals on his farm. Another crisis was reached in 1950, when there were only 91 Cape mountain zebras left alive. A population of about 400 was built up by 1984, rising to 1,200 by 1995; the zebras were then distributed among at least six wildlife reserves.

Hartmann's mountain zebra is slightly more numerous and widespread, and therefore appears to be more secure. However, since the 1920s it has faced a familiar problem: the expansion of cultivation on farms and grazing by domestic animals has taken over the best feeding areas to the exclusion of wild animals. The increased use of fencing on farmland is also a problem for the zebras, since it prevents them from moving around in search of water and alternative feeding places, and from making vital seasonal migrations between different grazing areas.

The mountain zebra *lives in inhospitable areas where the only moisture to support vegetation and freshwater springs is that carried in sea breezes.*

Glossary

Words in SMALL CAPITALS refer to other entries in the glossary.

Adaptation features of an animal that adjust it to its environment; may be produced by evolution—e.g., camouflage coloration

Adaptive radiation where a group of closely related animals (e.g., members of a FAMILY) have evolved differences from each other so that they can survive in different NICHES

Adhesive disks flattened disks on the tips of the fingers or toes of certain climbing AMPHIBIANS that enable them to cling to smooth, vertical surfaces

Adult a fully grown sexually mature animal; a bird in its final PLUMAGE

Algae primitive plants ranging from microscopic, single-celled forms to large forms, such as seaweeds, but lacking proper roots or leaves

Alpine living in mountainous areas, usually over 5,000 feet (1,500 m)

Ambient describing the conditions around an animal, e.g., the water temperature for a fish or the air temperature for a land animal

Amphibian any cold-blooded VERTEBRATE of the CLASS Amphibia, typically living on land but breathing in the water; e.g., frogs, toads, newts, salamanders

Amphibious able to live on both land and in water

Amphipod a type of CRUSTACEAN found on land and in both fresh and seawater

Anadromous fish that spend most of their life at sea but MIGRATE into fresh water for breeding, e.g., salmon

Annelid of the PHYLUM Annelida in which the body is made up of similar segments, e.g., earthworms, lugworms, leeches

Anterior the front part of an animal

Arachnid one of a group of ARTHROPODS of the CLASS Arachnida, characterized by simple eyes and four pairs of legs. Includes spiders and scorpions

Arboreal living in trees

Aristotle's lantern complex chewing apparatus of sea-urchins that includes five teeth

Arthropod the largest PHYLUM in the animal kingdom in terms of the number of SPECIES in it. Characterized by a hard, jointed EXOSKELETON and paired jointed legs. Includes INSECTS, spiders, crabs, etc.

Baleen horny substance commonly known as whalebone and growing as plates in the mouth of certain whales; used as a fringelike sieve for extracting plankton from seawater

Bill often called the beak: the jaws of a bird, consisting of two bony MANDIBLES, upper and lower, and their horny sheaths

Biodiversity the variety of SPECIES and the variation within them

Biome a major world landscape characterized by having similar plants and animals living in it, e.g., DESERT, jungle, forest

Biped any animal that walks on two legs. See QUADRUPED

Blowhole the nostril opening on the head of a whale through which it breathes

Breeding season the entire cycle of reproductive activity, from courtship, pair formation (and often establishment of territory) through nesting to independence of young

Bristle in birds a modified feather, with a bare or partly bare shaft, like a stiff hair; functions include protection, as with eyelashes of ostriches and hornbills, and touch sensors to help catch INSECTS, as with flycatchers

Brood the young hatching from a single CLUTCH of eggs

Browsing feeding on leaves of trees and shrubs

Cage bird A bird kept in captivity; in this set it usually refers to birds taken from the wild

Canine tooth a sharp stabbing tooth usually longer than the rest

Canopy continuous (closed) or broken (open) layer in forests produced by the intermingling of branches of trees

Carapace the upper part of a shell in a CHELONIAN

Carnivore meat-eating animal

Carrion rotting flesh of dead animals

Casque the raised portion on the head of certain REPTILES and birds

Catadromous fish that spend most of their life in fresh water but MIGRATE to the sea for SPAWNING, e.g., eels

Caudal fin the tail fin in fish

Cephalothorax a body region of CRUSTACEANS formed by the union of the head and THORAX. See PROSOMA

Chelicerae the first pair of appendages ("limbs") on the PROSOMA of spiders, scorpions, etc. Often equipped to inject venom

Chelonian any REPTILE of the ORDER Chelonia, including the tortoises and turtles, in which most of the body is enclosed in a bony capsule

Chrysalis the PUPA in moths and butterflies

Class a large TAXONOMIC group of related animals. MAMMALS, INSECTS, and REPTILES are all CLASSES of animals

Cloaca cavity in the pelvic region into which the alimentary canal, genital, and urinary ducts open

Cloud forest moist, high-altitude forest characterized by a dense UNDERSTORY and an abundance of ferns, mosses, and other plants growing on the trunks and branches of trees

Clutch a set of eggs laid by a female bird in a single breeding attempt

Cocoon the protective coat of many insect LARVAE before they develop into PUPAE or the silken covering secreted to protect the eggs

Colonial living together in a colony

Coniferous forest evergreen forests found in northern regions and mountainous areas, dominated by pines, spruce, and cedars

Costal riblike

Costal grooves grooves running around the body of some TERRESTRIAL salamanders; they conduct water from the ground to the upper parts of the body

Coverts small feathers covering the bases of a bird's main flight feathers on the wings and tail, providing a smooth, streamlined surface for flight

Crustacean member of a CLASS within the PHYLUM Arthropoda typified by five pairs of legs, two pairs of antennae, a joined head and THORAX, and calcerous deposits in the EXOSKELETON; e.g., crabs, shrimps, etc.

Deciduous forest dominated by trees that lose their leaves in winter (or in the dry season)

Deforestation the process of cutting down and removing trees for timber or to create open space for growing crops, grazing animals, etc.

Desert area of low rainfall typically with sparse scrub or grassland vegetation or lacking it altogether

Diatoms microscopic single-celled ALGAE

Dispersal the scattering of young animals going to live away from where they were born and brought up

Diurnal active during the day

DNA (deoxyribonucleic acid) the substance that makes up the main part of the chromosomes of all living things; contains the genetic code that is handed down from generation to generation

Domestication process of taming and breeding animals to provide help and useful products for humans

Dormancy a state in which—as a result of hormone action—growth is suspended and METABOLIC activity is reduced to a minimum

Dorsal relating to the back or spinal part of the body; usually the upper surface

Down soft, fluffy, insulating feathers with few or no shafts found after hatching on young birds and in ADULTS beneath the main feathers

Echolocation the process of perception based on reaction to the pattern of reflected sound waves (echos); occurs in bats

Ecology the study of plants and animals in relation to one another and to their surroundings

Ecosystem a whole system in which plants, animals, and their environment interact

Ectotherm animal that relies on external heat sources to raise body temperature; also known as "cold-blooded"

Edentate toothless; also any animals of the order Edentata, which includes anteaters, sloths, and armadillos

Endemic found only in one geographical area, nowhere else

Epitoke a form of marine ANNELID having particularly well developed swimming appendages

Estivation inactivity or greatly decreased activity during hot weather

Eutrophication an increase in the nutrient chemicals (nitrate, phosphate, etc.) in water, sometimes occurring naturally and sometimes caused by human activities, e.g., by the release of sewage or agricultural fertilizers

Exoskeleton a skeleton covering the outside of the body or situated in the skin, as found in some INVERTEBRATES

Explosive breeding in some AMPHIBIANS when breeding is completed over one or a very few days and nights

Extinction process of dying out at the end of which the very last individual dies, and the SPECIES is lost forever

Family a group of closely related SPECIES that often also look quite

GLOSSARY

similar. Zoological FAMILY names always end in -idae. Also used to describe a social group within a SPECIES comprising parents and their offspring
Feral domestic animals that have gone wild and live independently of people
Flagship species A high-profile SPECIES, which (if present) is likely to be accompanied by many others that are typical of the habitat. (If a naval flagship is present, so is the rest of the fleet of warships and support vessels)
Fledging period the period between a young bird hatching and acquiring its first full set of feathers and being able to fly
Fledgling young bird that is capable of flight; in perching birds and some others it corresponds with the time of leaving the nest
Fluke either of the two lobes of the tail of a whale or related animal; also a type of flatworm, usually parasitic

Gamebird birds in the ORDER Galliformes (megapodes, cracids, grouse, partridges, quail, pheasants, and relatives); also used for any birds that may be legally hunted by humans
Gene the basic unit of heredity, enabling one generation to pass on characteristics to its offspring
Genus (**genera**, pl.) a group of closely related SPECIES
Gestation the period of pregnancy in MAMMALS, between fertilization of the egg and birth of the baby
Gill Respiratory organ that absorbs oxygen from the water. External gills occur in tadpoles. Internal gills occur in most fish

Harem a group of females living in the same territory and consorting with a single male
Hen any female bird
Herbivore an animal that eats plants (grazers and BROWSERS are herbivores)
Hermaphrodite an animal having both male and female reproductive organs
Herpetologist ZOOLOGIST who studies REPTILES and AMPHIBIANS
Hibernation becoming inactive in winter, with lowered body temperature to save energy. Hibernation takes place in a special nest or den called a hibernaculum
Homeotherm an animal that can maintain a high and constant body temperature by means of internal processes; also called "warm-blooded"
Home range the area that an animal uses in the course of its normal activity
Hybrid offspring of two closely related SPECIES that can breed; it is sterile and so cannot produce offspring

Ichthyologist ZOOLOGIST specializing in the study of fish
Inbreeding breeding among closely related animals (e.g., cousins), leading to weakened genetic composition and reduced survival rates
Incubation the act of keeping the egg or eggs warm or the period from the laying of eggs to hatching
Indwellers ORGANISMS that live inside others, e.g., the California Bay pea crab, which lives in the tubes of some marine ANNELID worms, but do not act as PARASITES
Indigenous living naturally in a region; native (i.e., not an introduced SPECIES)
Insect any air-breathing ARTHROPOD of the CLASS Insecta, having a body divided into head, THORAX, and abdomen, three pairs of legs, and sometimes two pairs of wings
Insectivore animal that feeds on INSECTS. Also used as a group name for hedgehogs, shrews, moles, etc.
Interbreeding breeding between animals of different SPECIES, varieties, etc. within a single FAMILY or strain; Interbreeding can cause dilution of the GENE pool
Interspecific between SPECIES
Intraspecific between individuals of the same SPECIES
Invertebrates animals that have no backbone (or other bones) inside their body, e.g., mollusks, INSECTS, jellyfish, crabs
Iridescent displaying glossy colors produced (e.g., in bird PLUMAGE) not as a result of pigments but by the splitting of sunlight into light of different wavelengths; rainbows are made in the same way

Joey a young kangaroo living in its mother's pouch
Juvenile a young animal that has not yet reached breeding age

Keel a ridge along the CARAPACE of certain turtles or a ridge on the scales of some REPTILES
Keratin tough, fibrous material that forms hair, feathers, nails, and protective plates on the skin of VERTEBRATE animals
Keystone species a SPECIES on which many other SPECIES are wholly or partially dependent
Krill PLANKTONIC shrimps

Labyrinth specialized auxiliary (extra) breathing organ found in some fish
Larva an immature form of an animal that develops into an ADULT form through METAMORPHOSIS
Lateral line system a system of pores running along a fish's body. These pores lead to nerve endings that allow a fish to sense vibrations in the water and help it locate prey, detect PREDATORS, avoid obstacles, and so on. Also found in AMPHIBIANS
Lek communal display area where male birds of some SPECIES gather to attract and mate with females
Livebearer animal that gives birth to fully developed young (usually refers to REPTILES or fish)

Mammal any animal of the CLASS Mammalia—warm-blooded VERTEBRATE having mammary glands in the female that produce milk with which it nurses its young. The class includes bats, primates, rodents, and whales
Mandible upper or lower part of a bird's beak or BILL; also the jawbone in VERTEBRATES; in INSECTS and other ARTHROPODS mandibles are mouth parts mostly used for biting and chewing
Mantle cavity a space in the body of mollusks that contains the breathing organs
Marine living in the sea
Matriarch senior female member of a social group
Metabolic rate the rate at which chemical activities occur within animals, including the exchange of gasses in respiration and the liberation of energy from food
Metamorphosis the transformation of a LARVA into an ADULT
Migration movement from one place to another and back again; usually seasonal
Molt the process in which a bird sheds its feathers and replaces them with new ones; some MAMMALS, REPTILES, and ARTHROPODS regularly molt, shedding hair, skin, or outer layers
Monotreme egg-laying MAMMAL, e.g., platypus
Montane in a mountain environment
Natural selection the process whereby individuals with the most appropriate ADAPTATIONS are more successful than other individuals and therefore survive to produce more offspring. Natural selection is the main process driving evolution in which animals and plants are challenged by natural effects (such as predation and bad weather), resulting in survival of the fittest
Nematocyst the stinging part of animals such as jellyfish, usually found on the tentacles
Nestling a young bird still in the nest and dependent on its parents
New World the Americas
Niche part of a habitat occupied by an ORGANISM, defined in terms of all aspects of its lifestyle
Nocturnal active at night
Nomadic animals that have no fixed home, but wander continuously
Noseleaf fleshy structures around the face of bats; helps focus ULTRASOUNDS used for ECHOLOCATION

Ocelli markings on an animal's body that resemble eyes. Also, the tiny, simple eyes of some INSECTS, spiders, CRUSTACEANS, mollusks, etc.
Old World non-American continents
Olfaction sense of smell
Operculum a cover consisting of bony plates that covers the GILLS of fish
Omnivore an animal that eats a wide range of both animal and vegetable food
Order a subdivision of a CLASS of animals, consisting of a series of animal FAMILIES
Organism any member of the animal or plant kingdom; a body that has life
Ornithologist ZOOLOGIST specializing in the study of birds
Osteoderms bony plates beneath the scales of some REPTILES, particularly crocodilians
Oviparous producing eggs that hatch outside the body of the mother (in fish, REPTILES, birds, and MONOTREMES)

Parasite an animal or plant that lives on or within the body of another (the host) from which it obtains nourishment. The host is often harmed by the association
Passerine any bird of the ORDER Passeriformes; includes SONGBIRDS
Pedipalps small, paired leglike appendages immediately in front of the first pair of walking legs of spiders

and other ARACHNIDS. Used by males for transferring sperm to the females
Pelagic living in the upper waters of the open sea or large lakes
Pheromone scent produced by animals to enable others to find and recognize them
Photosynthesis the production of food in green plants using sunlight as an energy source and water plus carbon dioxide as raw materials
Phylum zoological term for a major grouping of animal CLASSES. The whole animal kingdom is divided into about 30 PHYLA, of which the VERTEBRATES form part of just one
Placenta the structure that links an embryo to its mother during pregnancy, allowing exchange of chemicals between them
Plankton animals and plants drifting in open water; many are minute
Plastron the lower shell of CHELONIANS
Plumage the covering of feathers on a bird's body
Plume a long feather used for display, as in a bird of paradise
Polygamous where an individual has more than one mate in one BREEDING SEASON. Monogamous animals have only a single mate
Polygynous where a male mates with several females in one BREEDING SEASON
Polyp individual ORGANISM that lives as part of a COLONY—e.g., a coral—with a saclike body opening only by the mouth that is usually surrounded by a ring of tentacles
Population a distinct group of animals of the same SPECIES or all the animals of that SPECIES
Posterior the hind end or behind another structure
Predator an animal that kills live prey
Prehensile capable of grasping
Primary forest forest that has always been forest and has not been cut down and regrown at some time
Primates a group of MAMMALS that includes monkeys, apes, and ourselves
Prosoma the joined head and THORAX of a spider, scorpion, or horseshoe crab
Pupa an INSECT in the stage of METAMORPHOSIS between a caterpillar (LARVA) and an ADULT (imago)

Quadruped any animal that walks on four legs

Range the total geographical area over which a SPECIES is distributed
Raptor bird with hooked beak and strong feet with sharp claws (talons) for seizing, killing, and dealing with prey; also known as birds of prey. The term usually refers to daytime birds of prey (eagles, hawks, falcons, and relatives) but sometimes also includes NOCTURNAL owls
Regurgitate (of a bird) to vomit partly digested food either to feed NESTLINGS or to rid itself of bones, fur, or other indigestible parts, or (in some seabirds) to scare off PREDATORS
Reptile any member of the cold-blooded CLASS Reptilia, such as crocodiles, lizards, snakes, tortoises, turtles, and tuataras; characterized by an external covering of scales or horny plates. Most are egg-layers, but some give birth to fully developed young
Roost place that a bird or bat regularly uses for sleeping
Ruminant animals that eat vegetation and later bring it back from the stomach to chew again ("chewing the cud") to assist its digestion by microbes in the stomach

Savanna open grasslands with scattered trees and low rainfall, usually in warm areas
Scapulars the feathers of a bird above its shoulders
Scent chemicals produced by animals to leave smell messages for others to find and interpret
Scrub vegetation dominated by shrubs—woody plants usually with more than one stem
Scute horny plate covering live body tissue underneath
Secondary forest trees that have been planted or grown up on cleared ground
Sedge grasslike plant
Shorebird Plovers, sandpipers, and relatives (known as waders in Britain, Australia, and some other areas)
Slash-and-burn agriculture method of farming in which the unwanted vegetation is cleared by cutting down and burning
Social behavior interactions between individuals within the same SPECIES, e.g., courtship
Songbird member of major bird group of PASSERINES
Spawning the laying and fertilizing of eggs by fish and AMPHIBIANS and some mollusks
Speciation the origin of SPECIES; the diverging of two similar ORGANISMS through reproduction down through the generations into different forms resulting in a new SPECIES
Species a group of animals that look similar and can breed with each other to produce fertile offspring
Steppe open grassland in parts of the world where the climate is too harsh for trees to grow
Subspecies a subpopulation of a single SPECIES whose members are similar to each other but differ from the typical form for that SPECIES; often called a race
Substrate a medium to which fixed animals are attached under water, such as rocks onto which barnacles and mussels are attached, or plants are anchored in, e.g., gravel, mud, or sand in which AQUATIC plants have their roots embedded
Substratum see SUBSTRATE
Swim bladder a gas or air-filled bladder in fish; by taking in or exhaling air, the fish can alter its buoyancy
Symbiosis a close relationship between members of two SPECIES from which both partners benefit

Taxonomy the branch of biology concerned with classifying ORGANISMS into groups according to similarities in their structure, origins, or behavior. The categories, in order of increasing broadness, are: SPECIES, GENUS, FAMILY, ORDER, CLASS, PHYLUM
Terrestrial living on land
Territory defended space
Test an external covering or "shell" of an INVERTEBRATE such as a sea-urchin; it is in fact an internal skeleton just below the skin
Thorax (**thoracic**, adj.) in an INSECT the middle region of the body between the head and the abdomen. It bears the wings and three pairs of walking legs
Torpor deep sleep accompanied by lowered body temperature and reduced METABOLIC RATE
Translocation transferring members of a SPECIES from one location to another
Tundra open grassy or shrub-covered lands of the far north

Underfur fine hairs forming a dense, woolly mass close to the skin and underneath the outer coat of stiff hairs in MAMMALS
Understory the layer of shrubs, herbs, and small trees found beneath the forest CANOPY
Ungulate one of a large group of hoofed animals such as pigs, deer, cattle, and horses; mostly HERBIVORES
Uterus womb in which embryos of MAMMALS develop
Ultrasounds sounds that are too high-pitched for humans to hear
UV-B radiation component of ultraviolet radiation from the sun that is harmful to living ORGANISMS because it breaks up DNA

Vane the bladelike main part of a typical bird feather extending from either side of its shaft (midrib)
Ventral of or relating to the front part or belly of an animal (see DORSAL)
Vertebrate animal with a backbone (e.g., fish, MAMMAL, REPTILE), usually with skeleton made of bones, but sometimes softer cartilage
Vestigial a characteristic with little or no use, but derived from one that was well developed in an ancestral form; e.g., the "parson's nose" (the fatty end portion of the tail when a fowl is cooked) is the compressed bones from the long tail of the reptilian ancestor of birds
Viviparous (of most MAMMALS and a few other VERTEBRATES) giving birth to active young rather than laying eggs

Waterfowl members of the bird FAMILY Anatidae, the swans, geese, and ducks; sometimes used to include other groups of wild AQUATIC birds
Wattle fleshy protuberance, usually near the base of a bird's BILL
Wingbar line of contrasting feathers on a bird's wing
Wing case one of the protective structures formed from the first pair of nonfunctional wings, which are used to protect the second pair of functional wings in INSECTS such as beetles
Wintering ground the area where a migrant spends time outside the BREEDING SEASON

Yolk part of the egg that contains nourishment for a growing embryo

Zooid individual animal in a colony; usually applied to corals or bryozoa (sea-mats)
Zoologist person who studies animals
Zoology the study of animals

Further Reading

Mammals

Macdonald, David, *The Encyclopedia of Mammals*, Barnes & Noble, New York, U.S., 2001

Payne, Roger, *Among Whales*, Bantam Press, U.S., 1996

Reeves, R. R., and Leatherwood, S., *The Sierra Club Handbook of Whales and Dolphins of the World*, Sierra Club, U.S., 1983

Sherrow, Victoria, and Cohen, Sandee, *Endangered Mammals of North America*, Twenty-First Century Books, U.S., 1995

Whitaker, J. O., *Audubon Society Field Guide to North American Mammals*, Alfred A. Knopf, New York, U.S., 1996

Birds

Attenborough, David, *The Life of Birds*, BBC Books, London, U.K., 1998

BirdLife International, *Threatened Birds of the World*, Lynx Edicions, Barcelona, Spain and BirdLife International, Cambridge, U.K., 2000

del Hoyo, J., Elliott, A., and Sargatal, J., eds., *Handbook of Birds of the World* Vols 1 to 6, Lynx Edicions, Barcelona, Spain, 1992–2001

Sayre, April Pulley, *Endangered Birds of North America*, Scientific American Sourcebooks, Twenty-First Century Books, U.S., 1977

Scott, Shirley L., ed., *A Field Guide to the Birds of North America*, National Geographic, U.S., 1999

Stattersfield, A., Crosby, M., Long, A., and Wege, D., eds., *Endemic Bird Areas of the World: Priorities for Biodiversity Conservation*, BirdLife International, Cambridge, U.K., 1998

Thomas, Peggy, *Bird Alert: Science of Saving*, Twenty-First Century Books, U.S., 2000

Fish

Bannister, Keith, and Campbell, Andrew, *The Encyclopedia of Aquatic Life*, Facts On File, New York, U.S., 1997

Buttfield, Helen, *The Secret Lives of Fishes*, Abrams, U.S., 2000

Reptiles and Amphibians

Corbett, Keith, *Conservation of European Reptiles and Amphibians*, Christopher Helm, London, U.K., 1989

Corton, Misty, *Leopard and Other South African Tortoises*, Carapace Press, London, U.K., 2000

Hofrichter, Robert, *Amphibians: The World of Frogs, Toads, Salamanders, and Newts*, Firefly Books, Canada, 2000

Stafford, Peter, *Snakes*, Natural History Museum, London, U.K., 2000

Insects

Borror, Donald J., and White, Richard E., *A Field Guide to Insects: America, North of Mexico*, Houghton Mifflin, New York, U.S., 1970

Pyle, Robert Michael, *National Audubon Society Field Guide to North American Butterflies*, Alfred A. Knopf, New York, U.S., 1995

General

Adams, Douglas, and Carwardine, Mark, *Last Chance to See*, Random House, London, U.K., 1992

Allaby, Michael, *The Concise Oxford Dictionary of Ecology*, Oxford University Press, Oxford, U.K., 1998

Douglas, Dougal, and others, *Atlas of Life on Earth*, Barnes & Noble, New York, U.S., 2001

National Wildlife Federation, *Endangered Species: Wild and Rare*, McGraw-Hill, U.S., 1996

Websites

http://www.abcbirds.org/ American Bird Conservancy. Articles, information about campaigns and bird conservation in the Americas

http://elib.cs.berkeley.edu/aw/ AmphibiaWeb information about amphibians and their conservation

http://animaldiversity.ummz.umich.edu/ University of Michigan Museum of Zoology animal diversity web. Search for pictures and information about animals by class, family, and common name. Includes glossary

www.beachside.org sea turtle preservation society

http://www.birdlife.net BirdLife International, an alliance of conservation organizations working in more than 100 countries to save birds and their habitats

http://www.surfbirds.com Articles, mystery photographs, news, book reviews, birding polls, and more

http://www.birds.cornell.edu/ Cornell University. Courses, news, nest-box cam

http://www.cites.org/ CITES and IUCN listings. Search for animals by scientific name of order, family, genus, species, or common name. Location by country and explanation of reasons for listings

www.ufl.edu/natsci/herpetology/crocs.htm crocodile site, including a chat room

www.darwinfoundation.org/ Charles Darwin Research Center

http://www.open.cc.uk/daptf DAPTF–Decllining Amphibian Population Task Force. Providing information and data about amphibian declines. (International Director, Professor Tim Halliday, is co-author of this set)

http://www.ucmp.berkeley.edu/echinodermata the echinoderm phylum—starfish, sea-urchins, etc.

http://endangered.fws.gov information about endangered animals and plants from the U.S. Fish and Wildlife Service, the organization in charge of 94 million acres of wildlife refuges

http://forests.org/ includes forest conservation answers to queries

www.traffic.org/turtles freshwater turtles

www.iucn.org details of species, IUCN listings and IUCN publications

http://www.pbs.org/journeytoamazonia the Amazonian rain forest and its unrivaled biodiversity

http://www.audubon.org National Audubon Society, named after the ornithologist and wildlife artist John James Audubon (1785–1851). Sections on education, local Audubon societies, and bird identification

www.nccnsw.org.au site for threatened Australian species

http://cmc-ocean.org facts, figures, and quizzes about marine life

http://wwwl.nature.nps.gov/wv/ The U.S. National Park Service wildlife and plants site. Factsheets on all kinds of animals found in the parks

www.ewt.org.za endangered South African wildlife

http://www.panda.org World Wide Fund for Nature (WWF). Newsroom, press releases, government reports, campaigns. Themed photogallery

http://www.greenchannel.com/wwt/ Wildfowl and Wetlands Trust (U.K.). Founded by artist and naturalist Sir Peter Scott, the trust aims to preserve wetlands for rare waterbirds. Includes information on places to visit and threatened waterbird species

http://wdcs.org/ Whale and Dolphin Conservation Society site. News, projects, and campaigns. Sightings database

List of Animals by Group

Listed below are the common names of the animals featured in the A–Z part of this set grouped by their class, i.e., Mammals, Birds, Fish, Reptiles, Amphibians, and Insects and Invertebrates.

Bold numbers indicate the volume number and are followed by the first page number of the two-page illustrated main entry in the set.

Mammals
addax **2**:4
anoa, mountain **2**:20
anteater, giant **2**:24
antelope, Tibetan **2**:26
armadillo, giant **2**:30
ass
   African wild **2**:34
   Asiatic wild **2**:36
aye-aye **2**:42
babirusa **2**:44
baboon, gelada **2**:46
bandicoot, western barred **2**:48
banteng **2**:50
bat
   ghost **2**:56
   gray **2**:58
   greater horseshoe **2**:60
   greater mouse-eared **2**:62
   Kitti's hog-nosed **2**:64
   Morris's **2**:66
bear
   grizzly **2**:68
   polar **2**:70
   sloth **2**:72
   spectacled **2**:74
beaver, Eurasian **2**:76
bison
   American **2**:86
   European **2**:88
blackbuck **2**:94
camel, wild bactrian **3**:24
cat, Iriomote **3**:30
cheetah **3**:40
chimpanzee **3**:42
   pygmy **3**:44
chinchilla, short-tailed **3**:46
cow, Steller's sea **3**:70
cuscus, black-spotted **3**:86
deer
   Chinese water **4**:6
   Kuhl's **4**:8
   Père David's **4**:10
   Siberian musk **4**:12
desman, Russian **4**:14
dhole **4**:16
dog
   African wild **4**:22
   bush **4**:24
dolphin
   Amazon river **4**:26
   Yangtze river **4**:28
dormouse
   common **4**:30
   garden **4**:32
   Japanese **4**:34
drill **4**:40
dugong **4**:46
duiker, Jentink's **4**:48
dunnart, Kangaroo Island **4**:50
echidna, long-beaked **4**:60
elephant
   African **4**:64
   Asian **4**:66
elephant-shrew, golden-rumped **4**:68
ferret, black-footed **4**:72
flying fox
   Rodrigues (Rodriguez) **4**:84
   Ryukyu **4**:86
fossa **4**:90
fox, swift **4**:92
gaur **5**:18
gazelle, dama **5**:20
gibbon, black **5**:26
giraffe, reticulated **5**:30
glider, mahogany **5**:32
gorilla
   mountain **5**:38
   western lowland **5**:40
gymnure, Hainan **5**:48
hare, hispid **5**:50
hippopotamus, pygmy **5**:52
horse, Przewalski's wild **5**:58
hutia, Jamaican **5**:64
hyena
   brown **5**:66
   spotted **5**:68
ibex, Nubian **5**:70
indri **5**:84
jaguar **5**:86
koala **6**:10
kouprey **6**:14
kudu, greater **6**:16
lemur
   hairy-eared dwarf **6**:22
   Philippine flying **6**:24
   ruffed **6**:26
leopard **6**:28
   clouded **6**:30
   snow **6**:32
lion, Asiatic **6**:34
loris, slender **6**:46
lynx, Iberian **6**:52
macaque
   barbary **6**:54
   Japanese **6**:56
manatee, Florida **6**:68
markhor **6**:72
marten, pine **6**:74
mink, European **6**:78
mole, marsupial **6**:80
mole-rat
   Balkans **6**:82
   giant **6**:84
monkey
   douc **6**:86
   Goeldi's **6**:88
   proboscis **6**:90
mouse, St. Kilda **6**:92
mulgara **6**:94
numbat **7**:14
nyala, mountain **7**:18
ocelot, Texas **7**:20
okapi **7**:22
orang-utan **7**:26
oryx
   Arabian **7**:28
   scimitar-horned **7**:30
otter
   European **7**:32
   giant **7**:34
   sea **7**:36
ox, Vu Quang **7**:44
panda
   giant **7**:48
   lesser **7**:50
pangolin, long-tailed **7**:52
panther, Florida **7**:54
pig, Visayan warty **7**:68
pika, steppe **7**:74
platypus **7**:82
porpoise, harbor **7**:86
possum, Leadbeater's **7**:88
potoroo, long-footed **7**:90
prairie dog, black-tailed **7**:92
pygmy-possum, mountain **8**:4
quagga **8**:8
rabbit
   Amami **8**:12
   volcano **8**:14
rat, black **8**:24
rhinoceros
   black **8**:26
   great Indian **8**:28
   Javan **8**:30
   Sumatran **8**:32
   white **8**:34
rock-wallaby, Prosperine **8**:36
saiga **8**:42
sea lion, Steller's **8**:62
seal
   Baikal **8**:70
   gray **8**:72
   Hawaiian monk **8**:74
   Mediterranean monk **8**:76
   northern fur **8**:78
sheep, barbary **8**:88
shrew, giant otter **8**:90
sifaka, golden-crowned **8**:92
sloth, maned **9**:6
solenodon, Cuban **9**:16
souslik, European **9**:18
squirrel, Eurasian red **9**:28
tahr, Nilgiri **9**:46
takin **9**:50
tamarin, golden lion **9**:52
tapir
   Central American **9**:56
   Malayan **9**:58
tenrec, aquatic **9**:64
thylacine **9**:66
tiger **9**:68
tree-kangaroo, Goodfellow's **10**:4
vicuña **10**:28
whale
   blue **10**:40
   fin **10**:42
   gray **10**:44
   humpback **10**:46
   killer **10**:48
   minke **10**:50
   northern right **10**:52
   sei **10**:54
   sperm **10**:56
   white **10**:58
wildcat **10**:62
wolf
   Ethiopian **10**:64
   Falkland Island **10**:66
   gray **10**:68
   maned **10**:70
   red **10**:72
wolverine **10**:74
wombat, northern hairy-nosed **10**:76
yak, wild **10**:90
zebra
   Grevy's **10**:92
   mountain **10**:94

Birds
akiapolaau **2**:6
albatross, wandering **2**:8
amazon, St. Vincent **2**:14
asity, yellow-bellied **2**:32
auk, great **2**:38
barbet, toucan **2**:54
bellbird, three-wattled **2**:82
bird of paradise, blue **2**:84
bittern, Eurasian **2**:90
blackbird, saffron-cowled **2**:92
bowerbird, Archbold's **3**:8
bustard, great **3**:10
cassowary, southern **3**:28
cockatoo, salmon-crested **3**:52
condor, California **3**:60
coot, horned **3**:62
cormorant, Galápagos **3**:64
corncrake **3**:66
courser, Jerdon's **3**:68
crane, whooping **3**:76
crow, Hawaiian **3**:82
curlew, Eskimo **3**:84
dipper, rufous-throated **4**:18

LIST OF ANIMALS BY GROUP

dodo **4**:20
duck
  Labrador **4**:42
  white-headed **4**:44
eagle
  harpy **4**:52
  Philippine **4**:54
  Spanish imperial **4**:56
finch
  Gouldian **4**:74
  mangrove **4**:76
firecrown, Juan Fernández **4**:78
flamingo, Andean **4**:80
flycatcher, Pacific royal **4**:82
fody, Mauritius **4**:88
grebe, Atitlán **5**:42
guan, horned **5**:44
gull, lava **5**:46
honeyeater, regent **5**:54
hornbill, writhed **5**:56
huia **5**:60
hummingbird, bee **5**:62
ibis, northern bald **5**:72
kagu **5**:88
kakapo **5**:90
kea **5**:92
kestrel
  lesser **5**:94
  Mauritius **6**:4
kite, red **6**:6
kiwi, brown **6**:8
lark, Raso **6**:18
lovebird, black-cheeked **6**:48
macaw
  hyacinth **6**:58
  Spix's **6**:60
magpie-robin, Seychelles **6**:62
malleefowl **6**:64
manakin, black-capped **6**:66
mesite, white-breasted **6**:76
murrelet, Japanese **7**:4
nene **7**:10
nuthatch, Algerian **7**:16
owl
  Blakiston's eagle **7**:38
  Madagascar red **7**:40
  spotted **7**:42
parrot, night **7**:58
peafowl, Congo **7**:60
pelican, Dalmatian **7**:62
penguin, Galápagos **7**:64
petrel, Bermuda **7**:66
pigeon
  pink **7**:70
  Victoria crowned **7**:72
pitta, Gurney's **7**:78
plover, piping **7**:84
quetzal, resplendent **8**:10
rail, Guam **8**:18
rockfowl, white-necked **8**:38
sandpiper, spoon-billed **8**:54

scrub-bird, noisy **8**:56
sea-eagle, Steller's **8**:64
siskin, red **8**:94
spatuletail, marvelous **9**:20
spoonbill, black-faced **9**:26
starling, Bali **9**:30
stilt, black **9**:32
stork, greater adjutant **9**:34
swallow, blue **9**:42
swan, trumpeter **9**:44
takahe **9**:48
tanager, seven-colored **9**:54
teal, Baikal **9**:62
tragopan, Temminck's **9**:94
turaco, Bannerman's **10**:10
vanga, helmet **10**:26
vireo, black-capped **10**:32
vulture, Cape griffon **10**:34
warbler
  aquatic **10**:36
  Kirtland's **10**:38
woodpecker
  ivory-billed **10**:78
  red-cockaded **10**:80
wren, Zapata **10**:86

Fish
anchovy, freshwater **2**:16
angelfish, masked **2**:18
archerfish, western **2**:28
barb, bandula **2**:52
caracolera, mojarra **3**:26
catfish, giant **3**:32
cavefish, Alabama **3**:34
characin, blind cave **3**:38
cichlids, Lake Victoria
  haplochromine **3**:48
cod
  Atlantic **3**:54
  trout **3**:56
coelacanth **3**:58
dace, mountain blackside **3**:90
danio, barred **3**:94
darter, watercress **4**:4
dragon fish **4**:36
eel, lesser spiny **4**:62
galaxias, swan **5**:16
goby, dwarf pygmy **5**:34
goodeid, gold sawfin **5**:36
ikan temoleh **5**:82
lungfish, Australian **6**:50
paddlefish **7**:46
paradisefish, ornate **7**:56
pirarucu **7**:76
platy, Cuatro Ciénegas **7**:80
pupfish, Devil's Hole **7**:94
rainbowfish, Lake Wanam **8**:20
rasbora, vateria flower **8**:22
rocky, eastern province **8**:40
salmon, Danube **8**:52
seahorse, Knysna **8**:68
shark
  basking **8**:80

  great white **8**:82
  silver **8**:84
  whale **8**:86
sturgeon, common **9**:36
sucker, razorback **9**:38
sunfish, spring pygmy **9**:40
toothcarp, Valencia **9**:80
totoaba **9**:92
tuna, northern bluefin **10**:8
xenopoecilus **10**:88

Reptiles
alligator
  American **2**:10
  Chinese **2**:12
boa
  Jamaican **3**:4
  Madagascar **3**:6
chameleon, south central lesser **3**:36
crocodile, American **3**:80
dragon, southeastern lined earless **4**:38
gecko, Round Island day **5**:22
gharial **5**:24
Gila monster **5**:28
iguana
  Fijian crested **5**:74
  Galápagos land **5**:76
  Galápagos marine **5**:78
  Grand Cayman blue rock **5**:80
Komodo dragon **6**:12
lizard
  blunt-nosed leopard **6**:36
  flat-tailed horned **6**:38
  Ibiza wall **6**:40
  sand **6**:42
python, woma **8**:6
racer, Antiguan **8**:16
skink, pygmy blue-tongued **9**:4
snake
  eastern indigo **9**:10
  leopard **9**:12
  San Francisco garter **9**:14
tortoise **9**:82
  Egyptian **9**:84
  Desert **9**:82
  Galápagos giant **9**:86
  geometric **9**:88
  plowshare **9**:90
tuatara **10**:6
turtle
  Alabama red-bellied **10**:12
  bog **10**:14
  Chinese three-striped box **10**:16
  hawksbill **10**:18
  pig-nosed **10**:20
  western swamp **10**:22
  yellow-blotched sawback map **10**:24
viper, Milos **10**:30
whiptail, St. Lucia **10**:60

Amphibians
axolotl **2**:40
frog
  gastric-brooding **4**:94
  green and golden bell **5**:4
  Hamilton's **5**:6
  harlequin **5**:8
  red-legged **5**:10
  tinkling **5**:12
  tomato **5**:14
mantella, golden **6**:70
newt, great crested **7**:12
olm **7**:24
salamander
  California tiger **8**:44
  Japanese giant **8**:46
  Ouachita red-backed **8**:48
  Santa Cruz long-toed **8**:50
toad
  golden **9**:70
  Mallorcan midwife **9**:72
  natterjack **9**:74
  western **9**:76
toadlet, corroboree **9**:78

Insects and Invertebrates
ant, European red wood **2**:22
beetle
  blue ground **2**:78
  hermit **2**:80
butterfly
  Apollo **3**:12
  Avalon hairstreak **3**:14
  birdwing **3**:16
  Hermes copper **3**:18
  large blue **3**:20
  large copper **3**:22
clam, giant **3**:50
crab
  California Bay pea **3**:72
  horseshoe **3**:74
crayfish, noble **3**:78
cushion star **3**:88
damselfly, southern **3**:92
earthworm, giant gippsland **4**:58
emerald, orange-spotted **4**:70
leech, medicinal **6**:20
longicorn, cerambyx **6**:44
mussel, freshwater **7**:6
nemertine, Rodrigues **7**:8
sea anemone, starlet **8**:58
sea fan, broad **8**:60
sea-urchin, edible **8**:66
snail, *Partula* **9**:8
spider
  great raft **9**:22
  Kauai cave wolf **9**:24
tarantula, red-kneed **9**:60
worm
  palolo **10**:82
  velvet **10**:84

Set Index

A **bold** number indicates the volume number and is followed by the relevant page number or numbers (e.g., **1**:52, 74).

Animals that are main entries in the A–Z part of the set are listed under their common names, alternative common names, and scientific names. Animals that appear in the data panels as Related endangered species are also listed under their common and scientific names.

Common names in **bold** (e.g., **addax**) indicate that the animal is a main entry in the set. Underlined page numbers (e.g., **2**:12) indicate the first page of the two-page main entry on that animal.

Italic volume and page references (e.g., *1:57*) indicate illustrations of animals in other parts of the set.

References to animals that are listed by the IUCN as Extinct (EX), Extinct in the Wild (EW), or Critically Endangered (CR) are found under those headings.

spp. means species.

A

Aceros spp. **5**:56
 A. leucocephalus **5**:5
Acestrura bombus **4**:78
Acinonyx jubatus **3**:40
Acipenser
 A. nudiventris **9**:36
 A. sturio **9**:36
Acrantophis madagascariensis **3**:6
Acrocephalus spp. **10**:36
 A. paludicola **10**:36
adaptation, reproductive strategies **1**:25
addax 2:4
Addax nasomaculatus **2**:4
Adelocosa anops **9**:24
Adranichthyis kruyti **10**:88
Aegialia concinna **2**:80
Aegypius monachus **10**:34
Aepypodius bruijnii **6**:64
Afropavo congensis **7**:60
Agapornis
 A. fischeri **6**:48
 A. nigrigenis **6**:48
Agelaius xanthomus **2**:92
Aglaeactis aliciae **4**:78
agricultural land use **1**:38, 61
agricultural practices **1**:52, 74; **2**:60, 63, 73, 92; **3**:10, 13, 67, 85; **4**:19, 24, 75; **5**:50, 94; **6**:6, 36, 38, 48, 82, 95; **7**:12, 19; **8**:95; **9**:4, 18; **10**:14, 34
Ailuroedus dentirostris **3**:8
Ailuropoda melanoleuca **7**:48
Ailurus fulgens **7**:50
akiapolaau 2:6
ala Balik **8**:52
Alabama **3**:34
alala **3**:82
Alauda razae **6**:18
albatross
 various **2**:9
 wandering 2:8
Algeria **7**:16
alien species **1**:71; **2**:7, 56, 77; **3**:27, 65, 83; **4**:15, 20, 50, 76, 78, 79, 88; **5**:6, 11, 17, 22, 36, 43, 46, 50, 61, 64, 74, 76, 88, 92; **6**:8, 19, 62, 65, 78, 80, 94; **7**:5, 9, 10, 14, 59, 66, 70, 82, 90; **8**:12, 19, 20, 40, 16; **9**:9, 16, 28, 32, 38, 48, 72, 81, 88; **10**:60, 87, 88
Alligator
 A. mississippiensis **2**:10
 A. sinensis **2**:12
alligator
 American 2:10
 Chinese 2:12
Allocebus trichotis **6**:22
Allotoca maculata **5**:36
Alsophis spp. **8**:16
 A. antiguae **8**:16
Alytes muletensis **9**:72
Amandava formosa **4**:74
amarillo **5**:36
amazon
 St. Vincent 2:14
 various **2**:14
Amazona spp. **2**:14
 A. guildingii **2**:14
Amblyopsis
 A. rosae **3**:34
 A. spelaea **3**:34
Amblyornis flavifrons **3**:8
Amblyrhynchus cristatus **5**:78
Ambystoma
 A. macrodactylum croceum **8**:51
 A. mexicanum **2**:40
Amdystoma spp. **8**:44
 A. californiense **8**:44
Ameca splendens **5**:36

Ammotragus lervia **8**:88
amphibians **1**:76
 diversity **1**:76
 risks **1**:78
 strategies **1**:76
 see also List of Animals by Group, page 100
Anas spp. **9**:62
 A. formosa **9**:62
 A. laysanensis **7**:10
 A. wyvilliana **7**:10
anchovy, freshwater 2:16
Andes **2**:74; **3**:46; **4**:80; **10**:28
Andrias
 A. davidianus **8**:46
 A. japonicus **8**:46
anemone see sea anemone
angelfish
 masked **2**:18
 resplendent pygmy **2**:19
Angola **10**:94
angonoka **9**:90
animal products **1**:46; **3**:28, 75; **10**:42, 58
anoa
 lowland **2**:20; **6**:14
 mountain 2:20
Anoa mindorensis **2**:20
Anodorhynchus spp. **6**:60
 A. hyacinthus **6**:58
Anser erythropus **7**:10
ant, European red wood 2:22
anteater
 banded **7**:14
 fairy **2**:25
 giant 2:24
 marsupial **7**:14
 scaly **7**:52
antelope **2**:4, 26; 94; **4**:48; **5**:20; **6**:16; **7**: 18, 28, 30; **8**:42
Anthornis melanocephala **5**:54
Anthracoceros
 A. marchei **5**:56
 A. montani **5**:56
Antigua **8**:16
Antilope cervicapra **2**:94
Antilophia bokermanni **6**:66
aoudad **8**:88
ape, barbary **6**:54
Aplonis spp. **9**:30
Apodemus sylvaticus hirtensis **6**:92
Apteryx spp. **6**:9
 A. mantelli **6**:8
aquaculture **8**:55
aquarium trade **1**:49; **4**:36; **8**:23, 69, 84
Aquila spp. **4**:56
 A. adalberti **4**:56
Aramidopsis pulteni **3**:66
arapaima **7**:76
Arapaima gigas **7**:76
archerfish
 few-scaled **2**:28
 large-scaled **2**:28

 western **2**:28
Archiboldia papuensis **3**:8
archipelagos **1**:32
 see also islands
Arctic **2**:70
Arctic Ocean **10**:58
Arctocephalus spp. **8**:62, 78
Ardeotis nigriceps **3**:10
Argentina **3**:46; 62; **4**:18
Arizona **3**:60
armadillo
 giant 2:30
 various **2**:30
arowana, Asian **4**:36
artificial fertilization **1**:88
Asia **3**:10, 66; **6**:20
asity
 Schlegel's **2**:32
 yellow-bellied 2:32
Aspidites ramsayi **8**:6
ass
 African wild 2:34; **8**:8
 Asiatic wild 2:36; **8**:8
 half- **2**:36
 Syrian wild *1:37*
Astacus astacus **3**:78
Asterina phylactica **3**:88
Astyanax mexicanus **3**:38
Atelopus varius **5**:8
Atlantic Ocean **3**:54, 88; **8**:72, 76, 80; **9**:36; **10**:8, 40, 43
Atlantisia rogersi **3**:66
Atlapetes flaviceps **4**:76
Atrichornis
 A. clamosus **8**:56
 A. rufescens **8**:56
auk, great 2:38
aurochs *1:37*
Australia **2**:16, 28, 48, 56; **3**:16, 28; **4**:38, 46, 50, 58, 74, 94; **5**:12, 32, 54; **6**:10, 51, 64, 80, 94; **7**:14, 58, 82, 88, 90; **8**:4, 6, 36, 56; **9**:4, 66, 78; **10**:20, 22, 77
Austroglanis barnardi **3**:32
avadavat, green **4**:74
avahi **5**:84; **8**:93
Avahi occidentalis **5**:84; **8**:93
Axis kuhlii **4**:8
axolotl 2:40; **8**:44
aye-aye 2:42

B

babirusa **2**:44
baboon, gelada 2:46
Babyrousa babyrussa **2**:44
baiji **4**:28
Balaenoptera
 B. acutorostrata **10**:50
 B. borealis **10**:54
 B. musculus **10**:40
 B. physalus **10**:42
Balantiocheilos melanopterus **8**:84
Balantiopteryx infusca **2**:64
Balearic Islands **6**:40; **9**:72

Bali **9**:30, 68
Baltic **8**:72; **9**:36
bandicoot
 eastern barred **2**:48
 golden **2**:48
 greater rabbit-eared *1:36*
 little barred **2**:48
 Shark Bay striped **2**:48
 western barred 2:48
Bangladesh **2**:72
banteng 2:50
barb
 bandula 2:52
 seven-striped **5**:82
 various **2**:52
barbet
 toucan 2:54
 various **2**:54
Barbus (Puntius) spp. **2**:52
 B. (P.) bandula **2**:52
bat
 Australian false vampire **2**:56
 ghost 2:56
 gray 2:58
 greater horseshoe 2:60
 greater mouse-eared 2:62
 Guatemalan **2**:62
 Indiana **2**:62
 Kitti's hog-nosed 2:64
 Morris's 2:66
 mouse-tailed **2**:64
 myotis, various **2**:66
 sheath-tailed **2**:64
 see also flying fox
Bawean Island **4**:8
bear
 Asian black **2**:68
 Asiatic black **2**:74
 brown 2:68
 grizzly 2:68
 Mexican grizzly *1:37*; **2**:68
 polar 2:70
 sloth 2:72
 spectacled 2:74
beaver, Eurasian 2:76
beetle
 blue ground **2**:78
 Ciervo scarab **2**:80
 delta green ground **2**:78
 Giuliani's dune scarab **2**:80
 hermit 2:80
 longhorn **6**:44
 scarab **2**:80
behavior studies **1**:85
bellbird
 bare-throated **2**:82
 Chatham Island **5**:54
 three-wattled 2:82
Belontia signata **7**:56
beloribitsa **8**:52
beluga **10**:58
Bering Sea **8**:62
Bermuda **7**:16
bettong, northern **7**:90
Bettongia tropica **7**:90
Bhutan **8**:28; **9**:50
big-game hunting **1**:47; **9**:68

SET INDEX

bilby **2**:48
bioaccumulation, toxins **1**:50, 51–52
biodiversity **1**:19
biogeographical areas **1**:19
Bioko Island **4**:40
biomes **1**:18–20
biosphere **1**:22
bird, elephant *1:37*
bird of paradise
  blue 2:84
  McGregor's **2**:84
  Raggiana *1:46*
BirdLife International (BI) **1**:12, 67
birds **1**:64–67
  conservation organizations for **1**:12–13, 67, 88
  diversity **1**:64
  flightless **1**:28, 64
  history **1**:64–65
  risks **1**:64–67
  see also List of Animals by Group, page 100
Bison
  B. bison **2**:86
  B. bonasus **2**:88
bison
  American *1:15*; **2**:86
  European 2:88
  wood *1:37*
bittern 2:90
  Australasian **2**:90
  Eurasian 2:90
  great **2**:90
Black Sea **8**:80; **9**:36
blackbird
  Jamaican **2**:92
  saffron-cowled 2:92
  yellow-shouldered **2**:92
blackbuck 2:94
bluebuck *1:37*
boa
  Cuban tree **3**:4
  Dumeril's **3**:6
  emerald tree *1:74*
  Jamaican 3:4
  Madagascar 3:6
  Madagascar tree **3**:6
  Mona Island **3**:4
  Puerto Rican **3**:4
  Virgin Islands **3**:4
Bolivia **2**:74; **3**:46, 62; **4**:18
bonobo **3**:44
bonytongue **4**:36
boom and bust **1**:21
Borneo **6**:30, 90; **7**:26; **8**:84
Bos
  B. frontalis **5**:18
  B. grunniens **10**:90
  B. javanicus **2**:50
  B. sauveli **6**:14
Bostrychia bocagei **5**:72
Botaurus
  B. poiciloptilus **2**:90
  B. stellaris **2**:90
Botswana **10**:34

bowerbird
  Archbold's 3:8
  various **3**:8
Brachylophus
  B. fasciatus **5**:74
  B. vitiensis **5**:74
Brachyramphus marmoratus **7**:4
Bradypus torquatus **9**:6
Branta
  B. ruficollis **7**:10
  B. sandvicensis **7**:10
Brazil **6**:58, 60, 66; **7**:76; **9**:6, 52, 54
British Columbia **5**:10
brush-turkey, Bruijin's **6**:64
Bubalus
  B. bubalis **2**:20
  B. depressicornis **2**:20; **6**:14
  B. quarlesi **2**:20
Bubo blakistoni **7**:38
Budorcas taxicolor **9**:50
buffalo **2**:87
  Indian water **2**:20
  see also bison
Bufo spp. **9**:70, 74, 76
  B. boreas **9**:76
  B. calamita **9**:74
  B. periglenes **9**:70
Bunolagus monticularis **8**:12, **8**:13
buntingi, various **10**:88
Burma *see* Myanmar
Burramys parvus **8**:4
bushdog **4**:93
bushmeat trade **1**:44
bustard
  great 3:10
  various **3**:10
Butan **7**:50
butterfly *1:83*
  Apollo 3:12
  Avalon hairstreak 3:14
  birdwing 3:16
  Hermes copper 3:18
  large blue 3:20
  large copper 3:22
  obi birdwing **3**:16
  Queen Alexandra's birdwing **3**:16
  Richmond birdwing **3**:16
  Rothschild's birdwing **3**:16
  swallowtail, various **3**:12

C

Cacatua spp. **3**:52
  C. moluccensis **3**:52
cachalot **10**:56
Cachorrito, various **7**:94
cage-bird trade **1**:49; **2**:14, 55; **3**:52; **4**:55, 74; **5**:44; **6**:48, 58; **7**:72, 78; **8**:94; **9**:30, 54
cahow **7**:66
Caimen, black **2**:10, 12
Calicalicus rufocarpalis **10**:27
California **3**:14, 18, 60; **9**:14

Callaeas cinerea **5**:60
catbird, tooth-billed **3**:8
callimico **6**:88
Callimico goeldii **6**:88
Callithrix
  C. flaviceps **6**:88
  C. nigriceps **6**:88
Callorhinus ursinus **8**:78
Calotes liocephalus **4**:38
Camarhynchus heliobates **4**:76
Cambodia **2**:50; **5**:26, 82; **6**:14, 86; **9**:34
camel, wild bactrian 3:24
Camelus
  C. bactrianus **3**:24
  C. dromedarius **3**:25
Cameroon **4**:40; **10**:10
Campephilus
  C. imperialis **10**:78
  C. principalis **10**:78
Camptorhynchus labradorius **4**:42
Canada **2**:70, 86; **3**:74, 76, 84; **4**:42; **5**:10; **7**:36, 42, 84; **9**:44, 76; **10**:74
canine distemper *1:56*
Canis
  C. lupus **10**:68
  C. rufus **10**:72
  C. simensis **10**:64
Cape Verde Islands **6**:18
Capito spp. **2**:54
Capra
  C. falconeri **6**:72
  C. nubiana **5**:70
  C. walia **5**:71; **6**:73
Caprolagus
  C. hispidus **5**:50
Capromys brownii **5**:64
captive breeding **1**:22, 57, 87; **2**:12, 15, 19, 34, 43, 53, 86, 88, 94; **3**:4, 7, 13, 27, 33, 42, 47, 49, 53, 56, 60, 77, 81, 83, 95; **4**:6, 10, 12, 24, 28, 31, 36, 45, 53, 55, 60, 66, 85, 88, 92; **5**:5, 15, 22, 24, 28, 37, 38, 41, 52, 58, 64, 75, 77, 80, 82, 88, 93; **6**:5, 12, 26; **31**; 47, 61, 65, 70, 78, 87, 89; **7**:11, 28, 46, 56, 70, 77, 81, 90; **8**:6, 14, 16, 19, 23, 53, 69, 85, 88, 95; **9**:9, 10, 15, 30, 33, 37, 41, 49, 52, 58, 68, 72, 79, 81, 85, 87, 91; **10**:7, 9, 14, 17, 21, 23, 25, 60, 70, 72, 88
captivity **10**:49
Carabus
  C. intricatus **2**:78
  C. olympiae **2**:78
caracolera, mojarra 3:26
Carcharhinus spp. **8**:86
Carcharias spp. **8**:86
Carcharodon carcharias **8**:82
Carcinoscorpius rotundicoruda **3**:74

Carduelis spp. **8**:94
  C. cucullata **8**:94
Carettochelys insculpta **10**:20
Caribbean **5**:80; **7**:84; **8**:16, 80; **10**:60
carp *1:52*
carpione del Garda **8**:52
Carpodectes antoniae **2**:82
cassowary
  Australian **3**:28
  common **3**:28
  double-wattled **3**:28
  dwarf **3**:28
  northern **3**:28
  southern 3:28
  two-wattled **3**:28
Castor fiber **2**:76
Casuarius
  C. bennetti **3**:28
  C. casuarius **3**:28
  C. unappendiculatus **3**:28
cat
  African wild *3:31*
  Asiatic golden *3:32*
  bay *3:30*
  black-footed *3:31*
  European wild *3:31*
  fishing *3:32*
  flat-headed **3**:30
  Iriomote 3:30
  jungle *3:32*
  leopard *3:32*
  margay *3:31*
  sand *3:32*
  tiger *3:31*
catfish
  Barnard's rock **3**:32
  giant 3:32
  Mekong **3**:32
  Thailand giant *3:32*
Catopuma badia **3**:30
cavefish
  Alabama 3:34
  various **3**:34
Centropyge resplendens **2**:19
Cephalophus
  C. adersi **4**:49
  C. jentinki **4**:48–49
  C. nigrifrons **4**:49
Cephalopterus glabricollis **2**:82
Cephalorhynchus hectori **10**:48
Cerambyx cerdo **6**:44
Ceratophora tennentii **4**:38
Ceratotherium simum **8**:34
Cercartetus macrurus **8**:4
cetaceans *see* dolphin; porpoise; whale
Cetorhinus maximus **8**:80
Chad **7**:30
Chaetophractus retusus **2**:30
chameleon
  Labord's **3**:36
  Madagascar forest **3**:36
  Senegal *1:72*
  south central lesser 3:36
chamois cattle **9**:50

characin
  blind cave 3:38
  naked **3**:38
characodon, black prince **5**:36
Characodon spp. **5**:36
Charadrius spp. **7**:84
  C. melodus **7**:84
cheetah *1:57*; **3**:40
Chile **3**:46, 62; **4**:78
chimpanzee 3:42
  common **3**:42
  dwarf **3**:44
  pygmy 3:44
China **2**:12, 26, 36; **3**:12, 24, 32; **4**:6, 10, 12, 16, 28; **5**:26, 58, 94; **6**:30, 32; **7**:32, 38, 48, 50; **9**:50, 62, 94; **10**:16, 90
chinchilla
  long-tailed **3**:46
  short-tailed 3:46
Chinchilla breviacaudata **3**:46
chiru **2**:26
Chlamydogobius squamigenus **5**:34
Chlamydotis undulata **3**:10
Chlamyphorus truncatus **2**:30
Chlorochrysa nitidissima **4**:76
Chloropipo flavicapilla **6**:66
Chocó Endemic Bird Area **2**:54
Choeropsis liberiensis **5**:52
Choloepus
  C. didactylus **9**:6
  C. hoffmanni **9**:6
Chondrohierax wilsoni **6**:7
Chrysocyon brachyurus **10**:70
Cichlasoma spp. **3**:26
  C. bartoni **3**:26
cichlid
  Barton's **3**:26
  Lake Victoria haplochromine 3:48
  Steindachner's **3**:26
Ciconia
  C. boyciana **9**:34
  C. stormi **9**:34
Cinclus schulzi **4**:18
Cistothorus apolinari **10**:86
CITES *see* Convention on International Trade in Endangered Species of Wild Fauna and Flora
clam, giant 3:50
class, taxonomic group **1**:58–59
classification
  animal kingdom **1**:58
  species **1**:26
  taxonomic **1**:58–59
Clemmys spp. **10**:14
  C. muhlebergii **10**:14
climate change **1**:8, 53, 78; **2**:56; **3**:13; **6**:48; **7**:30, 48, 66, 88; **8**:36; **9**:70
cloning **5**:19
Cnemidophorus
  C. hyperythrus **10**:61

103

C. vanzoi **10**:60
cochin **6**:86
cockatoo
　salmon-crested 3:52
　various **3**:52
cod
　Atlantic 3:54
　blue-nosed **3**:56
　Clarence River **3**:56
　Mary River **3**:56
　northern **3**:54
　rock **3**:56
　trout 3:56
coelacanth 3:58
　Sulawesi **3**:58
Coelingena prunellei **9**:20
Coenagrion
　C. hylas freyi **3**:92
　C. mercuriale **3**:92
Coleura seychellensis **2**:64
collecting **2**:80; **3**:13, 63, 82; **6**:21; **7**:24; **8**:23; **10**:78
Colombia **2**:54
colugo **6**:24–25
　Malayan **6**:22
Columba spp. **7**:71
　C. mayeri **7**:70
Columbia **2**:74
combtail **7**:56
Commander Islands **8**:78
commensalism **3**:34
communities **1**:22
Comoro Islands **3**:58
competition **2**:7, 34, 48, 55, 56, 77; **3**:13, 24, 27, 29, 31, 44; **4**:15, 19, 24, 32, 45, 79, 89; **5**:6, 11, 19, 31, 36, 43, 66, 74, 76, 92; **6**:62, 72, 78, 84; **7**:30, 59, 65, 66, 88; **8**:21, 25, 34, 36, 63, 88; **9**:9, 28, 49, 66, 72, 86; **10**:55, 72, 77, 90, 95
computer modeling **1**:8
condor
　Andean **3**:60
　California *1:86;* **3**:60
coney **5**:64
Congo **7**:60
Conolophus
　C. pallidus **5**:76
　C. subcristatus **5**:76
conservation **1**:10–13, 67, 84–95
Conservation Dependent *see* Lower Risk, Conservation Dependent
Conservation International (CI) **1**:12
conservation research **1**:84–86
Convention on International Trade in Endangered Species of Wild Fauna and Flora (CITES) **1**:11, 16–17
coot
　Caribbean **3**:62
　Hawaiian **3**:62
　horned 3:62
　Mascarene **3**:62
cooter, Rio Grande **10**:12

Copsychus
　C. cebuensis **6**:62
　C. sechellarum **6**:62
coral
　red **3**:51
　reef *1:82*
　see also sea fan
Corallium rubrum **3**:51; **8**:60, 61
cormorant
　Galápagos 3:64
　Pallas's *1:36*
　various **3**:64
corncrake 3:66
Corvus spp. **3**:82
　C. hawaiiensis **3**:82
Costa Rica **8**:10; **9**:70
costs, conservation **1**:87–89
cotinga
　turquoise **2**:82
　yellow-billed **2**:82
Cotinga ridgwayi **2**:82
courser, Jerdon's 3:68
cow
　golden fleeced **9**:50
　sea **4**:46
　Steller's sea *1:36;* **3**:70
crab
　California Bay pea 3:72
　California fiddler *3:73*
　horseshoe 3:74
　king **3**:74
crane
　various **3**:76
　whooping 3:76
Craseonycteris thonglongyai **2**:64
crawfish, noble **3**:78
crayfish
　noble 3:78
　Tennessee cave **3**:78
creeper, Hawaii **2**:6
Crex crex **3**:66
crimson-wing, Shelley's **4**:74
Critically Endangered (CR), IUCN category, definition, **1**:14; **2**:4, 12, 34, 52, 80; **3**:34, 46, 58, 60, 68, 82, 84, 94; **4**:10, 28, 54, 76, 78, 84, 88, 94; **5**:12, 16, 34, 71, 72, 74, 80; **6**:14, 18, 34, 60, 62; **7**:6, 54, 58, 68, 78; **8**:20, 26, 30, 32, 76, 92; **9**:30, 32, 36, 52, 70, 72, 92; **10**:16, 18, 22, 30, 64, 72, 76, 78
crocodile *1:75*
　American 3:80
　various **3**:80
Crocodile Specialist Group (CSG) **3**:81
Crocodylus spp. **3**:80
　C. acutus **3**:80
Crocuta crocuta **5**:68
crossbreeding **1**:26
　see also interbreeding
crow
　Hawaiian 3:82
　various **3**:82
Cryptoprocta ferox **4**:90
Cryptospiza shelleyi **4**:74

Ctenophorus yinniertharra **4**:38
Cuba **5**:62; **10**:78, 86
culling **8**:72; 79
Cuon alpinus **4**:16
Cuora spp. **10**:16
　C. trifasciata **10**:16
curlew
　Eskimo 3:84
　slender-billed **8**:54
　various **3**:84
cuscus
　black-spotted 3:86
　various **3**:86
cushion star 3:88
Cyanopsitta spixii **6**:60
Cyanoramphus unicolor **5**:92
Cyclades Islands **10**:30
cyclones **7**:70
Cyclopes spp. **2**:25
Cyclura
　C. colleo **5**:80
　C. nubila lewisi **5**:80
　C. n. spp. **5**:80
Cygnus buccinator **9**:44
Cynocephalus
　C. varigatus **6**:22
　C. volans **6**:22
Cynomys spp. **7**:92
　C. ludovicianus **7**:92
Cynoscion macdonaldi **9**:92
cypriniformes **9**:80
Cyprinodon spp. **7**:94
　C. diabolis **7**:94
cyprinodontiformes **9**:80

D

dace
　mountain blackside 3:90
　Tennessee **3**:90
Dactilopsila tatei **5**:32; **7**:88
Dalatias licha **8**:86
dam building **1**:40; **2**:92; **4**:19, 26, 29; **5**:83; **7**:82; **8**:47, 53; **9**:37; **10**:37
damselfly
　Frey's **3**:92
　southern 3:92
danio, barred 3:94
Danio pathirana **3**:94
darter
　Maryland **4**:4
　watercress 4:4
Darwin, Charles **1**:28; **5**:76
Dasycercus cristicauda **6**:94
Data Deficient (DD), IUCN category, definition **1**:16
Daubentonia madagascariensis **2**:42
DDT **1**:50, 51–52
deer
　Bawean **4**:8
　black musk **4**:12
　Chinese water 4:6
　forest musk **4**:12
　Kuhl's 4:8
　Père David's 4:10
　Schomburgk's *1:36*
　Siberian musk **4**:12

deforestation **1**:38, 41, 73; **2**:7, 22, 31, 42, 44, 65, 72, 75, 83, 85; **3**:8, 29, 44, 87; **4**:34, 40, 48, 52, 55, 60, 61, 66, 84, 86, 88, 91; **5**:26, 38, 40, 44, 45, 49, 52, 57, 63, 83, 84, 86, 88; **6**:4, 8, 14, 22, 24, 26, 31, 46, 58, 63, 66, 70, 76, 86, 88, 91; **7**:26, 35, 38, 41, 51, 68, 70, 78, 89; **8**:11, 12, 23, 32, 38, 41, 47, 49, 65, 91; **9**: 7, 31, 34, 52, 54, 76; **10**:4, 21, 24, 26, 72, 78, 85
Delphinapterus leucas **10**:58
Democratic Republic of Congo **3**:42; **5**:38, 40; **7**:22; **8**:34
Dendrocopus dorae **10**:80
Dendroica spp. **10**:38
　D. kirtlandii **10**:38
Dendrolagus spp. **10**:4
　D. goodfellowi **10**:4
desertification **1**:38–40; **5**:20
desman
　Pyrenean **4**:14
　Russian 4:14
Desmana moschata **4**:14
developing countries, conservation **1**:89, 95
devilfish **10**:44
dhole 4:16
Dicerorhinus sumatrensis **8**:32
Diceros bicornis **8**:26
dinosaurs **1**:34–35
Diomedea spp. **2**:9
　D. amsterdamensis **2**:9
　D. antipodensis **2**:9
　D. dabbenena **2**:9
　D. exulans **2**:8
dipper, rufous-throated 4:18
disease **1**:40, 55–56, 65, 79; **2**:7, 50, 89; **3**:29, 42, 57, 78, 83; **4**:5, 22, 26, 57, 94; **5**:12, 38; **6**:10, 14, 46, 48, 56; **8**:28, 36; **9**:56, 66, 76, 82; **10**:64, 72
dispersal corridors *see* habitat corridors
dodo *1:28–29, 31, 37;* **4**:20
dog
　African wild 4:22
　Asian wild **4**:16
　bush 4:24
　red **4**:16
Dolomedes plantarius **9**:22
dolphin
　Amazon river 4:26
　boto **4**:26–27
　Chinese river **4**:28
　Ganges river **4**:26, 28
　Hector's **10**:48
　Indus river **4**:26, 28
　pantropical spotted **10**:48
　pink **4**:26
　striped **10**:48
　whitefin **4**:28
　Yangtze river 4:28
　see also porpoise
domestic animals **1**:38–40, 56

　see also alien species; grazing
dormouse
　common 4:30
　garden 4:32
　hazel *1:53;* **4**:30
　Japanese 4:34
　various **4**:30, 32, 34
dotterel, New Zealand **7**:84
dragon
　southeastern lined earless 4:38
　Yinnietharra rock **4**:38
　see also Komodo dragon
dragon fish 4:36
dragonfly
　orange-spotted emerald 4:70
　various **4**:70
drainage *see* wetland drainage
drift nets *see* fishing nets
drill 4:40
Driloleirus americanus **4**:58; **10**:82
Driloleirus macelfreshi **4**:58
drought **1**:52; **3**:38; **8**:51
Drymarchon corais couperi **9**:10
Dryomys nitedula **4**:30
Dryomys sichuanensis **4**:32, 34
duck
　Labrador **4**:42
　pink-headed **4**:44
　various **7**:10
　white-headed 4:44
dugong 4:46; **6**:69
Dugong dugon **4**:46
duiker
　Ader's **4**:49
　Jentink's 4:48
　Ruwenzori black-fronted **4**:49
　squirrel **4**:48
dunnart
　Kangaroo Island **1**:24, 50
　sooty 4:50
　various **4**:50
Durrell Wildlife Conservation Trust (DWCT) **1**:12
Dusicyon australis **10**:66
Dyscophus antongilii **5**:14

E

eagle
　Adalbert's **4**:56
　bald *1:94*
　greater spotted **4**:56
　harpy 4:52
　Imperial **4**:56
　monkey-eating 4:54
　New Guinea harpy **4**:53, 54
　Philippine 4:54
　Spanish imperial **4**:56
　white-tailed sea *1:94;* **8**:64
earthworm
　giant gippsland **4**:58
　Oregon giant **4**:58
　Washington giant **4**:58; **10**:82
echidna
　long-beaked 4:60

SET INDEX

short-beaked **4**:60
Echinus esculentus **8**:66
ecology **1**:18–37
ecosystems **1**:22–24
ecotourism **1**:90–92; **5**:38;
  6:27; **10**:39
Ecuador **2**:54, 74; **4**:82
education **1**:94
Edwardsia ivelli **8**:58
eel, lesser spiny 4:62
egg collectors **2**:38, 91
El Niño **3**:64; **5**:79; **7**:65; **8**:10
Elaphe situla **9**:12
Elaphrus
  E. viridis **2**:78
  E. davidianus **4**:10
Elassoma
  E. alabamae **9**:40
  E. boehlkei **9**:40
  E. okatie **9**:40
elephant
  African 4:64
  Asian *1*:95; **4**:66
  Indian **4**:66
elephant-shrew
  golden-rumped 4:68
  various **4**:68
Elephantulus revoili **4**:68
Elephas maximus **4**:66
Eliomys
  E. elanurus **4**:30, 32
  E. quercinus **4**:32
Elusor macrurus **10**:22
Emballonura semicaudata **2**:64
**emerald, orange-spotted
  4**:70
emperor fish **4**:36
Endangered (EN), IUCN
  category, definition **1**:15
endemic species, definition
  1:30
energy flow **1**:23–24
Enhydra lutris **7**:36
Ephippiorhynchus asiaticus **9**:34
Epicrates
  E. angulifer **3**:4
  E. inornatus **3**:4
  E. monensis grati **3**:4
  E. monensis monensis **3**:4
  E. subflavus **3**:4
Epimachus fastuosus **2**:84
Equus
  E. africanus **2**:34; **8**:8
  E. grevyi **10**:92
  E. hemionus **2**:36
  E. przewalskii **5**:58
  E. quagga **8**:8
  E. zebra **10**:94
  E. z. hartmannii **10**:94
  E. z. zebra **10**:94
Eretmochelys imbricata **10**:18
Eriocnemis mirabilis **4**:78
  E. nigrivestis **9**:20
Erythrura
  E. gouldiae **4**:74
  E. viridifacies **4**:74
Eschrichtius robustus **10**:44
Estrilda poliopareia **4**:74
Etheostoma

E. nuchale **4**:4
E. sellore **4**:4
ethics, conservation **1**:88,
  94–95
Ethiopia **2**:34, 46, 66; **6**:84;
  7:18; **10**:64, 92
Euathlus smithi **9**:60
Eubalaena
  E. australis **10**:52
  E. glacialis **10**:52
Eudyptes
  E. pachyrhynchus **7**:64
  E. robustus **7**:64
Eulidia yarrellii **4**:78
Eumetopias jubatus **8**:62
Eunice viridis **10**:82
Eunicella verrucosa **8**:60
Eupleres goudotii **4**:91
European Habitats Directive
  6:52
Euryceros prevostii **10**:26
Eurynorhynchus pygmeus **8**:54
evolution, speciation **1**:26–28
exploitation **1**:49, 62, 75
Extinct (EX), IUCN category,
  definition **1**:14; **2**:38; **3**:70;
  4:20, 42; **5**:42, 60; **8**:8; **9**:66;
  10:66
Extinct in the Wild (EW), IUCN
  category, definition, **1**:14;
  4:72; **5**:36, 58; **7**:30; **8**:19
extinction **1**:34, 36
  see also natural extinction

F

falanoka **4**:91
falanouc **4**:91
Falco spp. **5**:95
  F. araea **6**:5
  F. naumanni **5**:94
  F. punctatus **6**:4
falcon, various **5**:95
Falkland Island **10**:66
family, taxonomic group
  1:58–59
Fauna & Flora International (FFI)
  1:12, 88
feather products **1**:46; **2**:85;
  5:50
Federal Bureau of Land
  Management **9**:83
Felis
  F. iriomotensis **3**:30
  F. pardinis **7**:20
  F. silvestris **10**:62
Ferminia cerverai **10**:86
ferreret **9**:72
ferret, black-footed 4:72
field studies **1**:84
Fiji **5**:74; **10**:82
finback **10**:42
finch
  Cochabamba **4**:76
  Galápagos *1*:28
  Gouldian 4:74
  Hawaiian *1*:27
  mangrove **4**:76
  olive-headed brush **4**:76

painted **4**:74
purple-breasted **4**:74
rainbow **4**:74
finner **10**:42
  Japan **10**:54
**firecrown, Juan Fernández
  4**:78
fires **1**:57, 73; **2**:25, 33, 59, 62,
  92; **3**:19, 83; **4**:24, 68, 75;
  5:50; **6**:10, 42, 46, 65, 76,
  81, 86; **7**:14, 17, 55, 88;
  8:14, 56; **9**:82, 89, 90;
  10:32, 38, 86
fish **1**:68–71
  definition **1**:68–69
  diversity **1**:68
  history **1**:69–70
  risks **1**:70–71
  see also List of Animals by
  Group, page 100
fish-eagle, various **8**:64
fishing **1**:45; **3**:33, 55, 65;
  4:26, 28, 44; **7**:38; **8**:53, 62,
  72, 75, 76, 79, 80, 82, 85;
  10:9, 45, 48, 52
  see also overfishing; sports
  fishing
fishing controls **3**:55
fishing nets **4**:15; **5**:42; **6**:68;
  7:5, 86; **10**:46
fishing techniques **2**:8
fishing-owl, rufous **7**:42
flagship species *1*:9
flamingo
  Andean **4**:80
  various **4**:81
flightless birds **1**:28, 64
flooding **1**:40; **6**:38; **7**:66; **9**:56
florican
  Bengal **3**:10
  lesser **3**:10
flycatcher
  Atlantic royal **4**:82
  Pacific royal 4:82
  royal **4**:82
  tyrant **4**:82
flying fox
  Rodrigues (Rodriguez) **4**:84
  Ryukyu 4:86
fody
  Mauritius 4:88
  Rodrigues **4**:88
  Seychelles **4**:88
food chains/webs **1**:23–24
food shortage **4**:75; **7**:65
forest management **4**:30
Formica
  F. aquilonia **2**:22
  F. lugubris **2**:22
  F. polyctena **2**:22
fossa 4:90
Fossa fossa **4**:91
Foudia
  F. flavicans **4**:88
  F. rubra **4**:88
  F. seychellarum **4**:88
fox
  Simien **10**:64
  South American **10**:66

swift 4:92
fragmented distribution **1**:8
  see also habitat
  fragmentation
French Polynesia **9**:8
friarbird, dusty **5**:54
Friends of the Earth **1**:13
frog
  Archey's **5**:6
  corroboree **9**:78
  gastric-brooding 4:94
  golden mantella 6:70
  green and golden bell 5:4
  green and golden swamp
    5:4
  Hamilton's 5:6
  harlequin 5:8
  Maud Island **5**:6
  New England swamp **5**:4, 5
  northern timber **5**:12
  northern tinker **5**:12
  Palestinian painted *1*:37
  platypus **4**:94
  red-legged 5:10
  sharp-snouted day **5**:12
  tinkling 5:12
  tomato 5:14
  various **5**:10
fruit bat *see* flying fox
Fulica spp. **3**:62
  F. cornuta **3**:62
fund raising, conservation **1**:90
fur trade **1**:46; **2**:46, 74, 76;
  3:46; **4**:14, 92; **5**:86; **6**:28,
  31, 33, 75; **7**:20, 34, 36, 82;
  8:70, 72, 78, 90; **10**:28, 74
Furcifer
  F. campani **3**:36
  F. labordi **3**:36
  F. minor **3**:36

G

Gadus morhua **3**:54
Galápagos Islands **3**:64; **4**:76;
  5:46, 76, 78; **7**:64; **9**:80, 86
galaxias
  swan 5:16
  various **5**:16
Galaxias spp. **5**:16
  F. fontanus **5**:16
Galemys pyrenaicus **4**:14
Gallinula
  G. pacifica **9**:48
  G. sylvestris **9**:48
Gallirallus spp. **8**:18
  G. owstoni **8**:18
Gambelia silus **6**:36
gamekeeping **6**:74
garefowl **2**:38
gaur 5:18
gavial **5**:24
Gavialis gangeticus
  5:24
Gazella
  G. arabica **5**:20
  G. cuvieri **5**:20
  G. dama **5**:20
  G. leptoceros **5**:20

gazelle
  Arabian **5**:20
  Cuvier's **5**:20
  dama 5:20
  sand **5**:20
gecko
  fat-tailed *1*:74
  Namaqua day **5**:22
  Rodrigues day **5**:22
  Round Island day 5:22
  Standing's day **5**:22
genera, taxonomic **1**:58
generalist species **1**:29
genetics **1**:56
Genicanthus personatus **2**:18
Geocapromys
  G. brownii **5**:64
  G. ingrahami **5**:64
Geochelone spp. **9**:86, 89
  F. radiata **9**:90
  G. nigra **9**:86
  G. yniphora **9**:90
Geonemertes rodericana **7**:8
Geopsittacus occidentalis **7**:58
Geronticus
  G. calvus **5**:72
  G. eremita **5**:72
Ghana **8**:38
gharial 5:24
gibbon
  black 5:26
  concolor **5**:26
  crested **5**:26
  silvery **5**:26
Gibraltar **6**:54
Gila monster 5:28
*Giraffa camelopardalis
  reticulata* **5**:30
giraffe, reticulated 5:30
Girardinichthys spp. **5**:36
Glareola nordmanni **3**:68
glider, mahogany 5:32
Glirulus japonicus **4**:32, 34
Glis glis **4**:30
Globicephala macrorhynchus
  10:48
Glossolepis spp. **8**:20
  G. wanamensis **8**:20
glutton **10**:74
Glyphis gangeticus **8**:86
gnu-goat **9**:50
goat **9**:46
goby
  dwarf pygmy **5**:34
  Edgbaston **5**:34
Goodea spp. **5**:36
goodeid
  gold sawfin 5:36
  various **5**:36
goose
  Hawaiian *1*:87; **7**:10
  various **7**:10
Gopherus
  G. agassizii **9**:82
  G. flavomarginatus **9**:82
  G. polyphemus **9**:82
Gorilla
  G. gorilla beringei **5**:38
  G. g. gorilla **5**:40

G. g. graveri **5**:39, 40
gorilla *1:45*
   eastern lowland **5**:39, 40
   mountain *1:91*; **5**:38
   western lowland 5:40
Goura
   G. cristata **7**:72
   G. scheepmaker **7**:72
   G. victoria **7**:72
Grantiella picta **5**:54
Graphiurus ocularis **4**:34
Graptemys spp. **10**:24
   G. flavimaculata **10**:24
grassland destruction **2**:92
grayling, New Zealand *1:36*
grazing animals **1**:38–40; **7**:17
grebe
   Atitlán 5:42
   giant pied-billed **5**:42
   various **5**:42
Greece **9**:12; **10**:30
greenhouse gases **1**:53
Greenland **2**:70
Greenpeace **1**:13
greenshank, spotted **8**:54
griffon, Cape 10:34
ground squirrel
   European **9**:18
   various **9**:18
Grus spp. **3**:76
   G. americana **3**:76
Guam **8**:18
guan
   horned 5:44
   various **5**:44
guanaco **3**:25; **10**:28
Guatemala **5**:42, 44; **8**:10
Guinea **8**:38
gull
   black-billed **5**:46
   lava 5:46
   Olrog's **5**:46
   relict **5**:46
   Saunder's **5**:46
Gulo gulo **10**:74
Guyana, pirarucu **7**:76
Gymnobelideus leadbeateri **7**:88
Gymnocharacinus bergii **3**:38
Gymnogyps californianus **3**:60
Gymnomyza aubryana **5**:54
gymnure
   Hainan 5:48
   various **5**:48
Gyps spp. **10**:34
   G. coprotheres **10**:34

H

habitat conservation **1**:10, 88–92
habitat corridors **4**:67; **6**:36, 65; **7**:55; **10**:23
habitat creation **3**:13; **9**:53; **10**:38
habitat fragmentation **2**:69; **3**:18, 22, 29, 42; **4**:31, 34; **5**:32, 55; **6**:10, 42, 66, 82; **7**:48, 78; **8**:10, 12, 45; **9**:54; **10**:15, 26
habitat management **3**:61, 67; **4**:19; **8**:69
habitat restoration **3**:13, 93; **4**:79; **6**:65; **9**:15; **10**:23
Habroptila wallacii **9**:48
haddock **3**:54
Hainan Island **4**:10; **5**:26, 48
Haliaeetus spp. **8**:64
   H. pelagicus **8**:64
Halichoerus grypus **8**:70, 72
Hapalemur
   H. aureus **6**:26
   H. simus **6**:26
Haplochromis spp. **3**:48
hare
   Amami **8**:12
   bristly **5**:50
   bushman **8**:12, *8:13*
   harsh-furred **5**:50
   hispid 5:50, *8:13*
   mouse **7**:74
   Sumatran **8**:12, *8:13*
Harpia harpyja **4**:52
Harpyopsis novaeguineae **4**:53, 54
harvesting **10**:83
Hawaiian Islands **1**:36; **2**:6, 18; **3**:82; **7**:10; **8**:74; **9**:24
heat pollution **1**:52
Heliangelus spp. **9**:20
   H. zusii **4**:78
Heloderma
   H. horridum **5**:28
   H. suspectum **5**:28
Hemignathus munroi **2**:6
Hemitragus
   H. hylocrius **9**:46
   H. jayakari **9**:46
   H. jemlahicus **9**:46
Herichthys spp. **3**:26
   H. bartoni **3**:26
Heteralocha acutirostris **5**:60
Heteromirafra ruddi **6**:18
Hexanchus griseus **8**:86
Hexaprotodon liberiensis **5**:52
hibernation **1**:53
hide trade *see* fur trade; skin trade
Himalayas **5**:50; **6**:32, 73; **7**:50; **9**:94
Himantopus novaezelandiae **9**:32
Hippocampus capensis **8**:68
hippopotamus
   common **5**:53
   pygmy 5:52
Hippopotamus amphibius tschadensis **5**:53
Hirudo medicinalis **6**:20
Hirundo
   H. atrocaerulea **9**:42
   H. megaensis **9**:42
hog
   pygmy **2**:45
   see also pig
Honduras **8**:10
honeycreeper, Hawaiian **2**:6

honeyeater
   crow **5**:54
   painted **5**:54
   regent 5:54
hornbill
   Mindanao wrinkled **5**:56
   various **5**:56
   writhed 5:56
horns **6**:16, 72; **8**:26, 28, 32, 34
horse, Przewalski's wild 5:58
Houbaropsis bengalensis **3**:10
Hubbsina turneri **5**:36
Hucho hucho **8**:52
huia 5:60
human competition **1**:61–62
human disturbance **2**:4, 59, 63; **3**:41, 75; **4**:28, 56; **5**:43; **6**:42, 84; **7**:63, 84; **8**:38, 74, 76; **10**:34, 46
hummingbird
   bee 5:62
   sapphire-bellied **4**:78
hunting **1**:42–49
   see also big-game hunting; fur trade; persecution; skin trade; traditional medicine
hutia
   Bahamian **5**:64
   Jamaican 5:64
Hyaena brunnea **5**:66
Hydrodamalis gigas **3**:70
Hydropotes inermis **4**:6
hyena
   brown 5:66, 69
   laughing **5**:68
   spotted 5:68
   striped **5**:69
Hylobates
   H. concolor **5**:26
   H. moloch **5**:26
Hylomys
   H. hainanensis **5**:48
   H. parvus **5**:48

I

ibex
   Nubian 5:70
   Portuguese *1:37*
   walia **5**:71; **6**:73
ibis
   crested **9**:26
   northern bald 5:72
   scarlet *1:21*
   various **5**:72
Iceland **8**:72
Ichthyophaga
   I. humilis **8**:64
   I. ichthyaetus **8**:64
iguana
   Barrington Island **5**:76
   Cuban ground **5**:80
   Fijian banded **5**:74
   Fijian crested 5:74
   Galápagos land 5:76
   Galápagos marine *1:28*; **5**:78
   Grand Cayman blue rock 5:80

   Jamaican **5**:80
   Little Cayman **5**:80
ikan temoleh 5:82
inbreeding **1**:56, 87; **2**:75, 89; **3**:41, 42, 89; **4**:26, 34, 72; **5**:6, 19, 37, 58, 74; **6**:46, 92; **7**:28; **8**:88; **9**:68, 79; **10**:77
inca, black **9**:20
India **2**:72, 94; **3**:68; **4**:16, 44, 62; **5**:18, 24; **6**:30, 34, 46; **8**:28; **9**:34, 46, 50, 68; **10**:90
Indian Ocean **3**:58; **4**:47; **8**:80
Indian Ocean islands **4**:84
Indochina **5**:18; **6**:86
Indonesia **2**:16, 20, 28, 44, 50; **3**:8, 28, 52; **4**:8, 36, 67; **5**:34; **6**:12, 30; **7**:26, 72; **8**:30, 32, 84; **9**:30, 58; **10**:88
indri 5:84
Indri indri **5**:84
industrial development **1**:40; **5**:11; **8**:55, 65; **9**:27; **10**:22, 31
   see also mining; quarrying
Inia geoffrensis **4**:26
insects *see* invertebrates
interbreeding **1**:26, 40, 57; **2**:50, 88; **3**:27, 38; **4**:45; **5**:37, 58; **6**:79; **7**:69; **9**:33, 38, 79; **10**:62, 64, 68, 72, 90
International Union for the Conservation of Nature (IUCN) **1**:11, 88–89
   categories **1**:14
internet trade **2**:80
introductions **1**:54–55
   see also alien species
invertebrates
   diversity **1**:80
   history **1**:81–83
   risks **1**:83
   see also List of Animals by Group, page 100
Iran **2**:36
Irian Jaya **10**:20
irrigation **1**:40; **2**:36; **3**:11; **4**:19, 26; **7**:55, 81; **8**:53; **9**:84
islands **1**:20
islands *see* individual island names
isolation **1**:26–28; **6**:92; **10**:94
Isoodon auratus **2**:48
IUCN *see* International Union for the Conservation of Nature
ivory *1:16*; **4**:64, 67
Ivory Coast **4**:48; **8**:38

J

jackal, Simien **10**:64
jaguar 5:86
jaguarundi *3:31*
Jamaica **3**:4; **5**:64; **10**:85
Japan **3**:30; **4**:34, 86; **6**:56; **7**:4, 38; **8**:12, 46, 64
Java **4**:16; **6**:30; **9**:68

Jersey Zoo **1**:86
Juan Fernández archipelago **4**:78
junco, Guadalupe **4**:76
Junco insularis **4**:76

K

"K" reproductive strategy **1**:25
kagu 5:88
kaka **5**:51, 92
kakapo 5:90
Kalmykia, saiga **8**:42
Kazakhstan **2**:36; **8**:42
kea 5:92
Kenya **4**:68; **10**:92
kestrel
   lesser 5:94
   Mauritius **6**:4
   Seychelles **5**:95; **6**:5
kite
   Cuban **6**:7
   red 1:56; **6**:6
   white-collared **6**:7
kittiwake, red-legged **5**:46
kiwi
   brown *1:66*; **6**:8
   various **6**:9
koala 6:10
kokako **5**:60
Komodo dragon 6:12
Korea **4**:6, 12
kouprey 6:14
kudu, greater 6:16

L

Labrador **8**:72
Lacerta spp. **6**:42
   L. agilis **6**:42
Lake Wanam rainbowfish 8:20
Lama
   L. guanaco **10**:28
   L. guanicöe **3**:25
Lamma nasus **8**:86
land recamation *see* wetland drainage
langur, douc **6**:86
Laos **5**:82; **6**:86; **7**:44; **10**:16
lark
   Raso 6:18
   Razo **6**:18
   various **6**:18
Larus spp. **5**:46
   L. fuliginosus **5**:46
Lasiorhinus krefftii **10**:77
Lathamus discolor **7**:58
Latimeria
   L. chalumnae **3**:58
   L. menadoensis **3**:58
Latin names **1**:59
Least Concern *see* Lower Risk, Least Concern (LRlc)
leech, medicinal 6:20
Leeward Islands **8**:74
Leiopelma
   L. archeyi **5**:6

L. hamiltoni **5**:6
L. pakeka **5**:6
Leipoa ocellata **6**:64
lemming **1**:21
lemur
  broad-nosed gentle **6**:26
  Coquerel's mouse **6**:22
  golden bamboo **6**:26
  hairy-eared dwarf 6:22
  Philippine flying 6:24
  red-fronted *1*:33
  ruffed 6:26
  variegated **6**:26
  see also indri; sifaka
Leontopithecus spp. **9**:52
  L. chrysopygus **6**:88
  L. rosalia **9**:52
leopard 6:28
  clouded 6:30
  snow 6:32
Leopardus pardalis albescens **7**:20
Lepidopyga lilliae **4**:78
Leptodon forbesi **6**:7
Leptoptilos
  L. dubius **9**:34
  L. javanicus **9**:34
Lesotho **10**:34
Leucopsar rothschildi **9**:30
Liberia **4**:48; **8**:38
life strategies **1**:24–26
light pollution **1**:43, 53
Limnogale mergulus **9**:64
Limulus polyphemus **3**:74
Linnaeus **1**:58
linnet, Warsangli **8**:94
lion *1*:23; **9**:69
  Asiatic 6:34
  Barbary *1*:37
Lipotes vexillifer **4**:28
Litoria
  L. aurea **5**:4
  L. castanea **5**:4
live animal trade **1**:49; **3**:58; **7**:46
see also aquarium trade; cage-bird trade; medical research; pet trade; scientific research; zoos
lizard
  blunt-nosed leopard 6:36
  flat-tailed horned 6:38
  Gila monster 5:28
  Ibiza wall 6:40
  Komodo dragon 6:12
  Lilford's wall **6**:40
  Mexican beaded **5**:28
  Miles wall **6**:40
  ocellated green *1*:74
  sand 6:42
    Schreiber's green **6**:42
    Soutpansberg rock **6**:42
    spineless forest **4**:38
    Tennent's leaf-nosed **4**:38
locust, desert *1*:81
Loddigesia mirabilis **9**:20
longicorn
  cerambyx 6:44
  rosalia **6**:44

loris
  pygmy **6**:46
  slender 6:46
Loris tardigradus **6**:46
lovebird
  black-cheeked 6:48–49
  Fischer's **6**:48
Lower Risk (LR) IUCN category, definition **1**:16
Lower Risk, Conservation Dependent (LRcd), IUCN category, definition **1**:16
Lower Risk, Least Concern (LRlc), IUCN category, definition **1**:16
Lower Risk, Near Threatened (LRnt), IUCN category, definition **1**:16
Laxities bailout **2**:6
Loxodonta africana **4**:64
lungfish, Australian 6:50
Lutra spp. **7**:35
  L. lutra **7**:32
luxury products **1**:46; **7**:53; **8**:81
Lycaena
  L. dispar **3**:22
  L. hermes **3**:18
Lycaon pictus **4**:22
Lycosa ericeticola **9**:24
lynx, Iberian 6:52
Lynx pardinus **6**:52

M

Macaca spp. **6**:54, 57
  L. fuscata **6**:56
  L. sylvanus **6**:54
macaque
  barbary 6:54
  Japanese 6:56
  various **6**:54, 56
macaw
  black **6**:58
  blue **6**:58
  hyacinth 6:58
  hyacinthine **6**:58
  Jamaican green and yellow *1*:37
  little blue **6**:60
  Spix's 6:60
  various **6**:60
Maccullochella spp. **3**:56
  M. macquariensis **3**:56
Macgregoria pulchra **2**:84
mackerel, Spanish **10**:8
Macrocephalon maleo **6**:64
Macroderma gigas **2**:56
Macrognathus aral **4**:62
Macrotis lagotis **2**:48
Macrovipera schweizeri **10**:30
Macruromys elegans **6**:92
Maculinea arion **3**:20
Madagascar **1**:33; **2**:32, 42; **3**:6, 36; **4**:90; **5**:14, 84; **6**:22, 26, 70, 76; **7**:40; **8**:92; **9**:64, 90; **10**:26
magpie-robin, Seychelles 6:62

Malaysia **2**:50; **4**:16, 36; **5**:18, 82; **6**:30; **7**:26; **8**:32, 84; **9**:58
maleo **6**:64
malleefowl 6:64
Malpulutta kretseri **7**:56
mammals **1**:60–63
  definition **1**:60
  diversity **1**:60
  history **1**:60–61
  risks **1**:61–63
  see also List of Animals by Group, page 100
manakin
  black-capped 6:66
  various **6**:66
manatee
  African **3**:70
  Amazon **3**:70
  American **3**:70
  Florida 1:42; **6**:68
  various **4**:47; **6**:69
Manchuria **4**:12
mandrill **4**:40
Mandrillus
  M. leucophaeus **4**:40
  M. sphinx **4**:40
Manis spp. **7**:52
  M. tetradactyla **7**:52
Manorina melanotis **5**:54
mantella, golden 6:70
Mantella aurantiaca **6**:70
Margaritifera spp. **7**:6
  M. auricularia **7**:6
  M. margaritifera **7**:6, 7
Mariana Islands **8**:18
markhor 6:72
marl **2**:48
Marmaronetta augustirostris **9**:62
marmoset
  black-headed **6**:88
  Goeldi's **6**:88
  golden-white tassel-ear **6**:88
marten, pine 6:74
Martes martes **6**:74
mass extinctions **1**:34
Mauritania **8**:76
Mauritius **1**:30–31; **4**:20, 88; **5**:22; **6**:4; **7**:8, 70
maxclapique **5**:36
Mayailurus iriomotensis **3**:30
medical research **2**:31, 41; **3**:42, 44; **6**:56
medical use, medicinal leech **6**:21
medicinal products **2**:12, 73, 75; **3**:42, 54; **4**:6, 12, 46, 80; **5**:24, 26; **6**:31, 46, 72; **7**:53; **8**:12, 26, 28, 30, 32, 42, 69, 81; **9**:21, 68; **10**:16, 21
Mediterranean **3**:88; **4**:44; **8**:76, 80; **9**:36
Megapodius spp. **6**:64
Megaptera novaeangliae **10**:46
Megascolides australis **4**:58
Melanogrammus aeglefinus **3**:54
Melanosuchus niger **2**:10, 12
melidectes, long-bearded **5**:54

Melidectes princeps **5**:54
Mellisuga helenae **5**:62
Melursus ursinus **2**:72
mesite
  brown **6**:77
  subdesert **6**:77
  white-breasted 6:76
Mesitornis
  M. unicolor **6**:77
  M. variegata **6**:76
Metallura
  M. baroni **4**:78
  M. iracunda **4**:78
metaltail
  Perijá **4**:78
  violet-throated **4**:78
metamorphosis **1**:76
Mexico **2**:40; **3**:26, 38, 74; **4**:53; **5**:10, 36, 44; **7**:42, 80, 84; **8**:10, 14; **9**:56, 60, 82, 92; **10**:32
Microgale spp. **9**:64
Micronesia **9**:8
Micropotamogale spp. **9**:64
  M. lamottei **8**:90
  M. ruwenzorii **8**:90
millerbird **10**:36
Milvus milvus **6**:6
Minimum Viable Population (MVP) **1**:21
mining **1**:40; **2**:56; **3**:25, 91; **4**:52, 55, 81; **7**:43, 61; **10**:4, 10:21
mink
  American *1*:54, 55
  European 4:72; **6**:78
minnow, Sarasin's **10**:88
minor, black-eared **5**:54
Mirafra ashi **6**:18
Mirza coquereli **6**:22
moa, giant **1**: 36, *1*:36
mole
  marsupial **6**:80
  northern marsupial **6**:80
  southern marsupial **6**:80
mole-rat
  Balkans 6:82
  giant 6:84
  various **6**:84
Monachus
  M. monachus **8**:76
  M. schauinslandi **8**:74
  M. tropicalis **8**:74, 76
Mongolia **2**:36; **3**:12, 24; **5**:58, 94; **8**:42
Monias benschi **6**:77
monkey
  China **6**:86
  douc **6**:86
  Goeldi's **6**:88
  grizzled leaf **6**:86
  Guizhou snub-nosed **6**:86
  pig-tailed snub-nosed **6**:86
  proboscis 1:40; **6**:90
Monodon monoceros **10**:58
montane biotype **1**:20
moonrat
  dinagat **5**:48
  Hainan **5**:48

moorhen
  Makira **9**:48
  Samoan **9**:48
Morocco **5**:72
Moschus
  M. berezovskii **4**:12
  M. chrysogaster **4**:12
  M. fuscus **4**:12
  M. moschiferus **4**:12
mountains, ecology **1**:20
mouse
  crest-tailed marsupial **6**:94
  Florida **6**:92
  St. Kilda 6:92
Mozambique **10**:34
mulgara 6:94
murrelet
  Japanese 7:4
  various **7**:4
Muscardinus avellanarius **4**:30
mussel
  freshwater 7:6
  freshwater pearl **7**:6
  Spengler's freshwater **7**:6
Mustela spp. **4**:72
  M. lutreola **6**:78
  M. nigripens **4**:72
MVP *see* Minimum Viable Population
Myanmar **4**:36; **6**:30; **7**:50; **8**:32; **9**:50, 94
Mycteria
  M. cinerea **9**:34
  M. leucocephala **9**:34
myna
  Bali **9**:30
  helmeted **9**:30
  Rothschild's **9**:30
Myomimus spp. **4**:34
Myotis spp. **2**:62
  M. cobanensis **2**:66
  M. grisescens **2**:58
  M. morrisi **2**:66
  M. myotis **2**:62
Myrmecobius fasciatus **7**:14
Myrmecophaga tridactyla **2**:24
myxomitosis **1**:55
myzomela, white-chinned **5**:54
Myzomela albigula **5**:54

N

Namibia **10**:94
Nandopsis
  N. bartoni **3**:26
  N. labridens **3**:26, 27
  N. steindachneri **3**:26
Nannoperca oxleyana **3**:56
narwhal **10**:58
Nasalis larvatus **6**:90
National Association of Audubon Societies for the Protection of Wild Birds and Animals **1**:12–13, 88
national parks **1**:13, 92; **2**:24, 46, 64, 69, 83, 89; **3**:4, 16, 25, 69, 76; **4**:16, 19, 24, 40, 48, 55, 60, 67, 68, 79; **5**:41, 46, 66, 69, 72, 77; **6**:30, 34,

107

47, 52, 94; **7:**17, 19, 26, 41, 61; **8:**14, 28, 31; **9:**7, 53, 64, 78, 87; **10:**21, 28, 64, 77, 87
national wildlife refuges **2:**7; **7:**94; **8:**75; **9:**15, 45
natural disasters **1:**57; **2:**15; **3:**63, 76; **4:**46, 55, 85; **5:**22, 35, 42, 46, 79; **6:**19; **7:**65, 75; **8:**77; **9:**88; **10:**94
natural extinction **4:**32; **7:**88
Natural Resources Conservation Service **9:**10
nature reserves see reserves
Near Threatened see Lower Risk, Near Threatened (LRnt)
Nematostella vectensis **8:**58
nemertine
  Rodrigues (Rodriguez) **7:**8
nene **1:**87; **7:**10
Neoceratodus forsteri **6:**50
Neodrepanis hypoxanthus **2:**32
Neofelis nebulosa **6:**30
Neopelma aurifrons **6:**66
Neophema chrysogaster **7:**58
Neotoma anthonyi **6:**92
Nepal **2:**72, 94; **5:**24; **6:**30; **7:**50; **8:**28
Nesolagus netscheri **8:**12, *8:*13
Nestor
  N. meridionalis **5:**51, 92
  N. notabilis **5:**92
New Caladonia **5:**88
New Guinea **3:**28, 86; **4:**60; **10:**20
New Mexico **3:**76
New Zealand **1:**89; **5:**6, 50, 60, 92; **6:**8; **9:**32, 48; **10:**6
newt
  Danube **7:**12
  great crested 7:12
  warty **7:**12
Nicaragua **8:**10
Nigeria **4:**40
Nipponia nippon **5:**72; **9:**26
noise pollution **1:**52
Norway **2:**70
Nosy Mangabe **2:**43; **6:**26
Not Evaluated (NE), IUCN category, definition **1:**16
Notiomystis cincta **5:**54
notornis **9:**48
Nova Scotia **8:**72
numbat **7:**14
Numenius spp. **3:**84
  N. borealis **3:**84
  N. tenuirostris **8:**54
nuthatch
  Algerian **7:**16
  various **7:**16
nyala, mountain 7:18
Nycticebus pygmaeus **6:**46

O

ocelot *3:*31
  Texas 7:20
Ochotona
  O. helanshanenesis **7:**74
  O. kolsowi **7:**74
  O. pusilla **7:**74
off-road vehicles **5:**29; **6:**38; **7:**84; **10:**12, 18
oil products **3:**33; **4:**27, 46; **8:**70, 81; **10:**56
oil spills **7:**5
okapi 7:22
Okapia johnstoni **7:**22
olm 7:24
Oncorhynchus ishikawai **8:**52
Onychorhynchus
  O. occidentalis **4:**82
  O. swainsoni **4:**82
oo, Kauai *1:*36
orang-utan 7:26
orca **10:**48
Orcinus orca **10:**48
Orconectes incomtus **3:**78
orders, taxonomic **1:**58
Oreomystis mana **2:**6
Oreophasis derbianus **5:**44
organizations **1:**11–13, 88
Oriolia bernieri **10:**27
Ornithoptera
  O. aesacus **3:**16
  O. alexandrae **3:**16
  O. richmondia **3:**16
  O. rothschildi **3:**16
Ornithorhynchus anatinus **7:**82
oryx, Arabian 7:28
Oryx
  O. dammah **7:**30
  O. leucoryx **7:**28
oryx
  scimitar-horned 7:30
  white **7:**28
Osmoderma eremita **2:**80
Other (O), category, definition **1:**16
Otis tarda **3:**10
otter
  European *1:*50; **7:**32
  giant 7:34
  sea **1:**24; **7:**36
  various **7:**35
otter shrew, various **9:**64
Otus
  O. hartlaubi **7:**42
  O. ireneae **7:**42
ou **2:**6
overfishing **1:**71; **3:**55, 56; **7:**46, 63; **8:**63, 65, 79; **9:**37, 93; **10:**41, 43
owl
  Blakiston's eagle 7:38
  Blakiston's fish **7:**38
  Madagascar grass **7:**40
  Madagascar red 7:40
  Rodrigues little *1:*37
  rufous fishing- **7:**42
  São Tomé scops- **7:**42
  Sokoke scops- **7:**42
  spotted *1:*85; **7:**42
  various **7:**40
owlet, long-whiskered **7:**42
ox
  Cambodian forest **6:**14
  Vu Quang 7:44
Oxygastra curtisii **4:**70

Oxyura leucocephala **4:**44
ozone layer depletion **1:**53–54, 79; **8:**51

P

Pacific islands **2:**6; **5:**76, 88; **8:**78
Pacific Ocean **3:**50; **4:**47; **8:**62, 78, 80; **9:**8, 86; **10:**40, 43, 44, 82
paddlefish *1:*88; **7:**46
  Chinese **7:**46
paiche **7:**76
Pakistan **2:**94
palila **2:**6
Pan
  P. paniscus **3:**44
  P. troglodytes **3:**42
Panama **8:**10
panda
  giant *1:*9; **7:**48
  lesser 7:50
  red **7:**50
Pandaka pygmaea **5:**34
Pangasianodon gigas **3:**32
pangolin
  long-tailed 7:52
  various **7:**52
panther
  eastern **7:**54
  Florida 7:54
Panthera
  P. leo **9:**69
  P. l. persica **6:**34
  P. onca **5:**86
  P. pardus **6:**28
  P. tigris **9:**68
Pantholops hodgsoni **2:**26
Papilio
  P. jordani **3:**12
  P. leucotaenia **3:**12
Papua New Guinea **2:**16, 28, 84; **3:**8, **7:**72; **8:**20; **10:**4
Paracentrotus lividus **8:**66
Paradisaea rudolphi **2:**84
paradisefish, ornate 7:56
parakeet
  Antipodes **5:**92
  Carolina *1:*37
  Guadeloupe *1:*37
Parapinnixa affinis **3:**72
parasites **3:**13; **4:**75, 94; **10:**33, 38, 72
Pardosa diuturna **9:**24
Parnassius
  P. apollo **3:**12
  P. autocrator **3:**12
parrot
  broad-billed *1:*31
  ground **5:**51
  night 7:58
  owl **5:**50
  St. Vincent **2:**14
  various **7:**58
  see also lovebird
parrotfinch, greenfaced **4:**74
Partula spp. **9:**8
Pavo muticus **7:**60

peacock, Congo **7:**60
peafowl
  Congo 7:60
  green **7:**60
pearl trade **7:**6
pearlshell
  Alabama **7:**6
  Louisiana **7:**6
peat extraction **10:**37
pedomorphism **2:**40; **8:**46
pelican
  Dalmatian **7:**62
  spot-billed **7:**62
Pelicanus
  P. crispus **7:**62
  P. philippensis **7:**62
Penelope spp. **5:**44
Penelopides
  P. mindorensis **5:**56
  P. panini **5:**56
penguin
  Galápagos 7:64
  various **7:**64
Pentalagus furnessi **8:**12
Perameles
  P. bourgainville **2:**48
  P. gunnii **2:**48
perch, oxleyan pygmy **3:**56
perfume **4:**12
perfume trade **10:**56
Peripatus spp. **10:**84
persecution **1:**40, 47; **2:**10, 42, 68, 72, 90; **3:**42; **4:**6, 16, 24, 40, 66; **5:**24, 28, 66, 93; **6:**4, 6, 24, 28, 33, 52, 54, 56, 74, 82; **7:**20, 38, 54, 75; **8:**7, 14, 25, 28, 77, 82; **9:**12, 34, 62, 66; **10:**31, 34, 48, 59, 64, 67, 70, 72, 74, 77
Peru **2:**74; **3:**46; **4:**82; **7:**76; **9:**20
pesticides **1:**50, 51–52; **2:**60; **3:**10, 19, 93; **4:**55; **5:**94; **6:**4, 6, 63; **8:**23, 65; **9:**24; **10:**49
pet trade **2:**22; **3:**42; **5:**15, 28, 38, 41; **6:**24, 26, 38, 70, 87; **7:**26, 53; **9:**14, 52, 60, 82, 84, 88, 91; **10:**12, 14, 16, 21, 24, 31
  see also aquarium trade; cage-bird trade
Petaurus gracilis **5:**32
petrel
  Bermuda *1:*55; **7:**66
  various **7:**66
Petrogale persephone **8:**36
Pezophaps solitaria **4:**20
Pezoporus wallicus **5:**51
Phalacrocorax spp. **3:**64
  P. harrisi **3:**64
Phalanger spp. **3:**86
  P. atrimaculatus **3:**86
  P. maculatus rufoniger **3:**86
Pharomachrus mocinno **8:**10
Phascolarctos cinereus **6:**10
pheasant **9:**94
Phelsuma spp. **5:**22
  P. guentheri **5:**22
Philemon fuscicapillus **5:**54

Philepitta schlegeli **2:**32
Philesturnus carunculatus **5:**60
Philippines **1:**23; **4:**36, 54; **5:**34, 56; **6:**24; **7:**68
Phoca
  P. caspica **8:**70, 72
  P. sibirica **8:**70
Phocarctos hookeri **8:**62
Phocoena
  P. phocoena **7:**86
  P. sinus **7:**86; **10:**56
  P. spinipinnis **7:**86
Phodilus prigoginei **7:**40
Phoenicoparrus
  P. andinus **4:**80
  P. jamesi **4:**81
Phoenicopterus
  P. chilensis **4:**81
  P. minor **4:**81
Phoxinus
  P. cumberlandensis **3:**90
  P. tennesseensis **3:**90
Phrynops
  P. dahli **10:**22
  P. hogei **10:**22
Phrynosoma m'callii **6:**38
phylum **1:**58–59
Physeter macrocephalus **10:**56
Picathartes
  P. gymnocephalus **8:**38
  P. oreas **8:**38
picathartes, white-necked **8:**38
Picoides
  P. borealis **10:**80
  P. ramsayi **10:**80
pig
  Javan warty **2:**45
  Visyan warty 7:68
  see also babirusa; hog
pigeon
  blue *1:*31
  chestnut-tailed **7:**70
  Mauritius pink **7:**70
  passenger *1:*22, 37
  pink 7:70
  southern crowned **7:**72
  various **7:**71
  Victoria crowned 7:72
  western crowned **7:**72
pika
  Helan Shan **7:**74
  Koslov's **7:**74
  steppe 7:74
Pinguinus impennis **2:**38
pintail, Eaton's **9:**62
Pipile spp. **5:**44
Pipra vilasboasi **6:**66
Piprites pileatus **6:**66
pirarucu 7:76
Pithecophaga jefferyi **4:**54
pitta
  black-breasted **7:**78
  Gurney's 7:78
  various **7:**78
Pitta spp. **7:**78
  P. gurneyi **7:**78
plants, nonnative invasions **9:**40, 42
Platalea minor **9:**26

108

SET INDEX

Platanista
  P. gangetica **4:**26, 28
  P. minor **4:**26, 28
platy
  Cuatro Ciénegas **7:**80
  Monterrey **7:**80
  Muzquiz **7:**80
  northern **7:**80
  red **5:**36
platypus 7:82
Plethodon spp. **8:**48
  P. serratus **8:**48
plover
  piping 7:84
  various **7:**84
Podarcis
  P. lilfordi **6:**40
  P. milensis **6:**40
  P. pityusensis **6:**40
Podiceps spp. **5:**42
Podilymbus gigas **5:**42
Podogymnura
  P. aureospinula **5:**48
  P. truei **5:**48
Podomys floridanus **6:**92
poisoning **4:**57, 92; **5:**93; **6:**63, 86; **7:**93; **8:**25, 65, 75; **9:**45; **10:**34
Poliocephalus rufopectus **5:**42
pollution **1:**40, 42, 50–53; **2:**10, 22, 40, 52, 77, 91; **3:**13, 35, 38, 49, 65, 76, 89, 95; **4:**5, 15, 19, 27, 29, 44, 70, 80; **5:**11, 15, 35, 43, 79; **6:**68, 78; **7:**24, 32, 35, 36, 46, 55, 63, 66, 77, 81, 82, 84; **8:**23, 41, 53, 55, 59, 62, 65, 69, 70, 75, 85, 91; **9:**14, 27, 34, 37, 38, 41, 45, 65, 75; **10:**12, 15, 21, 25, 41, 43, 45, 49, 52, 59
see also light pollution; noise pollution; oil spills; pesticides
Polyodon spathula **7:**46
Pongo pygmaeus **7:**26
Poospiza garleppi **4:**76
population modeling **1:**8
populations **1:**20–22
porbeagle **8:**86
Porphyrio mantelli **9:**48
porpoise
  Burmeister's **7:**86
  Gulf of California **7:**86
  harbor 7:86
  vaquita **10:**56
  Portugal **6:**52
possum, Leadbeater's 7:88
Potamogale velox **8:**90
potoroo
  Gilbert's **7:**90
  long-footed 7:90
Potorous
  P. gilbertii **7:**90
  P. longipes **7:**90
poverty **1:**89, 95; **3:**7, 37, 45; **8:**29, 34
power cables **4:**57; **7:**63; **10:**34

prairie dog
  black-tailed 7:92
  various **7:**92
pratincole, black-winged **3:**68
Presbytis comata **6:**86
pressure groups **1:**13
Prioailurus planiceps **3:**30
Priodontes maximus **2:**30
Prionailurus iriomotensis **3:**30
Probarbus spp. **5:**82
  P. jullieni **5:**82
Procnias
  P. nudicollis **2:**82
  P. tricarunculata **2:**82
Propithecus
  P. diadema **5:**84; **8:**93
  P. tattersalli **8:**92
  P. verreauxi **5:**84; **8:**93
Prosobonia cancellata **8:**54
Proteus anguinus **7:**24
Psammobates geometricus **9:**88
Psephotus chrysopterygius **7:**58
Psephurus gladius **7:**46
Pseudemydura umbrina **10:**22
Pseudemys
  P. alabamensis **10:**12
  P. gorzugi **10:**12
  P. rubriventris **10:**12
Pseudibis
  P. davisoni **5:**72
  P. gigantea **5:**72
Pseudocotalpa giulianii **2:**80
Pseudophryne spp. **9:**78
  P. corroboree **9:**78
Pseudoryx nghetinhensis **7:**44
Psittirostra psittacez **2:**6
Pterodroma spp. **7:**66
  P. cahow **7:**66
Pteronura brasiliensis **7:**34
Pteropus
  P. dasymallus **4:**86
  P. rodricensis **4:**84
puffleg
  black-breasted **9:**20
  colorful **4:**78
Puma concolor
  P. c. coryi **7:**54
  P. c. cougar **7:**54
pupfish
  Devil's Hole **7:**94
  various **7:**94
Pygathrix nemaeus **6:**86
pygmy-possum
  long-tailed **8:**4
  mountain 8:4
Pygopididae **1:**74
python
  Ramsay's **8:**6
  woma 8:6

Q

quagga *1:*37; **8:**8
  Bonte **8:**8
quarrying **1:**40; **2:**58; **3:**69; **6:**42; **10:**30
quetzal, resplendent 8:10

R

"r" reproductive strategy **1:**25
rabbit
  Amami 8:12
  Assam **5:**50
  Ryukyu **8:**12
  volcano *8:*13, 14
racer
  Antiguan **8:**16
  various **8:**16
racerunner **10:**60
rail *1:*31
  Guam **8:**18
  invisible **9:**48
  Owston's **8:**18
  various **3:**66; **8:**18
rainbowfish
  Lake Wanam **8:**20
  various **8:**20
Rallus antarcticus **3:**66
Rana spp. **5:**10
  R. aurora **5:**10
Ranthanbore National Park *1:*92
Raphus cucullatus **4:**20
Rare Animal Relief Effort (RARE) **2:**15
rasbora
  fire **8:**22
  golden **8:**22
  pearly **8:**22
  vateria flower 8:22
Rasbora vaterifloris **8:**22
rat
  Alexandrine **8:**24
  Asian black **1:**55
  black 8:24
  climbing **8:**24
  gray **8:**24
  roof **8:**24
  ship **8:**24
  various **6:**92
  see also mole-rat
rat kangaroo **7:**90
Rattus rattus **8:**24
razorback **10:**42
Red Data Book (IUCN) **1:**10–11, 14
reintroduction **1:**22, 56, 87, 92; **2:**69, 76, 79; **3:**33, 56, 60, 76, 83; **4:**15, 31, 53, 72, 92; **5:**58; **6:**5, 26, 61; **7:**11; **8:**19, 53; **9:**9, 38, 41, 49, 52, 87, 91; **10:**7, 23, 68, 73
relocation see translocation
reproductive strategies **1:**25–26
reptiles
  diversity **1:**72
  history **1:**73
  risks **1:**73–75
  see also List of Animals by Group, page 100
research see conservation research; medical research; scientific research
reserves **1:**33, 92; **2:**37, 43, 55, 59; **3:**69; **4:**16, 39; **5:**57; **6:**19, 26, 42, 47, 89; **7:**11, 41, 55, 73, 81, 89; **8:**41; **9:**7, 9, 53, 67, 85, 88, 89, 91; **10:**22, 25, 33, 37, 95
  see also national parks; wildlife refuges
reservoir building **2:**31; **7:**43; **9:**41; **10:**34
restricted distribution **1:**8
Rheobatrachus silus **4:**94
Rhincodon typus **8:**86
Rhinoceros
  R. sondaicus **8:**30
  R. unicornis **8:**28
rhinoceros
  black 8:26
  great Indian 8:28
  Javan 8:30
  Sumatran 8:32
  white 8:34
Rhinolophus ferrumequinum **2:**60
Rhinopithecus brelichi **6:**86
Rhinopoma macinnesi **2:**64
Rhinoptilus bitorquatus **3:**68
Rhodonessa caryophyllacea **4:**44
Rhynchocyon
  R. chrysopygus **4:**68
  R. petersi **4:**68
Rhynochetos jubatus **5:**88
Rissa breviostris **5:**46
ritual objects **2:**85; **3:**29; **5:**5
road building **2:**55; **3:**19; **4:**52, 67; **7:**54, 73, 90; **8:**5; **9:**84, 88; **10:**85
road kills **2:**77; **3:**29, 31; **4:**22, 92; **5:**80; **6:**10, 38, 52, 75; **7:**55; **8:**7, 36; **9:**10, 82; **10:**31
roatelo, white-breasted **6:**76
Robinson Crusoe Island **4:**78
rock-wallaby, prosperine 8:36
rockfowl
  bare-headed **8:**38
  gray-necked **8:**38
  white-necked 8:38
rocky, eastern province 8:40
Rodrigues (Rodriguez) Island **7:**8
Romania **6:**82
Romerolagus diazi **8:**13, 14
rorqual
  common **10:**42
  great northern **10:**40
Rosalia alpina **6:**44
Round Island **5:**22
Royal Society for the Protection of Birds (RSPB) **1:**13, 88
Russia **2:**70; **4:**32; **5:**94; **6:**78; **7:**32, 36, 38, 74; **8:**42, 54, 64; **10:**74
Rwanda **5:**38

S

saddleback **5:**60
Saguinus leucopus **6:**88
Sahara **2:**4
Sahel **5:**20

saiga **8:**42
Saiga tatarica **8:**42
St. Lucia **10:**60
salamander
  California tiger **8:**44
  Chinese giant **8:**46
  flatwood **8:**44
  Japanese giant **8:**46
  Lake Lerma **8:**44
  Ouachita red-backed **8:**48
  Santa-Cruz long-toed **8:**51
  southern red-backed **8:**48
  various **8:**48
  see also axolotl
Salmo spp. **8:**52
salmon
  Adriatic **8:**52
  Danube **8:**52
  European **8:**52
  Satsukimasa **8:**52
  various **1:**68
Salmothymus obtusirostris **8:**52
samaruc **9:**80
Samoa **10:**82
Sandelia bainsii **8:**40
sandpiper
  spoon-billed **8:**54
  Tuamotu **8:**54
Sanzinia madagascariensis **3:**6
sao la **7:**44
Sapheopipo noguchii **10:**78
Sapo Dorado **9:**70
saratoga
  southern **7:**77
  spotted **4:**36
Sarcogyps calvus **10:**34
sardina ciega **3:**38
Scandinavia **3:**12; **8:**72
scientific research **2:**46; **4:**62; **10:**50
Sciurus vulgaris **9:**28
Scleropages
  S. formosus **4:**36
  S. leichardi **7:**77
  S. leichardti **4:**36
Scomberomorus concolor **10:**8
scops-owl **7:**42
Scotopelia ussheri **7:**42
scrub-bird
  noisy **8:**56
  rufous **8:**56
scrubfowl, various **6:**64
sea anemone
  Ivell's **8:**58
  starlet **8:**58
sea cow 4:46
  Steller's **3:**70
sea fan, broad 8:60
sea lion
  Hooker's **8:**62
  northern **8:**62
  Steller's **8:**62
sea-eagle
  Pallas's **8:**64
  Steller's **8:**64
sea-urchin 1:24
  edible **8:**66
seahorse *1:*69
  Cape **8:**68

Knysna 8:68
seal
  Baikal 8:70
  Baltic gray 8:70
  Caribbean monk 1:37; 8:74, 76
  Caspian 8:70, 72
  fur, various 8:62
  Galápagos fur 8:78
  gray 8:72
  Guadaloupe fur 8:78
  Hawaiian monk 8:74
  Juan Fernandez fur 8:78
  Mediterranean monk 1:43; 8:76
  northern fur 8:78
seminatural habitats 1:38
Semnornis ramphastinus 2:54
Sephanoides fernandensis 4:78
Sepilok Rehabilitation Center 1:95
Sericulus bakeri 3:8
Seychelles 6:62
shama, black 6:62
shark
  basking 8:80
  great white 8:82
  silver 8:84
  various 8:86
  whale 8:86
shatoosh trade 2:26
sheep, barbary 8:88
shrew
  giant African water 8:90
  giant otter 8:90
  Nimba otter 8:90
  pygmy otter 8:90
Siberia 4:12; 8:54, 70; 9:62, 68; 10:74
sicklebill, black 2:84
Sierra Club 1:13
Sierra Leone 4:48; 8:38
sifaka
  Diadem 5:84; 8:93
  golden-crowned 8:92
  Verreaux's 5:84; 8:93
Simias concolor 6:86
sirenians 3:70; 4:46; 6:68
siskin
  red 8:94
  saffron 8:94
  yellow-faced 8:94
Sites of Special Scientific Interest 6:42
Sitta spp. 7:16
  S. ledanti 7:16
Skiffia francesae 5:36
skin trade 2:11, 36; 3:7, 70, 80; 4:46; 7:53; 8:9, 62, 74, 81, 88; 9:56; 10:58, 94
skink
  pygmy blue-tongued 9:4
  Réunion 1:37
  western 1:74
slash-and-burn agriculture 6:76
sloth
  Hoffmann's two-toed 9:6
  Linné's two-toed 9:6
  maned 9:6

slow reproduction 1:8, 25
Sminthopsis spp. 4:50
  S. aitkeni 4:50
snail, *Partula* 9:8
snake
  Cuban tree boa 3:4
  Cyclades blunt-nosed viper 10:30
  Dumeril's boa 3:6
  eastern indigo 9:10
  emerald tree boa 1:74
  Jamaican boa 3:4
  leopard 9:12
  Madagascar boa 3:6
  Madagascar tree boa 3:6
  Milos viper 10:30
  Mona Island boa 3:4
  Puerto Rican boa 3:4
  racer, Antiguan 8:16
  Ramsay's python 8:6
  San Francisco garter 9:14
  sharp-snouted 1:74
  two-striped garter 9:14
  Virgin Islands boa 3:4
  woma python 8:6
solenodon
  Cuban 9:16
  Haitian 9:16
Solenodon
  S. cubanus 9:16
  S. paradoxus 9:16
solitaire
  Réunion 1:37
  Rodrigues (Rodriguez) 4:20
Solomys ponceleti 6:92
Somalia 2:34
Somatochlora
  S. calverti 4:70
  S. hineana 4:70
Sosippus placidus 9:24
souslik
  European 9:18
  European spotted 9:18
South Africa 3:40; 8:8, 40, 68; 9:89; 10:34, 94
South America 2:24, 30, 54, 74, 92; 3:46, 62, 80, 84; 4:18, 24, 26, 53, 78, 82; 5:86; 6:58, 66, 88; 7:35, 76; 8:94; 9:6, 20, 52, 54; 10:28, 70
Southern Ocean 2:8; 10:40, 43
souvenir trade 2:46; 3:6, 50, 75, 80; 4:67; 5:38, 41; 8:60, 66, 69, 82; 10:18
Spain 1:42–43; 4:56; 6:52; 9:80
Spalax spp. 6:82
  S. graecus 6:82
sparrow
  house 1:64
  Zapata 4:76
spatuletail, marvelous 9:20
specialization 1:28–30
speciation 1:26–28
species
  definition 1:26
  taxonomic groupings 1:58–59

Species Survival Commission (SSC) 1:10
specimen collectors 2:38; 5:60, 72
Speoplatyrhinus poulsoni 3:34
Speothos venaticus 4:24, 93
Spermophilus spp. 9:18
  S. citellus 9:18
Spheniscus
  S. demersus 7:64
  S. humboldti 7:64
  S. mendiculus 7:64
Sphenodon
  S. guntheri 10:6
  S. punctatus 10:6
spider
  great raft 9:22
  Kauai cave wolf 9:24
  red-kneed tarantula 9:60
  wolf, various 9:24
Spilocuscus rufoniger 3:86
Spizocorys fringillaris 6:18
spoonbill
  black-faced 9:26
  lesser 9:26
sport, exploitation of animals for 1:47–48
sports fishing 10:8
squirrel
  Arctic ground 1:24
  Eurasian red 9:28
  European red 9:28
  see also ground squirrel
Sri Lanka 2:52, 72; 3:94; 4:62, 67; 6:46; 7:56; 8:22
starling
  Bali 9:30
  various 9:30
steamerduck, Chubut 4:42
Stenella
  S. attenuata 10:48
  S. coeruleoalba 10:48
Stenodus leucichthys leucichthys 8:52
stilt, black 9:32
stitchbird 5:54
stork
  greater adjutant 9:34
  various 9:34
Strigops habroptilus 5:50
Strix occidentalis 7:42
Strymon avalona 3:14
sturgeon
  Baltic 9:36
  common 9:36
  ship 9:36
Sturnella defilippii 2:92
Sturnus spp. 9:30
sub-Antarctic islands 2:8
sucker
  harelip 9:38
  razorback 9:38
  sulphur-bottom 10:40
Sumatra 4:16; 6:30; 7:26
sunangel
  Bogotá 4:78
  various 9:20
sunbeam, purple-backed 4:78

sunfish
  blue-barred pygmy 9:40
  Carolina pygmy 9:40
  oceanic 1:68
  spring pygmy 9:40
superstition 1:47; 3:86
see also ritual objects; traditional medicine
Sus
  S. cebifrons 7:68
  S. salvanius 2:45
  S. verrucosus 2:45
swallow
  blue 9:42
  white-tailed 9:42
swan, trumpeter 9:44
Synthliboramphus spp. 7:4
  S. wumizusume 7:4
Sypheotides indica 3:10

T

Tachybaptus spp. 5:42
Tachyeres leucocephalus 4:42
Tachyglossus aculeatus multiaculeatus 4:60
Tachyoryctes spp. 6:84
  T. macrocephalus 6:84
Tachypleus
  T. gigas 3:74
  T. tridentatus 3:74
tagging see tracking and tagging
Tahr
  Arabian 9:46
  Himalayan 9:46
  Nilgiri 9:46
  Taiwan 6:30
takahe 9:48
Takin 9:50
tamaraw 2:20
tamarin
  golden lion 9:52
  golden-rumped 6:88
  various 9:52
  white-footed 6:88
Tanagara spp. 9:54
  T. fastuosa 9:54
tanager
  multicolored 4:76
  seven-colored 9:54
  various 9:54
Taphozous troughtoni 2:64
tapir
  Central American 9:56
  Malayan 9:58
  mountain 9:56, 58
Tapirus
  T. bairdii 9:56
  T. pinchaque 9:56, 58
tarantula, red-kneed 9:60
tarictic
  Mindoro 5:56
  Visayan 5:56
tarpan 1:37
Tasmania 5:16; 9:66
Taudactylus
  T. acutirostris 5:12
  T. rheophilus 5:12

Tauraco spp. 10:11
  T. bannermani 10:10
  T. fischeri 10:11
  T. ruspolii 10:11
taxonomic classification 1:26, 58
teal
  Baikal 9:62
  various 9:62
tenrec
  aquatic 9:64
  long-tailed 9:64
  web-footed 9:64
teporingo 8:14
Testudo spp. 9:84
  T. kleinmanni 9:84
tetra, Mexican 3:38
Tetrax tetrax 3:10
Texas 7:20; 10:32
Thailand 2:50, 64; 4:36; 5:82; 6:30; 7:78; 8:32, 84
Thamnophis
  T. gigas 9:14
  T. hammondi 9:14
  T. sirtalis tetrataenia 9:14
Theropithecus gelada 2:46
threat
  IUCN, categories of 1:14–17
threats, general 1: 38–57
Thryothorus nicefori 10:86
thryssa, New Guinea 2:16
Thryssa scratchleyi 2:16
Thunnus spp. 10:8
  T. thynnus 10:8
thylacine 1:36; 9:66
Thylacinus cynocephalus 9:66
Tibet 2:26; 9:50; 10:90
tiger 1:9, 95; 9:68
  Bali 1:36
  Tasmanian 9:66
Tiliqua adelaidensis 9:4
timber treatment chemicals 2:61, 62
toad
  boreal 9:76
  cane 1:54
  golden 9:70
  Mallorcan midwife 1:77; 9:72
  natterjack 9:74
  running 9:74
  Surinam 1:77
  various 9:70, 74, 76
  western 9:76
toadlet
  corroboree 9:78
  various 9:78
tokoeka 6:9
Tolypeutes tricinctus 2:30
toothcarp
  Corfu 9:80
  valencia 9:80
torgos tracheliotus 10:34
Torreornis inexpectata 4:76
tortoise
  Abingdon Island 1:37
  bolson 9:82
  Charles Island 1:37
  desert 9:82

SET INDEX

domed **1**:31
Egyptian 9:84
Galápagos giant 9:86
geometric 9:88
gopher **9**:82
Mauritian giant **1**:37
plowshare 9:90
radiated **9**:90
various **9**:84, 86, 89
tortoiseshell trade **10**:18
totoaba 9:92
Totoaba macdonaldi **9**:92
tourism **1**:42–43; **2**:4; **3**:41, 52, 65; **5**:38, 88; **6**:41; **7**:65; **8**:5, 14, 69, 76; **9**:12, 46, 56, 81, 84; **10**:18, 25, 31
see also ecotourism
toxins, bioaccumulation **1**:50, 51
Toxotes oligolepis **2**:28
tracking and tagging **1**:14–15, 85
traditional land management **1**:38
traditional medicine **1**:46; **10**:34
Tragelaphus
  T. buxtoni **7**:18
  T. strepsiceros **6**:16
tragopan
  Temminck's 9:94
  various **9**:94
Tragopan spp. **9**:94
  T. temminckii **9**:94
translocation **5**:17; **10**:60
tree-kangaroo
  Goodfellow's 10:4
  various **10**:4
Tremarctos ornatus **2**:74
Trichechus spp. **3**:70; **4**:47; **6**:69
  T. manatus latirostris **6**:68
Tridacna gigas **3**:50
Tringa guttifer **8**:54
triok, Tate's **5**:32; **7**:88
Triturus
  T. cristatus **7**:12
  T. dobrogicus **7**:12
trogon, resplendent **8**:10
trout
  Danube **8**:52
  European river **8**:52
  Ohrid **8**:52
  rainbow **1**:71
tuatara 10:6
  Cook Strait **10**:6
Tubulanus superbus 7.9
tuna
  Atlantic bluefin **10**:8
  northern bluefin 10:8
  various **10**:8
Tunisia **7**:30
turaco
  Bannerman's 10:10
  Fischer's **10**:11
  Prince Ruspoli's **10**:11
  various **10**:11
turtle 1:43
  Alabama red-bellied 10:12
  American red-bellied **10**:12

bog 10:14
box, various **10**:16
Chinese three-striped box 10:16
Fly River **10**:20
green **1**:72
hawksbill 10:18
map, various **10**:24
New Guinea softshell **10**:20
pig-nosed 10:20
various **10**:14, **10**:22
western swamp 10:22
yellow-blotched sawback map 10:24
Tympanocryptis lineata pnguicolla **4**:38
Typhlichthys subterraneus **3**:34
Tyto
  T. inexspectata **7**:40
  T. nigrobrunnea **7**:40
  T. soumagnei **7**:40

U

Uganda **5**:38
ultraviolet (UV) radiation damage **8**:51; **9**:76
umbrellabird, bare-necked **2**:82
Uncia uncia **6**:32
United States **2**:10, 58, 68, 70, 86; **3**:14, 15, 18, 34, 60, 72, 74, 76, 80, 90, 84; **4**:4, 42, 72, 93; **5**:10, 28; **6**:36, 38, 68; **7**:20, 36, 42, 46, 54, 84, 92, 94; **8**:45, 48, 51, 58; **9**:10, 14, 38, 40, 44, 60, 76, 82; **10**:12, 14, 24, 32, 38, 72, 74, 80
United States Fish and Wildlife Service **3**:81
urban development **3**:16, 19, 21, 31; **4**:38; **5**:11, 49; **6**:31, 41, 42, 72, 86; **7**:35, 43; **8**:45, 59, 65, 76; **9**:14, 84, 88; **10**:12, 22, 24, 31, 33, 62
Ursus
  U. arctos **2**:68
  U. a. nelsoni **2**:68
  U. maritimus **2**:70
  U. thibetanus **2**:68, 74
UV radiation *see* ultraviolet radiation

V

Valencia
  V. hispanica **9**:80
  V. letourneuxi **9**:80
vanga
  helmet **10**:26
  various **10**:27
Varanus komodoensis **6**:12
Varecia variegata **6**:26
Venezuela **2**:74; **8**:94
Vicugna vicugna **10**:28
vicuña 10:28
Vietnam **2**:50; **4**:36; **5**:26, 82; **6**:14, 30, 86; **7**:44; **8**:30, 32; **9**:94; **10**:16

viper
  Cyclades blunt-nosed **10**:30
  Milos 10:30
  various **10**:30
Vipera spp. **10**:30
vireo
  black-capped 10:32
  Chocó **10**:32
  St. Andrew **10**:32
  San Andrés **10**:32
Vireo
  V. atricapillus **10**:32
  V. caribaeus **10**:32
  V. masteri **10**:32
Viverridae **4**:90
Vulnerable, definition **1**:15–16
Vulpes velox **4**:92
Vultur gryphus **3**:60
vulture
  Cape **10**:34
  Cape griffon 10:34
  various **10**:34

W

wallaby
  prosperine rock **8**:36
  Toolache **1**:36
walpurti **7**:14
war **1**:47; **4**:48, 55, 67; **5**:38, 41, 42, 52; **6**:16, 86; **7**:22, 44; **8**:31, 34
warbler
  aquatic 10:36
  Kirtland's 10:38
  Manchurian reed **10**:36
  streaked reed **10**:36
  various **10**:38
Washington Convention *see* Convention on International Trade in Endangered Species of Wild Fauna and Flora
water balance **1**:40
water buffalo, Indian **2**:20
water extraction **8**:53; **10**:21, 22
water shortages **2**:34, 36; **8**:34; **10**:92
waxbill, Anambra **4**:74
weasel
  black-striped **4**:72
  Colombian **4**:72
  Indonesian mountain **4**:72
weaverbirds **4**:88
West Indies **2**:14
wetland drainage **1**:40, 74; **2**:11, 40, 90; **3**:11, 22, 63, 92; **4**:26, 44, 70; **5**:5, 35; **6**:21, 91; **7**:63; **8**:30, 53, 55, 59; **9**:14, 22, 27, 33, 34, 63; **10**:14, 22, 25, 37, 86
whale
  blue 10:40
  California gray **10**:44
  coalfish **10**:54
  fin 10:42
  gray **1**:62, 90; **10**:44
  herring **10**:42
  humpback 10:46

killer **10**:48
minke **1**:44; **10**:50
northern right 1:25; **10**:52
pollack **10**:54
right **1**:25
Rudolphi's **10**:54
sardine **10**:54
scrag **10**:44
sei **10**:54
short-finned pilot **10**:48
southern right **10**:52
sperm **10**:56
spermaceti **10**:56
white **10**:58
whaling **1**:45
whiptail
  Colorado checkered **1**:74
  orange-throated **10**:61
  St. Lucia, *1*:86, **10**:60
white eye, Lord Howe Island **1**:36
wildcat 10:62
wildlife refuge **3**:76; **10**:33, 73
wildlife surveys **1**:84
Williamsonia lintneri **4**:70
Windward Islands **10**:60
wolf **1**:47
  Antarctic **10**:66
  Ethiopian 10:64
  Falkland Island **1**:37; **10**:66
  gray 10:68
  maned **10**:70
  marsupial **9**:66
  red *1*:93; **10**:72
  Simien **10**:64
  Tasmanian **9**:66
  timber **10**:68
wolverine 10:74
wombat
  northern hairy-nosed 10:77
  Queensland hairy-nosed **10**:76
  soft-furred **10**:76
woodpecker
  Arabian **10**:80
  imperial **10**:78
  ivory-billed 10:78
  Okinawa **10**:78
  red-cockaded 10:80
  Sulu **10**:80
woodstar
  Chilean **4**:78
  little **4**:78
wool trade **2**:26
World Bank **1**:89
World Conservation Union *see* International Union for the Conservation of Nature
World Parrot Trust **2**:15
World Wide Fund for Nature (WWF) **1**:13
World Wildlife Fund *see* World Wide Fund for Nature
worm
  Palolo **10**:82
  ribbon **7**:8
  velvet 10:84
  see also earthworm

wren
  Apolinar's **10**:86
  Fermina **10**:86
  Niceforo's **10**:86
  Stephen Island **1**:37
  Zapata 10:86

X

Xanthomyza phrygia **5**:54
Xanthopsar flavus **2**:92
Xenoglaux loweryi **7**:42
Xenoophorus captivus **5**:36
Xenopirostris damii **10**:27
xenopoecilus 10:88
Xenopoecilus spp. **10**:88
  X. saranisorum **10**:88
Xiphophorus spp.
  X. couchianus **7**:80
  X. gordoni **7**:80
  X. meyeri **7**:80
Xyrauchen texanus **9**:38

Y

yak, wild **10**:90
yamane **4**:34
yamion **10**:76
Yellowstone National Park **1**:10
Yugoslavia **7**:24

Z

zacatuche **8**:14
Zaglossus bruijni **4**:60
Zaire *see* Democratic Republic of Congo
Zambia **6**:48
zebra
  Burchell's **8**:8
  Cape mountain **10**:94
  Grevy's 10:92
  Hartmann's **10**:94
  mountain 10:94
zebu cattle **1**:38
Zimbabwe **4**:22
zoogeographic regions **1**:19, 20
zoos **1**:86; **5**:41; **8**:38
  see also captive breeding

111

Acknowledgments

The authors and publishers would like to thank the following people and organizations:
Aquamarines International Pvt. Ltd., Sri Lanka, especially Ananda Pathirana; Aquarist & Pond keeper Magazine, U.K.; BirdLife International (the global partnership of conservation organizations working together in over 100 countries to save birds and their habitats). Special thanks to David Capper; also to Guy Dutson and Alison Stattersfield; Sylvia Clarke (Threatened Wildlife, South Australia); Mark Cocker (writer and birder); David Curran (aquarist specializing in spiny eels, U.K.); Marydele Donnelly (IUCN sea turtle specialist); Svein Fossa (aquatic consultant, Norway); Richard Gibson (Jersey Wildlife Preservation Trust, Channel Islands); Paul Hoskisson (Liverpool John Moores University); Derek Lambert; Pat Lambert (aquarists specializing in freshwater livebearers); Lumbini Aquaria Wayamba Ltd., Sri Lanka, especially Jayantha Ramasinghe and Vibhu Perera; Isolda McGeorge (Chester Zoological Gardens); Dr. James Peron Ross (IUCN crocodile specialist); Zoological Society of London, especially Michael Palmer, Ann Sylph, and the other library staff.

Picture Credits

Abbreviations
AL   Ardea London
BBC BBC Natural History Unit
BCC Bruce Coleman Collection
FLPA Frank Lane Photographic Agency
NHPA Natural History Photographic Agency
OSF Oxford Scientific Films
PEP Planet Earth Pictures
b = bottom; **c** = center; **t** = top; **l** = left; **r** = right

Jacket
Ibiza wall lizard, illustration by Denys Ovenden from *Collins Field Guide: Reptiles and Amphibians of Britain and Europe*; Grevy's zebra, Stan Osolinski/Oxford Scientific Films; Florida panther, Lynn M. Stone/BBC Natural History Unit; silver shark, Max Gibbs/Photomax; blue whale, Tui de Roy/Oxford Scientific Films

5 Daniel J. Cox/OSF; **6–7** Survival Anglia/Mike Linley/OSF; **9** Richard Herrmann/OSF; **11** Roger Fotso/BirdLife International; **14–15** Animals Animals/Zig Leszczynski/OSF; **16–17** David M. Dennis/OSF; **19** Mark Webster/OSF; **21** David M. Dennis/OSF; **23** Reg Morrison/AL; **25** David M. Dennis/OSF; **27** Nick Garbutt/PEP; **29** Pete Oxford; **31** R. Gibson; **33** G. Lasley/Vireo; **34–35** Survival Anglia/Janeen R. Walker/OSF; **37** Nigel Bean/BBC; **39** R. Austing/FLPA; **40–41** & **42–43** Tui de Roy/OSF; **45** François Gohier/AL; **47** Daniel J. Cox/OSF; **48–49** Jeff Foott/OSF; **51** Ben Osborne/OSF; **52–53** Doug Allan/OSF; **55** Doug Perrine/PEP; **56–57** Howard Hall/OSF; **58–59** Animals Animals/Zig Leszczynski/OSF; **61** R. Gibson; **62–63** Michael Callan/FLPA; **64–65** Charlie Hamilton James/BBC; **68–69** Anthony Cooper/Ecoscene; **71** T. Whittaker/FLPA; **72–73** Mark Newman/FLPA; **74–75** M. Watson/AL; **77** A.N.T./NHPA; **79** P. Morris/AL; **81** S. Maka/Vireo; **83t** Pete Atkinson/PEP; **83** inset Ken Lucas/PEP; **84–85** J.A.L. Cooke/OSF; **86–87** Göran Altstedt/Windrush Photos; **89** D.J. Lambert; **90–91** Pete Oxford/BBC; **92–93** & **95** Stan Osolinski/OSF.

Artists
Graham Allen, Norman Arlott, Priscilla Barrett, Trevor Boyer, Ad Cameron, David Dennis, Karen Hiscock, Chloe Talbot Kelly, Mick Loates, Michael Long, Malcolm McGregor, Denys Ovenden, Oxford Illustrators, John Sibbick, Joseph Tomelleri, Dick Twinney, Ian Willis

While every effort has been made to trace the copyright holders of illustrations reproduced in this book, the publishers will be pleased to rectify any omissions or inaccuracies.

R
333.95
END
V.10